SPSS

for you

MJP
PUBLISHERS

MJP Publishers

No. 44, Nallathambi Street,
Triplicane, Chennai 600 005

MJP 080   © Publishers, 2024

Publisher : C. Janarthanan

SPSS

for you

A. Rajathi

Associate Professor in Zoology

Holy Cross College

Tiruchirappalli, Tamil Nadu

P. Chandran

Professor

Center for Population Studies

Annamalai University

Chidambaram, Tamil Nadu

Preface

Statistics has its applications in diversified fields and it is rather impossible to see any field where statistics does not creep in. Owing to the importance of statistics, this subject has become a part of the general curriculum of many academic and professional courses. In olden days, researchers spent months in completing a statistical task manually. With the advent of computers, a few programs were made available to analyse statistical data. SPSS, earlier termed as Statistical Package for the Social Sciences, is one of the oldest statistical programs on the market, which was originally written for mainframe computers and designed to be used in the social sciences, hence the name. Nowadays, this package is used by researchers from every discipline as the software contains powerful tools for automated analysis of data.

Our experience of more than two and a half decades of teaching SPSS from the earlier version to the latest version, our practical experience in guiding researchers in their statistical analyses and our experience in conducting courses in SPSS in various institutions gave us the interest and confidence to write this self-study book on SPSS.

The scope of this book is to introduce the reader to the SPSS for Windows and to enable them enter and format data, run the analysis, draw different kinds of diagrams and graphs and interpret data. This book is prepared for use in the teaching of statistics in colleges and for those who work independently in research, for analysis and interpretation of data.

This book is written in a simple systematic way. The subject matter is arranged in chapters and sections, numbered by the conventional decimal numbering system. All chapters have been written like a tutorial. Each chapter has instructions that guide the learner through a series of exercises, as well as graphics showing how the screen should look like at various steps in the process.

This book has nine chapters. Chapter 1 gives a brief account of statistical data, sample and population and the basics of hypothesis testing. The rest of the chapters contain chapter- specific materials with exercises. Chapter 4 exclusively deals with a versatile way of producing graphs such as clustered bar chart with error bars with the aid of Chart builder and Interactive graphs. Chapters on comparing averages, analysis of variance, correlation, regression and chi-square are written in a very simple way with specific examples, to enable the reader to understand the concept and carry out the analysis easily, and interpret the results.

Throughout the book, we have used screen snapshots of SPSS Data Editor with Variable view and Data view, Dialog boxes and Outputs to illustrate finer aspects of the technique. The revision exercises are chapter-specific to enable the novice to have a personal hands-on training. We have also included a glossary for easy reference.

We would like to thank the faculty and the research scholars who approached us to have some clarification on the choice of the statistical test, running the analysis and interpreting data.

We are grateful to the authors of various books on SPSS which we have referred to while writing this book, especially Andy Field who has authored *Discovering Statistics using SPSS*, for the topics on 'Matched-Pairs Signed Rank test and Mann–Whitney's test".

We are grateful to Prof. P. Shanmugavadivel, Department of Statistics, St. Josephs College, Tiruchirapalli, India, for his spontaneous help and for his valuable comments. Finally, we would like to thank Mr. C. Sajeesh Kumar, Managing Editor, MJP Publishers, Chennai, for scrutinizing the manuscript with perfection, and for his valuable suggestions.

We hope that this book will be of great help to the readers in carrying out analysis with SPSS. If you would like to make suggestions, correct errors, or give us feedback, you are most welcome. Please send your suggestions and criticisms to c_rajathi@yahoo.com, to enable us to improve the contents in the next editions.

A. Rajathi
P. Chandran

Contents

1 INTRODUCTION

A scientist, an engineer, an economist or a physician is interested in discovering about a phenomenon that he assumes or believes to exist. Whatever phenomenon he desires to explain, he tries to explain it by collecting data from the real world and then using these data he draws conclusions. The available data areby him with the help of statistical tools by building statistical models of the phenomenon. This chapter gives a brief overview of some important statistical concepts and tools that help us to analyze the data to answer scientific questions.

POPULATION AND SAMPLE

Biologists might be interested in finding the effect of a certain drug on rat metabolism; psychologist might want to discover processes that occur in all human beings, an economist might want to build a model that apply to all salary groups and so on. In all these situations, it is impossible to study the entire unit on which the researcher is interested. Instead he studies only a handful of observations and based on this he draws conclusion for the entire unit on which he was originally interested. In this connection two terms are often used in statistical investigation, one is "population" and the other is "sample". The term population refers to all possible observations that can be made on a specific characteristic. In the first example of the biologist, the term "population" could mean all the rats now living and all rats yet to be born or it could mean all rats of a certain species now living in a specific area. A biologist cannot collect data from every rat and the psychologist cannot collect data from every human being. Therefore, he collects data from a small subset of the population known as "sample" and use these data to infer on the population as a whole.

If engineers want to build a dam, they cannot make a full-size model of the dam they want to build; instead they build a small-scale model and tests this model under various conditions. These engineers infer how the full-sized bridge will respond from the results of the small-scale model. Therefore, in real life situations we never have access to the entire population so we collect smaller samples and use the characteristics of the sample to infer the characteristics of the population. The larger the sample, the more likely it is to represent the whole population. It is essential that a sample should be representative of the population from which it is drawn.

OBSERVATIONS AND VARIABLES

In statistics, we observe or measure characteristics called variables. The study subjects are called observational units. For example, if the investigator is interested in studying systolic and diastolic blood pressure among 100 college students,the systolic and diastolic blood pressures are the variables, the blood pressure readings are the observations and the students are the observational units. If the investigator records the student's age, height and weight in addition to systolic and diastolic blood pressure readings, then he has a data set of 100 students with observations recorded on each of five variables (systolic pressure, diastolic pressure, age, height and weight) for each student or observation unit.

VARIABLES AND SCALES

Quantitative or Measurement Variable on Interval Scale

There are numerous characteristics found in the world which can be measured in some fashion. Some characteristics like height, weight, temperature, salary etc. are quantitative variables. Since these variables are capable of exact measurements and assume, at least theoretically, infinite number of values between any two fixed points. The data collected on such measurements are called continuous data and we use interval scale for these data. For example, height of individuals can be fixed on some interval like 2–3; 3–4; 4–5; 5–6 feet. On the other hand, number of children in a family can be counted as 0, 1, 2, 3, 4, 5, … and the number of families having these many children can be counted and given. In this example the number of children is 1, 2, 3,…. . and not any intermediate value as 1.5 or 2.3. Such a variable is called discrete variable.

Qualitative Variable on Nominal Scale

Here the units are assigned to specific categories in accordance with certain attributes. For example, gender is measured on a nominal scale, namely male and female. Qualitative variable is an attribute and is descriptive in nature. For example, colour of a person like fair, whitish and dark.

Ranked Variable on Ordinal Scale

Some characteristics can neither be measured nor counted, but can be either ordered or ranked according to their magnitude. Such variables are called ranked variables. Here the units are assigned an order or rank. For example, a child in a family is referred by its birth order such as first, second, third or fourth child. Similarly,it may be possible to categorize the income of people into three categories as low income, middle income and high income. The only requirement is that the order is maintained throughout the study.

Thus based on these there are three different scales and there are three types of data namely nominal (categorical), ordinal (ordered) and measurement (interval or ratio).

FREQUENCY DISTRIBUTION

Once the data collection is over, the raw data appear very huge and it is not possible to infer any information. Therefore, it is important to reduce the data by formulating a frequency distribution. It could be done either by classification and tabulation or by plotting the values on a graph sheet. These procedures reduce a huge amount of data into a mind capturing data. When the variables are arranged on an interval scale and the number of items (frequency) against each class, then the resulting distribution of that particular variable is called frequency distribution (Table 1.1.).

Table 1. 1 Freqency distribution

Marks	Number of students
10 – 20	5
20 – 30	10
30 – 40	20
40 – 50	30
50 – 60	50
60 – 70	30
70 – 80	20
80 – 90	10
90 – 100	5

Properties of Frequency Distribution

Alternatively, when the variable is plotted in X-axis and the number of observations against each class-interval in the Y-axis, then the resulting graph is known as histogram, and when the mid-points of the class intervals are connected in the form of a smooth curve, the resulting curve is a frequency curve (Figure 1.1). From this histogram and frequency curve, we could study the nature of distribution. By looking at the tallest bar one can say which mark is repeated the maximum number of times or occurs most frequently in a data set. On either side of the class interval 50–60, the frequencies are distributed equally. The curve is also bell-shaped and symmetrical. Such as symmetrical curve is called a normal curve.

If we draw a vertical line through the centre, the distribution on either side of the vertical line should look the same. This curve implies that the majority of the scores lie around the centre of the distribution. As one moves away from the centre, the bars get smaller, implying that the marks start to deviate from the centre or the frequency is decreasing. As one moves still further away from the centre, the bars become very short. In an ideal world our data would be symmetrically distributed around the centre of all scores. But natural phenomena ar not always ideal.

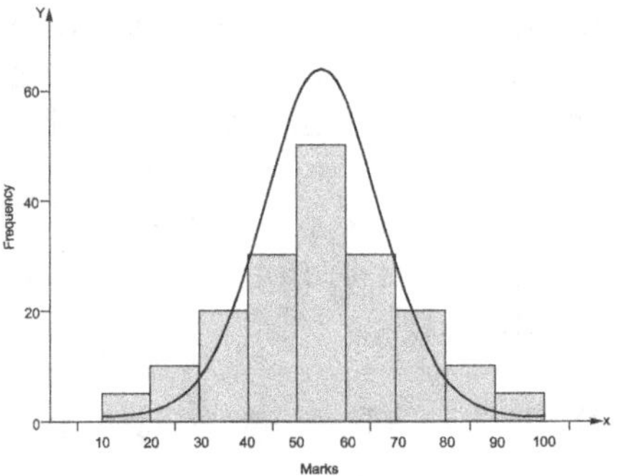

Figure 1.1 Histogram

Most frequently, in real life situations the frequency distributions deviate from an ideal world. As a law of nature, ideal world does not exist. Everywhere we always see deviations. There are two main ways in which a distribution can deviate from normal. In statistics we call these as skewness where there is lack of symmetry, and kurtosis which is the peakedness of the distribution.

Skewness Skewness implies asymmetry in a distribution. Skewed distributions are not symmetrical and the most frequent values are clustered at one end of the scale. So, the typical pattern is cluster of frequent values at one end of the scale and the frequency tailing off towards the other end of the scale. There are two kinds of skewed distribution:

i. *Positively skewed* In Figure 1.2, the number of students obtaining low marks is clustered at the lower end indicating that more number of students are getting low marks. The tail points towards higher marks.

ii. *Negatively skewed* In Figure 1.3, more number of students is clustered at the higher end indicating that there are more students getting high marks. In this graph the tail points towards the low marks indicating that there are only a few stuents getting low marks.

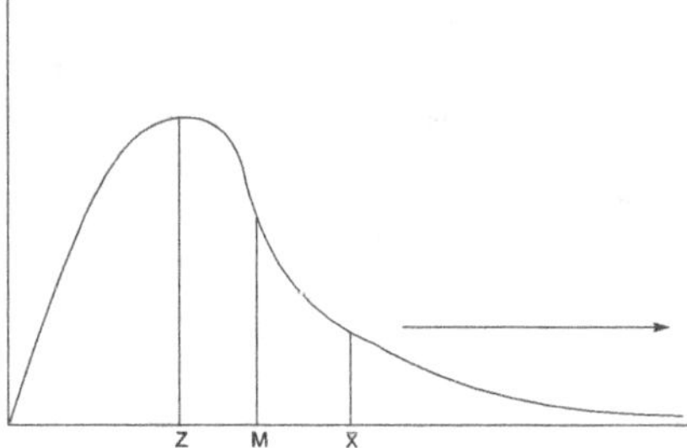

Figure 1.2 Positive skew (Elongated tail at the right, more items in the left)

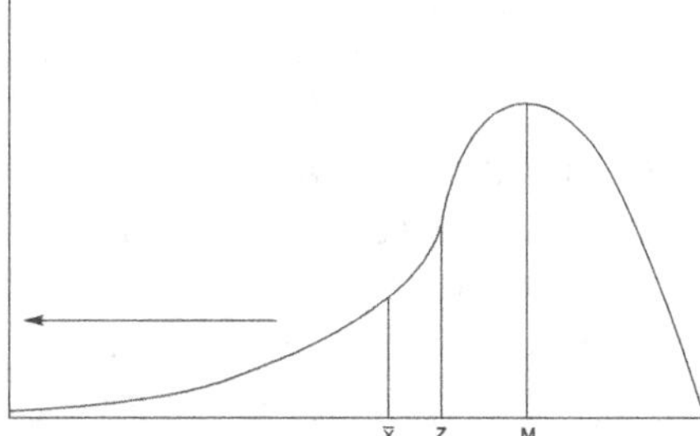

Figure 1.3 Negative skew (Elongated tail at the left, more items in the right)

Kurtosis Two or more distributions may be symmetrical and yet different from each other in the extent of concentration of items close to the peak. This characteristic is shown by how flat or peaked a distribution is. This aspect of the study is called kurtosis. A platykurtic distribution is the one that has many items in the tails and so the curve is quite flat. In contrast, leptokurtic distributions have relatively a fewer items towards the tail and have thin tails and so look quite pointed or peaked (Figure 1.4). To remember easily, "the leptokurtic distribution leaps up in air and the platykurtic distribution is like a plateau". Ideally, an investigator wants his data to be normally distributed, that is, not too much skewed or nt too much flat or peaked.

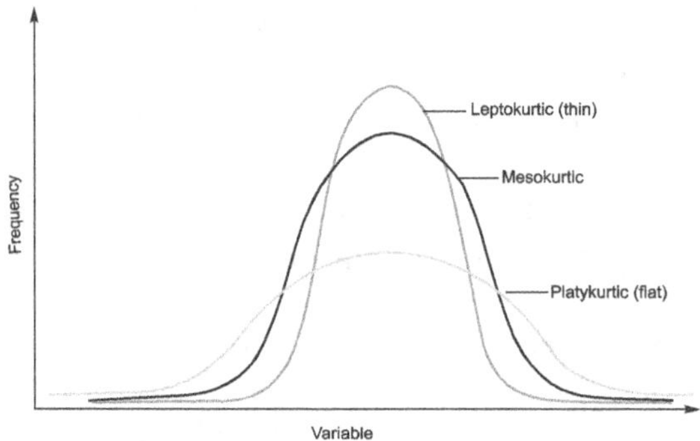

Figure 1.4 Frequency Distribution Curve

In a normal distribution the values of skewness and kurtosis are 0 and 3 respectively. If the distribution has values of skew or kurtosis above or below 0 then this indicates a deviation from normal. Thus skewness and kurtosis give an idea to the investigator whether the distribution is close to or deviate from the ideal condition.

Standard deviation and shape of the distribution In a distribution, if the mean represents the data well then most of the scores will cluster close to the mean and the resulting standard deviation will be small relative to the mean. When the mean is not a good representative of the data, then the values or items cluster more widely around the mean and the standard deviation is large. This distinction is a key point in inferential statistics. Since, lesser the standard deviation the more consistent is your data and the greater the standard deviation the less consistent is your data. When the standard deviation gets larger the sample mean may not be a good representative of the population.

NORMAL DISTRIBUTION

To understand and to make use of statistical tools to infer the salient features of data, it is essential for anyone to think of frequency distribution in terms of probability. In the previous example on marks obtained by the students, consider for example that someone is interested to find how likely is it that a boy getting a mark of 70. Based on the frequencies of different marks, the probability could be calculated. A probability value can range from 0 to 1.

For any distribution it is possible to calculate the probabilities of obtaining that event, but it is very tedious, statisticians have identified several common distributions after studying a large number of actual distributions. For each one they have worked out mathematical formulae that specify the idealized version of the distributions. These idealized distributions are known as "Theoretical distributions" or "probability distributions". Like frequency distribution, the probability distributions could be either continuous or discrete. The discrete distributions are binomial and Poisson. The continuous distribution is the normal distribution. To understand the basic concept of standard normal distribution it is important to learn the properties of normal curve and the transformation of normal distribution into standard normal distribution.

Properties of Normal Curve

i.   The normal curve is unimodal, perfectly bell-shaped and symmetrical. The tails of the curve are asymptotic, that is, the curve gets closer and closer to the X-axis but they never touch it. The two tails of the distribution extend indefinitely and never touch the horizontal axis.

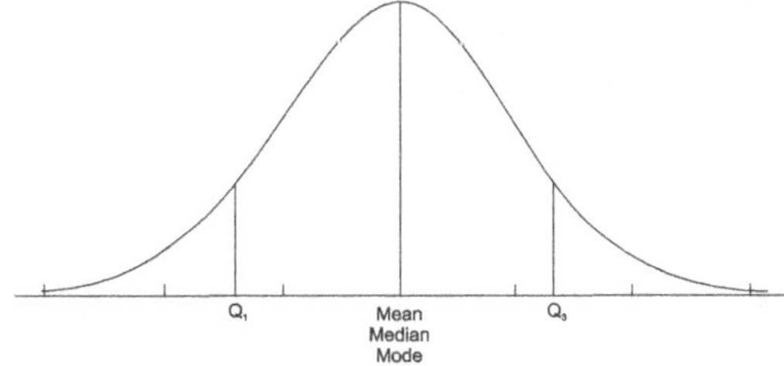

Figure 1.5   Normal curve—symmetrical around mean

ii.   The mean (average) lies at the centre of the distribution and the distribution is symmetrical round the mean (Figure 1.5).

iii.   Mean, median and mode coincide or mean = median = mode.

iv.   The quartiles are equidistant from the mean.

v.   Coefficient of skewness $\beta_1 = 0$.

vi.   Coefficient of kurtosis $\beta_2 = 3$.

vii.   The total area under the normal curve is equal to the total probability, that is 1.

viii.   The ordinate drawn through the mean divides the total area under the curve into two equal parts. The area under the curve is unity and therefore 0.5 to the right and 0.5 to th left of the mean (Figure 1.6).

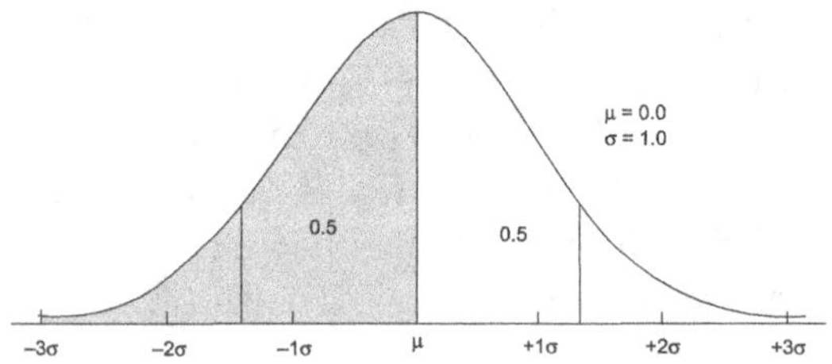

Figure 1.6 Normal curve—total area under curve is = 1

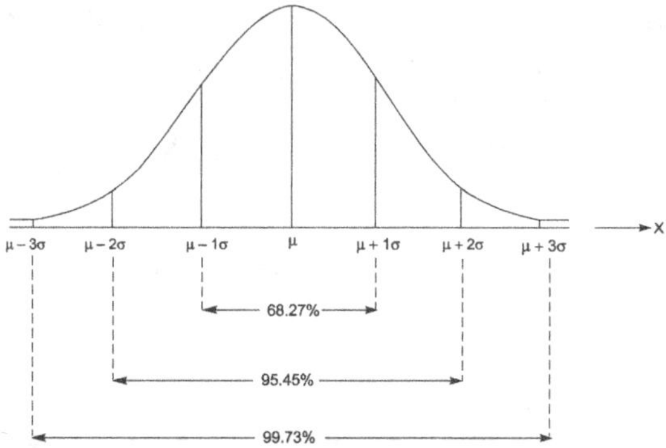

Figure 1.7 Normal curve—area under the curve in relation to μ and σ

ix. About 68.27% of the items lie between the values of $\mu - 1\sigma$ and $\mu + 1\sigma$. About 95.45% of the items lie between the values of $\mu - 2\sigma$ and $\mu + 2\sigma$. About 99.73% of the items lie between the values of $\mu - 3\sigma$ and $\mu + 3\sigma$ (Figure 1. 7).

Standard Normal Distribution

The probability of the normal distribution as given above is difficult to work with. In determining areas under the curve, for a given set of data. Therefore, each set of X values (means and standard deviations) are translated to a new axis, a Z-axis. These values are called as Z-score. Z-score is the value of an observation expressed in standard deviation units. It is calculated by taking the observations and subtracting from it the mean and dividing the result by the standard deviation. By converting a distribution into Z-score, one can create a new distribution that has a mean of 0 and a standard deviation of 1.

$$Z = \frac{X - \mu}{\sigma}$$

It is called the standard normal variate. The resulting curve is called standard normal curve.

The standard normal curve The standard normal curve is a member of the family of normal curves with $\mu = 0.0$ and $\sigma = 1.0$. The value of 0. 0 was selected because the normal curve is symmetrical around μ and the number system is symmetrical around 0. 0. The value of 1. 0 for σ is simply a unit value. The X-axis on a standard normal curve is often relabelled and called *Z*-scores.

There are three areas on a standard normal curve that all introductory statistics students should know. The first is that the total area below 0.0 is 0.50, as the standard normal curve is symmetrical like all normal curves. This result generalizes to all normal curves in that the total area below the value of μ is 0. 50 on any member of thefamily of normal curves (Figure 1.8).

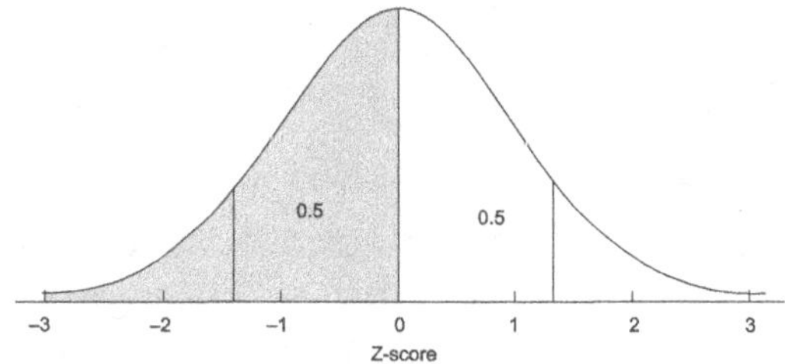

Figure 1.8 Standard normal curve—the area below 0.0 is 0.5

The second area is between *Z*-scores of −1.00 and 1.00. It is 0. 68 or 68% (Figure 1.9).

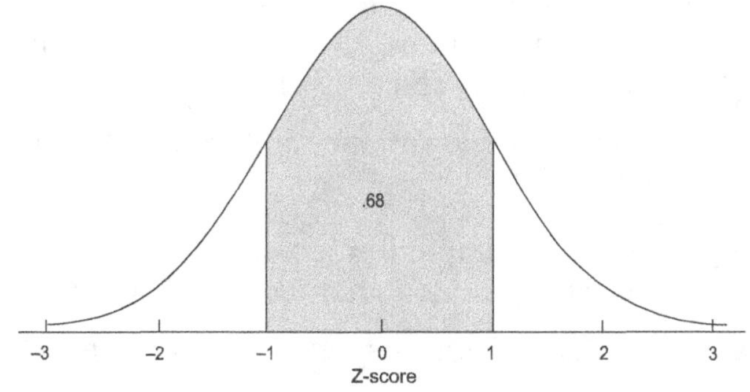

Figure 1.9 Standard normal curve—the area between +1 and −1 is 0. 68

The total area between plus and minus one Z-score on any member of the family of normal curves is also 0.68.

The third area is between Z-scores of −2.00 and +200 and is 0.95 or 95% (Figure 1.10).

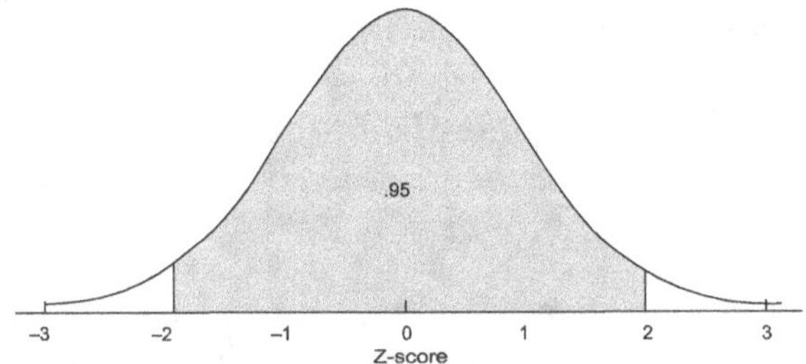

Figure 1.10 Standard normal curve—the area between –2. 00 and 2. 00 is 0. 95

The fourth area is between Z-scores of –3.00 and +3.00 and is 0.9973 or 99.73%.

STATISTICS AND PARAMETERS

Values of means and standard deviations obtained from the samples are called statistics. In other words, sample attributes are called statistics. For example, if we say sample mean, it is a sample statistic. On the other hand, the values of mean and standard deviation of the population are called parameters. Thus in statistical inference, we draw samples from the population, derive sample statistics and use these sample statistics as the basis for estimating unknown population parameters. In other words, unknown population attributes are derived from the characteristics of the samples drawn from that population.

Generally statisticians use Greek letters to designate population parameters and Roman letters to designate statistics. Thus, μ(mu) is population mean σ (sigma) is the standard deviation and σ^2 is the variance. The sample mean is given the symbol $\overline{X}$ and the sample variance and standard deviation are written as S^2 and S respectively.

Since the population is too large or impossible to measure directly, we can assume that we do not know μ and σ^2, but it is possible for us to estimate the same on the basis of our samples statistics $\overline{X}$ and S^2. Then $\overline{X}$ and S^2 are the estimators of population parameters. Then the sample mean $\overline{X}$, is called an unbiased estimate of population mean μ. This is so because, if we draw an infinite number of samples of a certain number N from the populations, with replacement, the mean of these sample means would be equal to μ. On the other hand, the mean of all S^2 of an infinite number of samples would not equal σ. Infact it would be smaller than σ^2. For this reason, the sample variance S^2 is called a biased estimate of σ^2.

It is important to understand biased nature of S. For example, if a sample of 50 males were drawn randomly from the population, logically the degree of dispersion of different items around $\overline{X}$ would be greater than it would be from μ. In this case, the sample may not have extreme values (like a man $4'5''$ tall and another man $6'8''$ tall). Therefore, we are not likely to find the various extremes of the population adequately represented in the sample.

If we want to use S^2 as an unbiased estimate of σ^2 it is apparent to do something to make S as an unbiased estimate of σ. The formula to calculate variance is

$$S^2 = \frac{\Sigma d^2}{N}$$

The value of S would be increased if 1 is taken away from N in the denominator. Further, it is important to recall that sum of the deviations from the true mean of a distribution will always be equal to "0", but sum of the deviations from some number other than the mean will not equal to "0". If the sample size is smaller, then the denominator should be $N-1$. On the other hand, it is not that important for a large sample, for example, if the denominator is 500, changing this from 500 to 499 will hardly make any difference.

If we want to use statistics derived from a sample as estimates of population parameters, S^2 should be calculated as

$$S^2 = \frac{\Sigma d^2}{N-1}$$

The square root of S^2 will yield σ which is more reliable.

SAMPLING DISTRIBUTION

Suppose we collect samples from a population and compute the mean of every sample drawn. This would yield a distribution of sample means which would take the form of a normal distribution of sample means. In this case, most of the sample means, $\overline{X}$ would tend to cluster around μ, the mean of the population from which the samples were drawn. This is one of most basic and important principles in statistics. The distribution of sample mean is called a sampling distribution and it is of critical importance to inferential statistics. The sampling distribution is a purely hypothetical concept. The mean of the sample means would be equal to μ. Therefore, the mean of a sampling distribution and the mean of the population from which the samples were drawn are one and the same. Thus, μ may refer to either mean of a population or its sampling distribution. The second important characteristic of any distribution is the variance or standard deviation.

Let us suppose that a person is interested in finding out the average of how much of money is spent by a student staying in a hostel in every month. Of course he cannot collect information relating to expenditure from all students staying in the hostel throughout the country; rather he could select a few hostels as samples. For each of these he can calculate the average expenditure or sample mean. Let us consider that he has taken nine different samples. There will be nine different means for nine different samples and a population mean (obtained by adding all values and dividing by the total of all samples). In this case, some of the samples have the same mean as the population but some have different means. There are three samples that have a mean of 3000, two samples with means of 2000 and 4000 each and one sample each have means of 1000 and 5000. If we plot mean values of all nine samples as a frequency distribution or histogram, it will result in a symmetrical distribution known as sampling distribution. A sampling distribution is simply the frequency distribution of sample means from the same population. For practicality and simplification, nine samples are cited as examples. Theoretically we can have as large as hundreds and thousands. The sampling distribution thus tells us about the behaviour of samples from population. The average of the sample means is the same value as the population mean.

Sampling Distribution of Mean

To have clarity in understanding, recollect the relationship between mean and standard deviation of a sample. The small standard deviation tells us that most of the data points are close to the mean, a large standard deviation represents, a situation in which data points are widely spread from the mean. Similarly, if we want to a calculate the standard deviation between sample means then this would give us a measure of how much variability occurs between the means of different samples. The standard deviation of sample means is known as the standard error of the mean (*SE*). The standard error could be calculated by taking the difference between each sample mean from overall mean (population mean), squaring these differences, adding them and then dividing by the number of samples.

Since, in reality we cannot collect hundreds and thousands of samples, we rely on approximation of standard error done by statisticians. The standard error is calculated by dividing the sample standard deviation by the square root of the sample size *N*.

$$SE = \frac{S}{\sqrt{N}}$$

SE—Standard error of sampling distribution of means
S—Standard deviation of means from population mean
N—Number of items in the sample

In this, standard error is simply a standard deviation of sample mean of a sampling distribution instead of a distribution of individual measurements. The sampling distribution concept is useful in understanding inferential statistics and decision making or hypothesis testing.

To sum up, the standard error is the standard deviation of sample means. If the value of standard error is large then there is a lot of variability between the means of different samples and therefore the samples we have may not be the representative of the population. If the value of standard error is small, then the sample means are similar to population mean and the samples would be the true representative of the population.

The accuracy of sample mean as an estimate of the population means is assessed by calculating boundaries within which the true value of the mean lies. Such boundaries are called confidence intervals. The basic idea behind confidence interval is to construct a range of values within which we think the population values fall. The confidence intervals are limits constructed such that at a certain percentage of the time the true value of the population mean will fall within these limits. In most of the statistical analysis we say at 95% confidence interval or 99%. When we say 95% confidence interval, the explanation goes like this: if we had collected 100 samples, calculated the mean and then calculated a confidence interval for that mean, then for 95 of these samples, the confidence intervals would contain the true value of the mean in the population.

To calculate the confidence interval, we need to know the limits within which 95% of means will fall. Therefore, the confidence interval can easily be calculated once the standard deviation (S in the equations below) and mean ($\overline{X}$) in the equation) are known. However, we use the standard error and not the standard deviation because we are interested in the variability of sample means, not the variability in observations within the sample as stated above.

The lower boundary of the confidence interval is, therefore, the mean minus 1. 96 times the standard error, and the upper boundary is the mean plus 1. 96 $\overline{X}$ times the standard error.

Lower boundary of confidence interval = $\overline{X} - (1. 96 \times SE)$.

Upper boundary of confidence interval = $\overline{X} + (1. 96 \times SE)$

The mean is always in the centre of the confidence interval. Therefore, if the confidence interval is small, the sample mean must be very close to the true mean. Conversely, if the confidence interval is very wide then the sample mean could be very different from the true mean, indicating that it is a bad representative of the population.

When the confidence limit is set as 68% ($\mu \pm 1SE$ covers $\overline{X}$ 68% observations), then μ would range between ± 1 standard erro. If $\overline{X}$ – sample mean $= 50$, SE – Standard error of mean $= 0.50$, then

$$\mu = \overline{X} \pm SE \times (1) = 50 \pm 0.50 \,(1) = 49.50 \pm 0.50$$

i. e. , the μ will lie between 49.50 and 50.50.

If the confidence limit is changed to 95%, the total area under the limits is 95% or 47.50% on each side of μ. An area of 47.50% is equivalent to a standard score of 1.96 time SE. Therefore, at 95% confidence,

$$\mu = \overline{X} \pm SE \times (1.96) = 50 \pm 0.50 \,(1.96) = 50 \pm 0.98$$

The μ will lie between 49.02 to 50.98. This new confidence interval is larger than before.

Since SE is equal to S divided by square root N, it can be seen that as N increases, SE decreases. A look at the estimation formula reveals that as SE decreases, the confidence interval also decreases. Decrease in confidence limit increases precision.

It is therefore apparent that there are two ways to increase the precision of an estimate. First, we can use a lower confidence limit, and second, we can increase the sample size. Precision, therefore, depends only on the sample size and confidence limits used; accuracy depends on proper sampling as well as the care and skill used in performing experiments from which data are derived. The confidence limit can be lowered to 99% to have higher precision and the interpretation is similar as explained above for 95% confidence limit.

HYPOTHESIS TESTING

The difference between the sample statistic and population parameter, should be a statistically significant difference. What is meant by a statistical difference?Differences may be due to "error" that occurs naturally. "Error" does not refer to "mistake". No two random samples from a population will be "identical".

Some differences are bound to occur. For example, if we take 10 random samples from a population, the arithmetic means of these samples will not be the same. The differences among them are due to "random error". Random error is also called as "sampling error" contributed mainly by chance, due to the fact of studying a small sample to represent a population. This is not due to error in the procedure or computation. This random error is not accounted for "real differences". Therefore, it is important to distinguish differences due to "chance" and "real differences". There are a number of real life situations where we want to make statements regarding the real differences.

In biology, scientists are often required to make decisions or judgements. The physiologists may be interested in finding out the effectiveness of some drug on blood pressure or heart attack. The taxonomists may wish to know whether certain morphological differences between populations are large enough to suggest speciation. In all these situations the differences should be large enough to make decisions. Mostly, it is necessary to make these judgements based on the samples drawn from the population. When we draw samples from the population, the different measures like mean, standard deviation etc. of the samples differ from each other and they also "differ" from such measures of the population. Under such situations, an investigator proposes a hypothesis and tests the hypothesis.

Null and Alternate Hypothesis

A hypothesis is a statement made by the investigator on the problem under investigation. There are two kinds of hypothesis:

   i.   Null hypothesis and
  ii.   Alternative hypothesis.

***Null hypothesis* (H_0)** A null hypothesis is a statement of "no difference". The H_0 states that there is no significant difference between sample mean and population mean, or between means of two populations, or between means of more thantwo populations, that may be represented as follows.

$$H_0 : \overline{X} = \mu \text{ or } H_0 : \overline{X} - \mu = 0$$

$$\text{or } H_0 : \mu_1 = \mu_2 = \mu_3 = \mu_4$$

***Alternate hypothesis* (H_A)** Any statement (hypothesis) which is complementary to null hypothesis is called as an alternative hypothesis. This states that the sample mean and population mean are not equal or in other words there is significant difference between sample mean and population mean.

$$H_A : \overline{X} \neq \mu$$

In other words the mean of three or more different populations are not equal, that is.

$$H_A : \mu_1 \neq \mu_2 \neq \mu_3 \neq \mu_4$$

Though we could propose a hypothesis in either null form or in an alternative form, it is always customary to propose in null form, since the null hypothesis could either be accepted or rejected without much difficulty and ambiguity. After proposing a null hypothesis, the confidence level with which an investigator accepts or rejects the same is set up.

Percentiles and Confidence Interval

Any distribution could be described in terms of percentiles. 10th percentile is the value in a distribution below which 10% of the values lie. 90th percentile is the value below which 90% of the values lie. So, 50th percentile is the median in a distribution. If we say 97.5th percentile, then it is the value below which 97.5% of the values lie but it is also the value above which 2.5% of value lies. 2.5th percentile is the value below which 2. 5% of the values lies. Therefore, if we want to find how, 5% of the values in a distribution are distributed on either side of the tail then these values lie below 2.5th percentile and above 97. 5 percentile. To make it clear 5% of the values lie on either side of the tail in a distribution.

In any scientific study, a small fixed probability known as a significance level is decided before the data is collected. Conventionally the significance level is set as 0.05 (or) 0.01. If the significance level has been set at 0.05, the critical region will be above 97.5th percentile; in the upper tail and, below the 2.5th percentile in the lower tail. If the value of the test statistics falls within the critical (tail) region, the result is said to be significant, then the null hypothesis is rejected and alternate hypothesis is accepted.

A statistical test is said to be significant if the *p*-value is less than the significance level. This also means that the value of test statistics falls within the critical region. Therefore, *p*-value of a test statistics is the probability of obtaining a value in the tail of the distribution (as extreme values not covered under 95 %).

Levels of Significance

In the formal hypothesis testing procedure, an experimenter decides, prior to performing the test, the maximum probability of a difference (between two groups taken) by chance alone. The experimenter should preset the maximum probability that he will reject a null hypothesis. The maximum probabilities, or level of significance, have been arbitrarily established as 0.05 and 0. 01. These two values are conventional levels of significance. Therefore, when an experimenter says that the level of significance is 0.05 or 5%, it implies that in 5 out of 100 is likely to reject a true null hypothesis. In other words, he is 95% confident that his decision to reject a null hypothesis is correct.

Two-Tailed Test and One-Tailed Test

In any hypothesis testing, we have to answer the questions, "Is there a significant difference between the observed statistic (e. g. $\bar{X}$) and the population parameter (μ)?" or Is the observed statistics greater or lesser than population parameter? The first question does not specify the direction of the test. We are not interested whether the statistic is greater or lesser than the parameter; all that we want to know is whether the sample statistic is different from the population parameter. In such instances the level of significance (0.05 or 0.01) is equally distributed in the two-tails of the sampling distribution as 0.025 and 0.025 for 0.05 level of significance and 0.005 and 0.005 for 0.01. In the second question, when we say the observed statistic (e. g. $\bar{X}$) is significantly lesser than the population parameter (μ), then the level of significance 0.05 is on one tail.

Two-tailed test   A two-tailed test means that the level of significance 0.05, is equally distributed on both the sides of the tail. 0.025 is in each tail of the distribution of test statistic. When using a two-tailed test, hypothesise is tested for the possibility of the relationship in both directions. For example, we may wish to compare the mean of a sample to a given valueusing a t-test. Our null hypothesis is that the sample mean is equal to μ. A two-tailed test will test if the mean is significantly greater than μ and also if the mean is significantly less than μ. The mean is considered significantly different from μ if the test statistic is in the top 2.5% or bottom 2.5% o its probability distribution, resulting in a p-value less than 0.05 (Figure 1.11).

One-tailed test   If we are interested in finding out whether the observed statistic is greater or lesser than the parameter, the test we apply is a one-tailed test, meaning that the level of significance (0.05 or 0.01) is restricted to only one of the two tails of the sampling distribution. If the question is about "greater than" the level of significance is in the tail on the right side (Figure 1.12) of the sampling distribution and if it is about "lesser than" , then the level of significance is in the tail on the left side (Figure 1.13) of sampling distribution. A one-tailed test will test either the mean is significantly greater than X or the mean is significantly less than X, but not both. The one-tailed test provides more power to detect an effect in one direction by not testing the effect in the other direction. So, when is a one-tailed test appropriate? If one considers the consequences of missing an effect in the untested direction and conclude that they are negligible, then one can proceed with a one-tailed test.

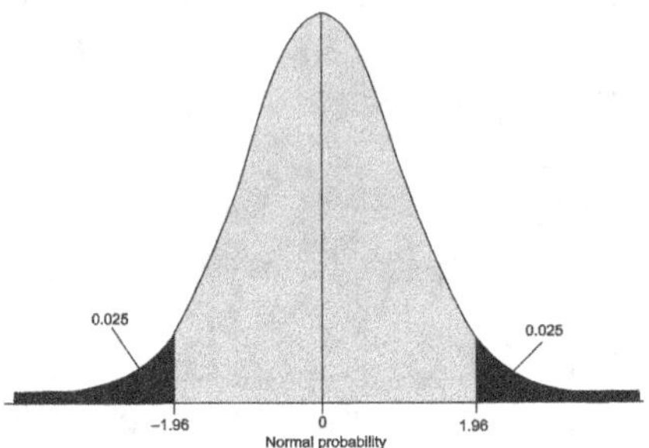

Figure 1.11   Two-tailed test—0.05 level of significance is distributed on both tails

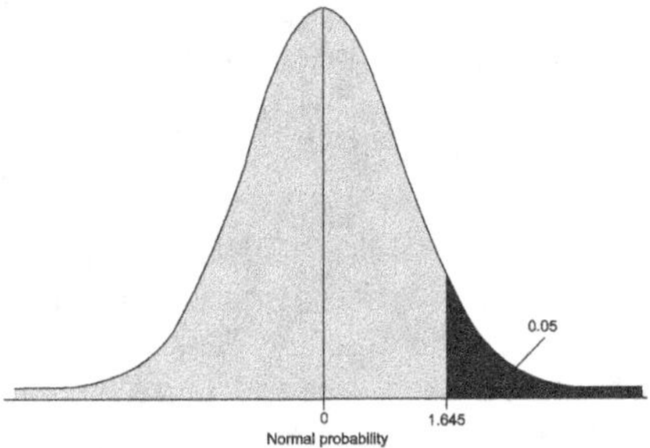

Figure 1.12   One-tailed test—level of significance in the right tail

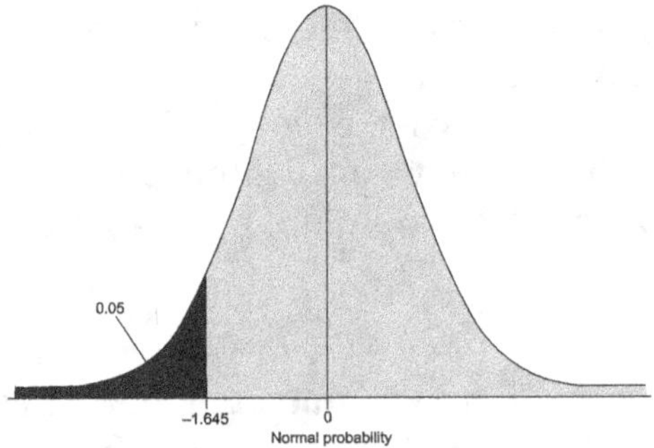

Figure 1.13   One-tailed test—level of significance in the left tail

Type I and Type II Errors

The logic of selecting 0.05 or 0.01 as the level of significance is to keep the probability of rejecting a H_0 reasonably at low level. If H_0 is true it should not be rejected. Suppose we made a decision to reject it. Then, we have committed an error called Type I error. The probability of committing such an error is specified by the level of significance. If we set a high level of significance such as 0.1 or 0.2, we might be rejecting many H_0 that should not have been rejected. That is the reason why fairly low levels of significance are selected. Suppose we select a level of significance much lower than the conventional levels, such as 0.005 or 0.001, then we will be failing to reject H_0 many of which hould have been rejected because they were false.

Table 1. 2 Type I and Type II errors

Null Hypothesis	Reject	Fail to reject
True	Type I error (α)	
False		Type II error (β)

When we fail to reject a false null hypothesis and accept it when it should be rejected, we have committed an error called Type II error. The area in the sampling distribution that lies between the levels of significance in the tails represents the probability of Type II error. Whenever we reduce the levels of significane, the probability of Type II error increases. That is the reason why we should not set unreasonably very low level of significance. A practical approach to decrease the probability of Type II error is to increase the size of the sample so that the standard error of the sampling distribution would become lower and consequently the area representing the probability of Type II error becomes smaller while the Type I error probability area remains the same.

p-values

When we compare the calculated probability (p) (area in the tail) with thelevel of significance, if it is less than 0.05 ($p < 0.05$) or less than 0.01 ($p < 0.01$), we reject the H_0. Then there is significant difference between sample statistics and population parameter. If the calculated p is equal to or greater than 0.05 ($p \geq 0.05$) or ($p \geq 0.01$), we fail to reject (accept) the H_0. Then there is no significant difference between the two. Thus we have only two options regarding our decision about the null hypothesis, either reject it or fail to reject it. A statistical test is said to be significant if the p-value is less than the significance level (0.05 or 0.01).

2

SPSS DATA FILE

OPENING A DATA FILE IN SPSS

There are several ways of opening a data file in SPSS. One way is by clicking the SPSS icon. An introductory window will appear with the title **SPSS statistics 17.0** (Figure 2.1). Read and click the radio button labelled **Type in data** and then click **OK**.

Now the **Data Editor** appears with the **Variable View** under display. At the foot of the Data Editor, **Data View** appears along with **Variable View**. There is also a status bar showing the line, **SPSS Processor is ready**. One should check this while working. Data is typed directly in the SPSS data file created already in the **Data Editor**. Data can also be imported from Excel and STATISTICA. In the SPSS data set, each row represents only one case and each column represents a variable or a character of the case measured. Before entering data in the Data Editor, it is essential to understand the terms used in data editor.

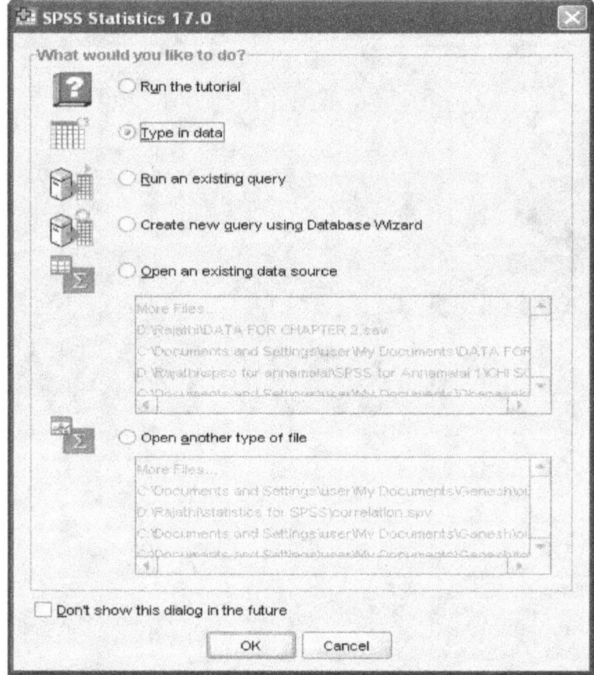

Figure 2.1   Opening a data file in SPSS

SPSS DATA EDITOR

SPSS data editor has two spreadsheets like an array. One is the **Data View**, inwhich new data is entered and the other is the **Variable View** that contains the names and details of the variables of the data (Figure 2.2)

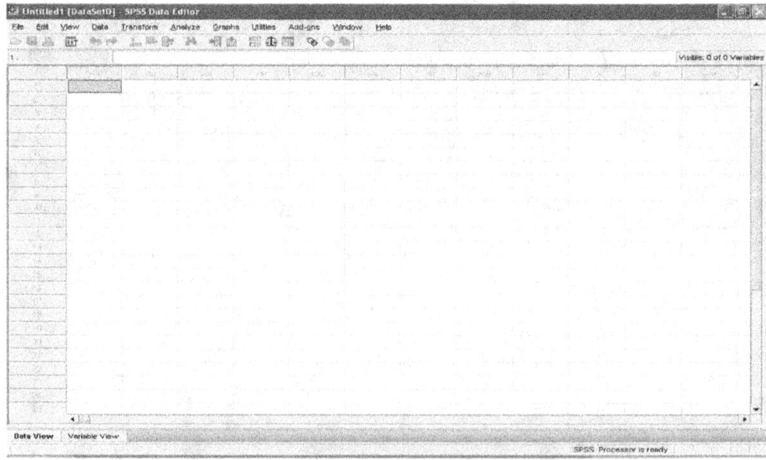

Figure 2. 2   SPSS data editor

Variable View

To get the Variable View click **Variable View** at the left hand bottom of the window. Now the data sheet appears with the title **Variable View** as in Figure 2.3.

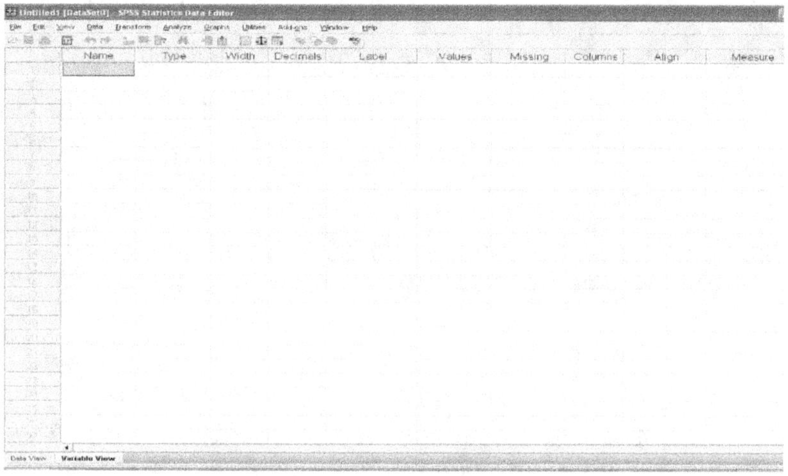

Figure 2.3 Variable View

This Variable View data sheet has 10 columns namely:

1. **Name**   It is a string character (normally, letters and spaces, and sometimes digits). It appears at the head of a column in Data View but not in the output. It is a shortened view that appears only within the data view. It should be a continuous sequence with no space. Though 64 letters can be entered it is desirable to keep it short. It can be a mixture of cases.

2. **Type**   It accepts eight different types of variables. Two important ones are the numeric, i. e. , numeral with decimal point and string, names of participants, cites or any non-numeric characters.

3. **Width**   It is the width of the variable. The default setting for the width of the variable is 8. But it can be changed by choosing **Edit**, clicking options and then selecting **Data**.

4. **Decimals**   It is the number of decimals that will be displayed in the **Data View**. The default setting displays 2 decimals. If required it could be changed by clicking twice on the upward/downward arrow.

5. **Label**   Label is a meaningful phrase with spaces in between words. It describes the variable and also appears in the output. It is important to assign meaningful labels for the variables.

6. **Values**   This column is meant for grouping variables. It gives the keys to the meanings of code numbers. The value dialog box is opened by clicking the grey area. The value and value labels are given in the value dialog box.

7. **Missing value**   It specifies the missing values in a data set.

8. **Columns**   It denotes the width of all variables that appear in the Data View.

9. **Align**   This coloumn determines whether the data are left, right or centre aligned. The default is right alignment.

10. **Measure**   This tells about the type of measurement scale, whether the data are on the **ordinal** or **nominal** scale.

Data View

Data View of the **Data Editor** when accessed gives the variable names at the head of the columns which are labelled in the **Variable View**. The rest of the columns contain the default name **var**, indicating that these columns have not yet been labelled with specific variables(Figure 2.4).

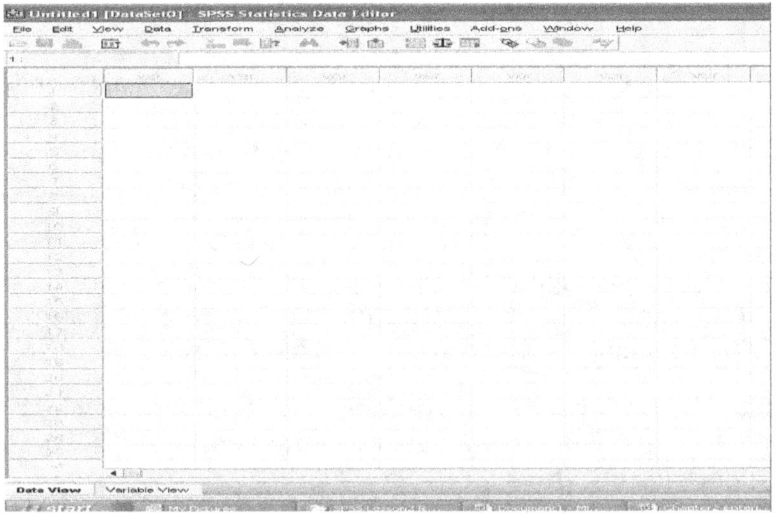

Figure 2.4   Data View

Entering Data into the Data Editor

Naming variables in Variable View   For naming of the variables and their properties, click **Variable View**. Naming of variables is left to the preference of the individual. But you should remember to use exactly the same variable names to a data set.

Naming numeric variables in Variable View

Step 1 Enter the name of the variable under the **Name** in the **Variable View**. For example, if you want to enter the height of the individuals in a class, type HEIGHT, under Name (Figure 2.5). (It should be remembered that it is a continuous sequence with no space in between characters. Whatever we type, it appears at the head of a column in Data View but not in the output).

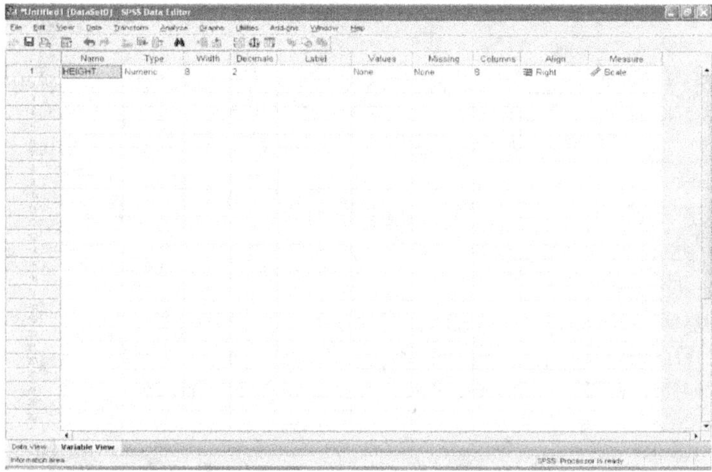

Figure 2.5   Naming numeric variable in Variable View

Step 2 Next go to **Type**, and right click anywhere in the cell of the **Type** column. A **Variable Type** dialog box opens (Figure 2.6).

Step 3 Retain the **Numeric** format (default type). Decide and enter the **Width** and **Decimal Places**. Since the variable is "**HEIGHT**" we shall select onl two decimals.

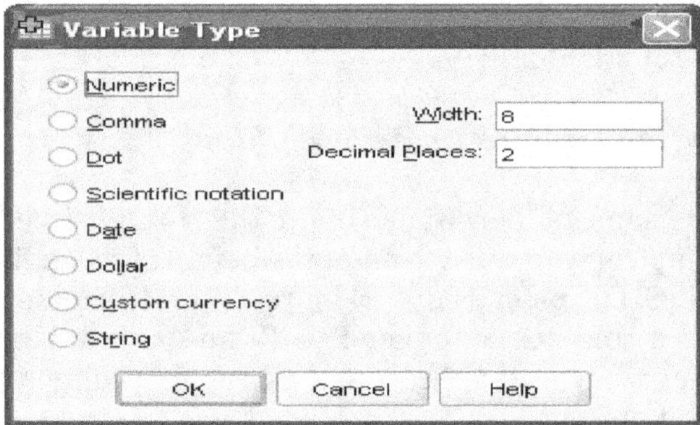

Figure 2.6   Selecting variable type and decimal places

Step 4 **Under the Label** column, describe the variable by a phrase or in a sentence. Take care to type correctly since this appears in the output. For example, we can type as "The height of the students in III B. Sc".

Step 5 Since height is a numerical variable we need to give the unit of expression.

Step 6 Next we can open **Data View** by clicking the same at the bottom. The **Data View** appears as given in Figure 2.7 with the variable label as "**HEIGHT**". Now we can start tping the data.

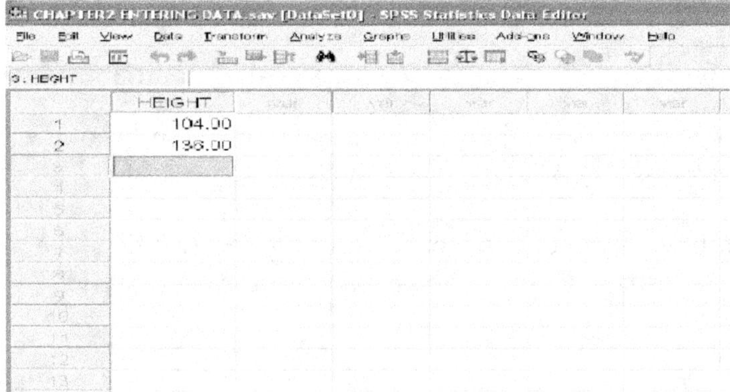

Figure 2.7   Entering data in Data View

Entering data for grouped or categorical variable and naming grouped or categorical variable in Variable View   If we are interested in finding out, for example, the significance of difference in blood pressure among age groups in a population, we can enter the variables as described in the following paragraph.

Measure the systolic pressure in mm mercury for different age groups and categorise the age (variable) into young, adult and old, before entering the data. Now, click on **Variable View** tab at the foot of the **Data Editor**. Enter the variable name as "age", then go to **Type** column, retain **Numeric format** (default type) and decide the **Width** and **Decimal Places**. Describe the variable under the Label column (as you want it to appear in the output. For example, the age in years of persons in Chennai). Go to **Values** column, click on the grey area, a pop up window oens (Figure 2. 8).

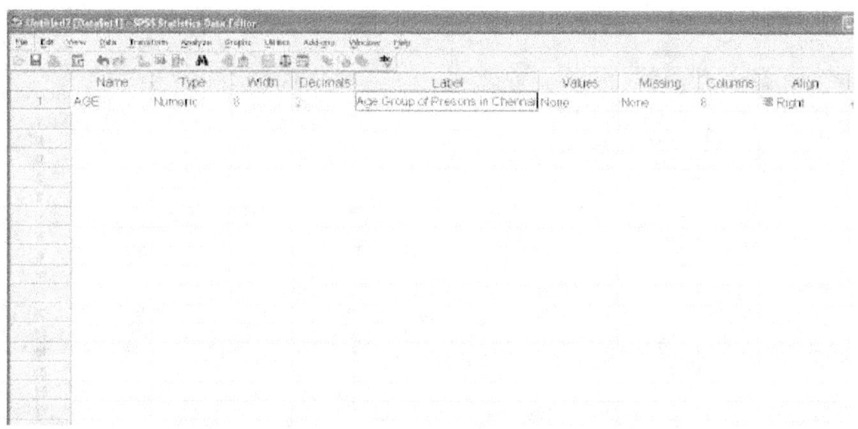

Figure 2.8   Naming categorical or grouping variable in variable view

You can give a code number in **Value** and a key to the code in **Label**. For example, type "**1**" in the **Value Box** and "young (age1–18), in the **Label** box" similarly "label "2" as adult (age19–50) and "3" "as "old (age 51 and above)" (Figure 2.9).

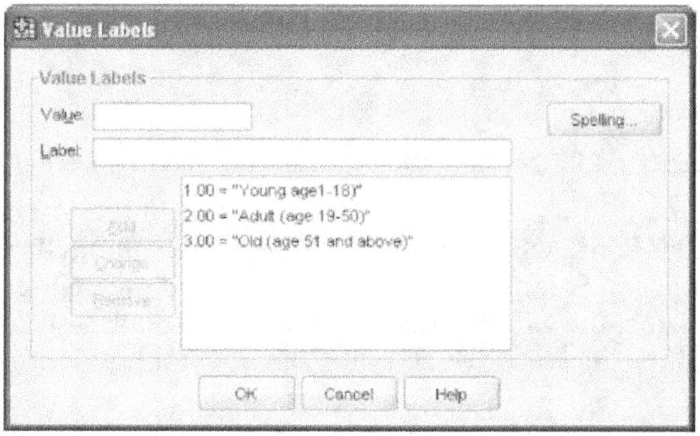

Figure 2.9   Naming categorical or grouping variable in Value labels dialog box

Then type the second variable as "Blood Pressure" under Name and complete the rest. Then click OK to return to Data View. Type the data under specific heads (Figure 2. 10).

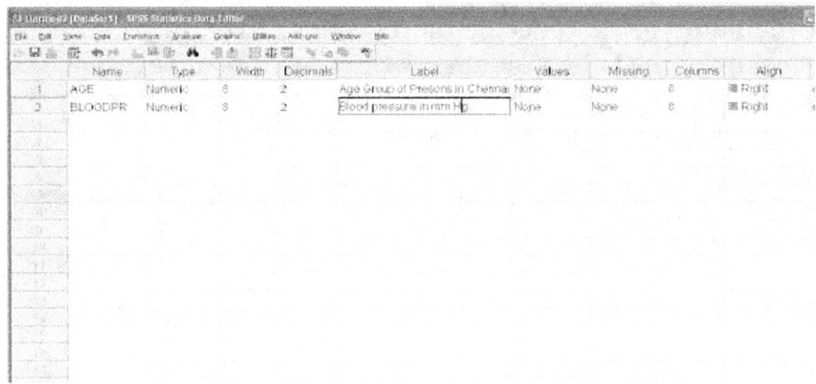

Figure 2.10   Variables named in Variable view with details for two variables

Naming qualitative variables in Variable View   If you want to type blood group of students in a class, click on **Variable View**, type Bloodgp under **Name** (Figure 2.11).

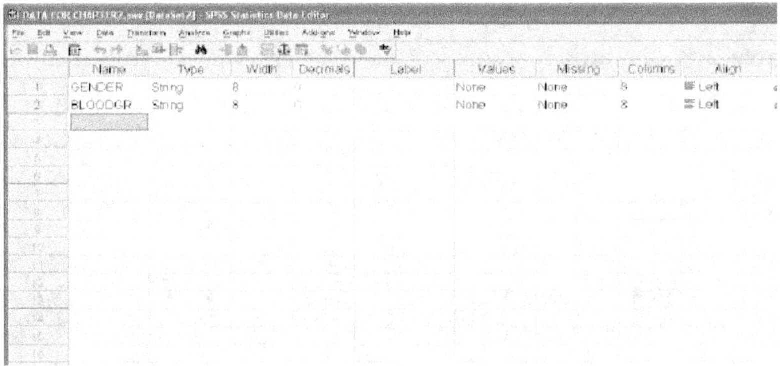

Figure 2.11   Naming Qualitative variable in Variable view

An attribute or a qualitative variable, is named in the **Variable View**. Go to **Type**, right click anywhere in the cell under the column **Type**, a **Variable dialog** box appears. Select **String** radio button and then click **OK** to return to variable view. Label the variable (as in the previous example). No need to name the **Values** column as you have chosen **String** varable (Figure 2.12).

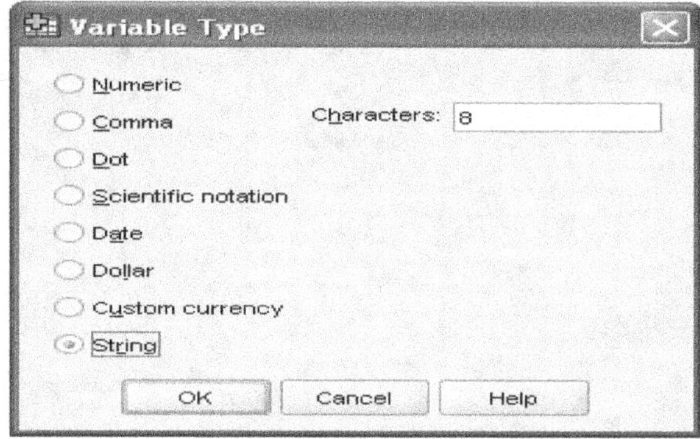

Figure 2.12 Selecting String from Variable Type dialog box (To type a qualitative variable in variable view)

Type the variables of any quality as in Figure 2.13.

Figure 2.13 Two qualitative variables named in Variable View

After specifying all the variables and their characteristics click **Data View** tab at the foot of Variable view to open the data file. Enter your data case by case.

Entering data in Data View   Once the specifications have been entered into **Variable View**, click the **Data View** tab at the bottom of the **Variable View**. When the Data View opens, the variable names will be seen at the colum heads (Figure 2.14).

	GENDER	BLOODGROUP	var	var	var	var
1	Male	A				
2	Male	B				
3	Male	A				
4	Male	B				
5	Male	O				
6	Male	AB				
7	Male	O				
8	Male	AB				
9	Male	B				
10	Male	A				
11	Male	A				
12	Female	B				
13	Female	O				
14	Female	AB				
15	Female	O				
16	Female	AB				
17	Female	B				

Figure 2.14   Data entered for two Qualitative variables in Data View

(***Note:*** Check at the bottom of the data view window, where a horizontal bar appears with the message: SPSS Processor is ready. This horizontal band is known as the Status Bar. It is named so because it reports on the stage that a procedure has reached in addition to whether SPSS is ready to begin).

The contents of the cell you are typing are also displayed in a white area known as the **Cell Editor** just above the column headings. The values in the cell can be changed by clicking in the cell editor, then by selecting the present value and replacing it with new value.

The new value will appear in the grid. It is either possible to highlight a cell or whole block of cells or entire row or the column. This will help you to copy the values from one column and paste them to another. Similarly entries can be removed by pressing delete keys.

Saving the Data File

Once the data entry is over and checked for accuracy, select **File** from the main menu, and click **Save as**. **Save as** dialog box opens. Decide a suitable destination for this file (like disc C or D). Always it is good to save the data in a folder created earlier with a name such as **SPSS 17.0 exercises**. Type the file name in the **File name** box and click **Save**. Close SPSS and any other open windows before logging off the computer. If you do not do this you need to give the file name when you terminate or close the SPSS.

STATISTICAL ANALYSIS

Let as consider an example of computing mean for categorical variable given in Figure 2.10.

Step 1 From the main menu select **Analyze**. From the drop down menu, choose compute means and thn **Means** (Figure 2.15).

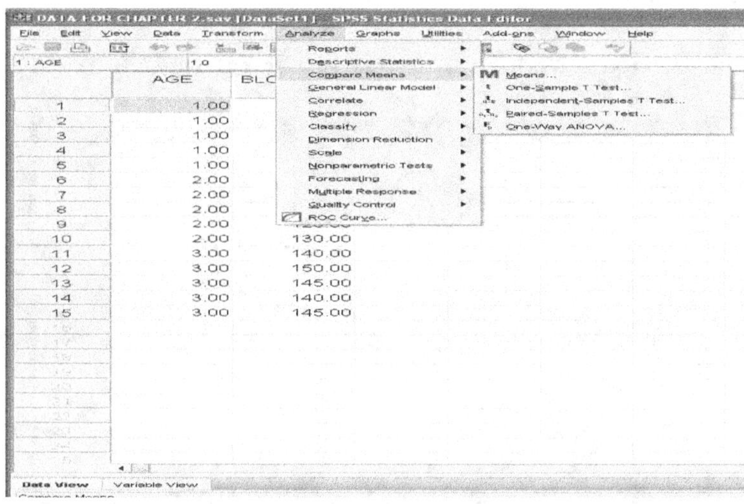

Figure 2.15　Selecting **Means** from main menu in **Data Editor**

Step 2 This opens the **Means** dialog box. In the left hand panel the variable names re seen (Figure 2.16).

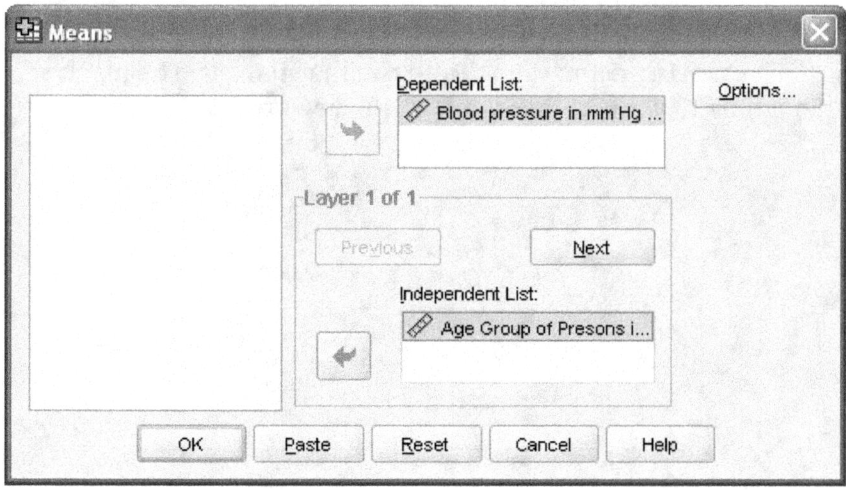

Figure 2.16　Selecting and transferring variable to dependent and independent list in **Means** Dialog box

Step 3 Click on the variable, "**Age group of person**", then on the arrow pointing to **Independent List text box** to transfer the variable to the appropriate box. Similarly, click on the variable, "Blood Pressure" then on the arrow pointing to **Dependent list text box** to transfer the variable.

Step 4 Click **Options** to open **Means: Options** dialog box (Figure 2.17).

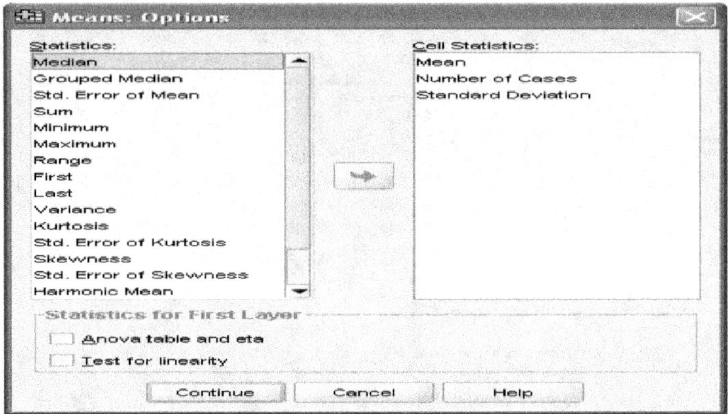

Figure 2.17   Selecting and transferring descriptives (like mean…) under **Statistics** to **Cell Statistics**

Step 5 Transfer **Mean**, **Number of Cases** and **Standard deviation** from left hand panel (**Statistics**) to the right hand panel (**Cell Statistics**).

Step 6 Click **Continue** and then **OK** to run the analysis. The result will appear in a new window called the Output Viewer (Figure 2.18).

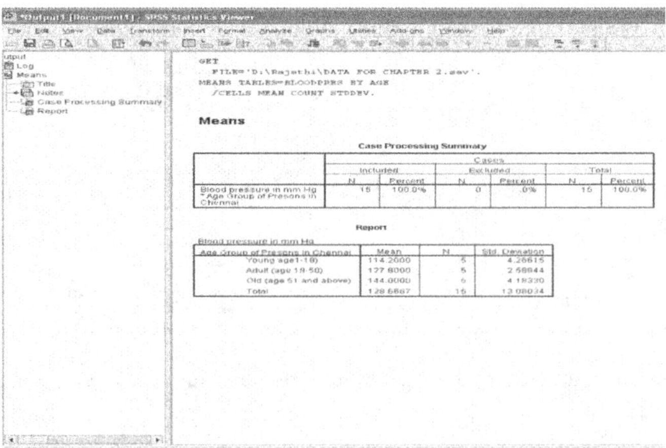

Figure 2. 18   SPSS output viewer showing the list of output items in the left pane and the output tables in the right pane

EDITING AND MANIPULATING DATA

After entering the data, it could be edited or manipulated like inserting new variables, rearranging the order of variables in **Variable View** or changing the type of variable.

Inserting a New Variable

An additional variable can be inserted in the **Variable View** by highlighting any row by clicking the grey cell on the left and choosing **Insert variable** (Figure 2.19).

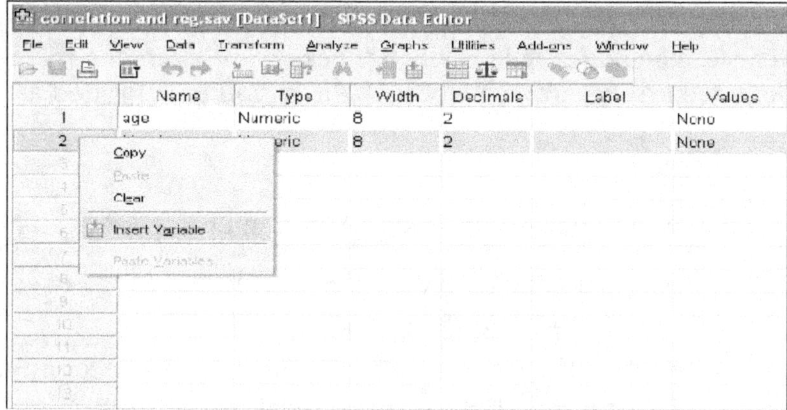

Figure 2.19   Inserting a new variable in **Variable View**

The new variable, with a default name "VAR00001" will appear above the row that has been highlighted (Figure 2.20).

Figure 2. 20   New variable inserted between the old ones

Now type the name of the **variable** in the **Variable View**.

Rearranging the Order of Variables in Variable View

As with inserting new variables, the sequence of the variables in the **Data View** can be changed. For this click the **Variable View** then click the grey box to the left of the score variable to highlight the whole row. By holding the left mouse button down, drag the screen pointer upward. A red line will appear above the group row. On releasing the mouse button, the variable score will appear immediately under case. In Data View, the variable score will now appear to the left of variable groups.

Deleting and Rearranging Items from the Viewer

Items are removed from the viewer by selecting them and pressing **Delete** button. Items can be rearranged easily by clicking and dragging them in the left hand pane, a red arrow showing where the item will be relocated as you drag.

Creating a Page Break

A page break between items that belong to different categories can be given.

Step 1   Click the item above which you want to create a page break

Step 2   Choose Insert and then click Page Break

Step 3   Return to the viewer and click outside the selection rectangle to cancel the selection. Check the pages in Print Preview.

Changing the Type of Variable

By default, the type of variable in the **Type column** is assumed to be numeric. To create a **string variable** you should proceed as follows

Step 1   After typing in the name of the variable, highlight the cell in the Type column. (*Refer* Steps 1–3 given in page 28).

Step 2   Click grey area with 3 dots to the right of **Numeric** to open the **Variable Type** dialog box.

Step 3   Click **String** radio button and the **Width** and **Decimal Places** box will immediately be replaced by a box labelled **Characters**.

Step 4   Change the default value 8 in the character box to some larger number such as 20 to accommodate the longest name. Do this by moving the cursor into the number box selecting 8 and then replacing it by typing 20.

Step 5   **Click OK**. Now the **Width column** will show 20. In the **Variable View**, the variable type String will appear under **Type** column.

Step 6 Click **Width column** and copy the specification either by choosing copy.

Step 7 Click on Column and paste the new **Width** specification (20) by choosing **Paste**. After this there will sufficient space in **Data View** to see the longest name in the data set.

MISSING VALUES

SPSS assumes that all data sets are complete. However, the user may not have entries for every case on every variable in the data set. Such missing entries are marked by SPSS with what is known as **system-missing value**, which is indicated in the **Data Editor** by a full stop. SPSS will exclude system-missing value from its calculations of means, standard deviations and other statistics.

In contrast to the above, sometimes the user might wish SPSS to treat certain responses actually present in the data set as missing data. This is called **user-missing value**. To define such user-missing values, perform the following steps:

Step 1 Go to **Variable View**, move the cursor to the **Missing** column and click on the appropriate cell of the variable concerned.

Step 2 Click the grey area with the ellipsis to the right of **None** to open **Missing Value** dialog box.

Step 3 There are three radio buttons. The **No missing values** radio button is marked default. For a quantitative variable, click the range plus one discrete missing value button. Enter the values 0 to 20 into the **Low** and **High** boxes respectively and 9 into **Discrete Value** box.

Step 4 Click **OK** and the values will appear in the **Missing** column cell.

EDITING SPSS OUTPUT

The SPSS output viewer window is divided into two panes by a vertical grey bar (Refer Figure 2. 18). **Left pane** shows hierarchical organisation of the contents. The right pane shows the results of statistical analysis. The contents of both sides can be edited, as it offers editing facilities.

Step 1 Right click on the table, a hatched border appears on the table and in the menu select **Edit Contents** and then select. **In a Separate Window** (Figure 2. 21), in which the categorical variable appears in rows and descriptives in columns.

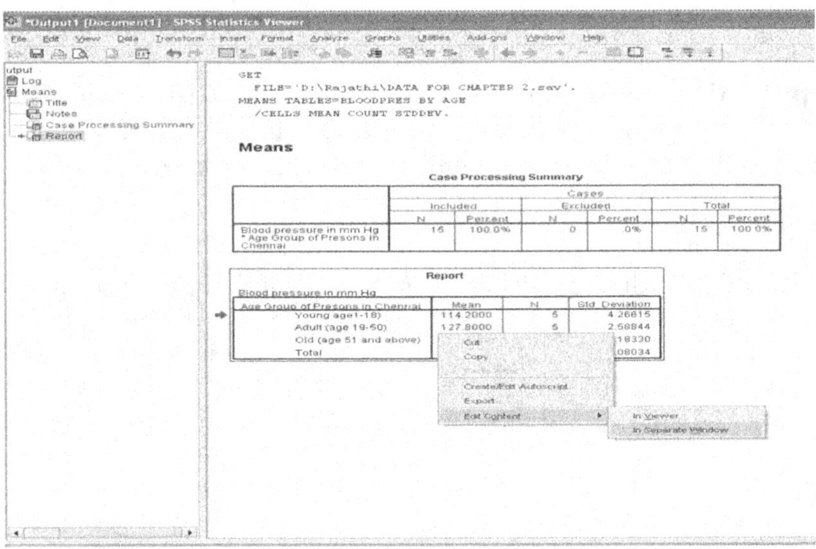

Figure 2.21 Selecting **Edit Contents** options in SPSS output

Step 2 **SPSS Pivot Table Report** appears on top. You can edit as you do in **Word**. If you want descriptive statistics in **rows**, then click on **Pivot** and then select **Transpose Rows and Columns** (Figure 2. 22).

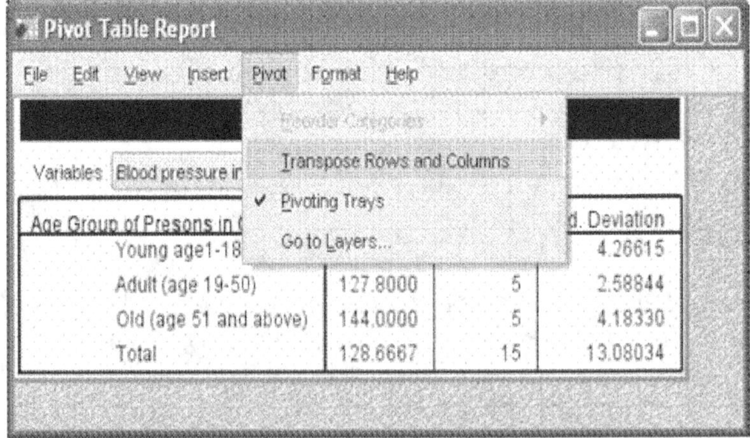

Figure 2. 22 Selecting Transpose Rows and Columns in **Pivot Table Report**

Step 3 Now the categorical variable is copied in column and the descriptves in rows (Figure 2. 23).

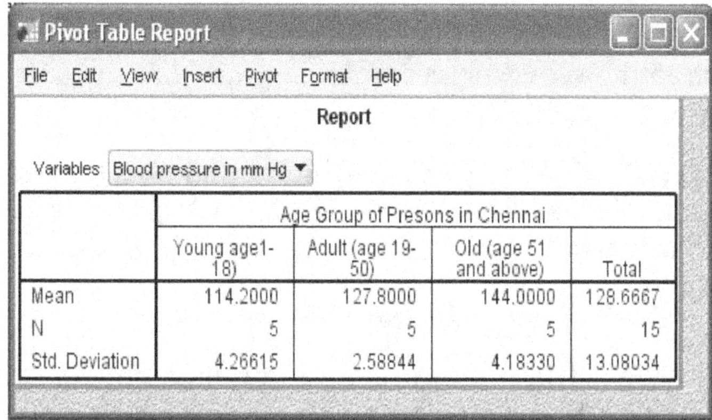

| | Age Group of Presons in Chennai | | | |
	Young age1-18)	Adult (age 19-50)	Old (age 51 and above)	Total
Mean	114.2000	127.8000	144.0000	128.6667
N	5	5	5	15
Std. Deviation	4.26615	2.58844	4.18330	13.08034

Figure 2.23   Changed row and column heads after editing in SPSS output

COPYING SPSS OUTPUT

The optimal procedure for copying items in the viewer differs slightly for tables and graphs.

Copying aTable

Step 1 If you intend to copy a table from the **output viewer in SPSS**, keep the cursor anywhere within the table and click on, now the table is boxed.

Step 2 Click copy in the **Edit** menu.

Step 3 Go to the **word** processor, select **Paste Special** from **Edit Menu** and then select **Picture** from the **Pop up window**,

or

if you wish to copy more than one table, then ensure that all the desired tables are boxed by holding down the **Ctrl key** while clicking on each table in turn and then copy.

Select **Paste special** in the **Edit** menu, select **Picture** and select **Paste Special** from the pop up window.

Copying a Graph

Step 1 Keep the cursor anywhere within the graph and click. Now the graph has a box around it. If more than one graph are to be copied, hold **Ctrl** key and click on each graph.

Step 2 Click **Copy** in the **Edit** menu.

Step 3 Switch to the **word** processor and ensure that the cursor is located at the insertion point.

Step 4 Click **Edit** and choose **Paste special** and select **Picture** (Enhanced Metafile). The item can then be centred, enlarged or reduced by clicking it so that it acquires a box around it with the usual tabs.

CHANGING FROM PORTRAIT TO LANDSCAPE

If your table is wide it will not fit in portrait orientation. For printing purpose landscape orientation that can accommodate wide tables is used. In order to change from portrait to landscape the following steps are followed.

Step 1 Click the Page setup button at the top of the Print preview dialog box. Look in the Orientation panel, the radio button is set in Portrait default. Change to Landscape.

Step 2 Click OK to return to the viewer.

Step 3 Access the viewer's Print dialog box by choosing File and then click Print. Note the Print Range selection in the lower left area of the box. Choose the desired option either All visible output or Selection and click OK. If you select the former, entire content of the viewer will be printed indiscriminately. In the latter case, you will get only the selected output.

PRINTING FROM SPSS

Both data and output can be printed in SPSS. There are differences between printing output from the **SPSS Viewer** and printing data from the Data Editor.

Printing the Output from the Viewer

SPSS output is very extensive and indiscriminate printing results in printing of irrelevant material also. Therefore, one should make full use of the viewer's editing facility to remove all irrelevant material. One can select the items and print. There are two ways of selecting items, by clicking the **items** icon in the **left pane** of the viewer, or by clicking the item itself in the right pane. Either way, a rectangle with a single continuous border will appear around the item. Then choose **Print Preview** to see the SPSS viewer (selected output) window, which will display only the items selected. Then return to print dialog box, see that **Selection** radio button in the **Print range** pane is activated and then Click **OK**. Only the selected item will be printed. To select more items, click the first and press the Ctrl key and click the other items you wish to select. Now choose **Print Preview** to see the selected items. Return to the **Print** dialog box and give the printing option.

CLOSING SPSS

SPSS is closed by choosing **Exit** from the **File** menu. If the data or output is not yet saved, a default dialog box will appear with the question. Save contents of Data Editor to Untitled? or Save contents or Output Viewer to Output1? Click **Yes**, **No** or **Cancel** button. You are given a final opportunity to save your contents. Select the output file needed and save. Otherwise they may be too large to be accommodated.

TUTORIALS IN SPSS

SPSS package has tutorials on various aspects of the system including the use of viewer and the manipulation of pivot tables. Tutorial could be accessed by choosing **Help** and selecting **Tutorial** and **double-clicking** to open the **Tutorial** menu. The button in the right hand bottom corner of each page of the tutorial enables the user to see the list of items (magnifier) and to navigate forward and backward through the tutorial (right and left arrows).

IMPORTING DATA

It is possible to import data into SPSS from other platforms like **Microsoft**, **Excel** and **SPSS** for **Macintosh**. It can also read fixed format files with variables recorded in the same column locations for each case. It is also possible to export SPSS data and output into other applications such as word processors and spread sheets.

Importing Excel Files

Following are the steps to import the Excel file stored in a folder:

Step 1 Click directory of files.

Step 2 Select the file type from the box named as **Files of types**: and highlight **Excel (*. xls)**.

Step 3 Click the appropriate file from the list of file names that appear in the panel in **File name**: box.

Step 4 Click open to get the **Opening File Options** dialog box. Select Read Variable Names box to transfer the excel variable names into the SPSS **Data Editor.**

Step 5   If an error message appears stating that SPSS cannot load an Excel worksheet, it may be necessary to return to Excel and re-save the file in the format of a different version of Excel, to copy and paste column of data directly into SPSS data view.

Step 6   **Click OK** to transfer the file into SPSS. **Variable view** will list the variable names and their types and **Data View** will show the transferred data and variable names. The **SPSS Viewer** will list the names, types and format of variable. The file can then be saved as a SPSS data file.

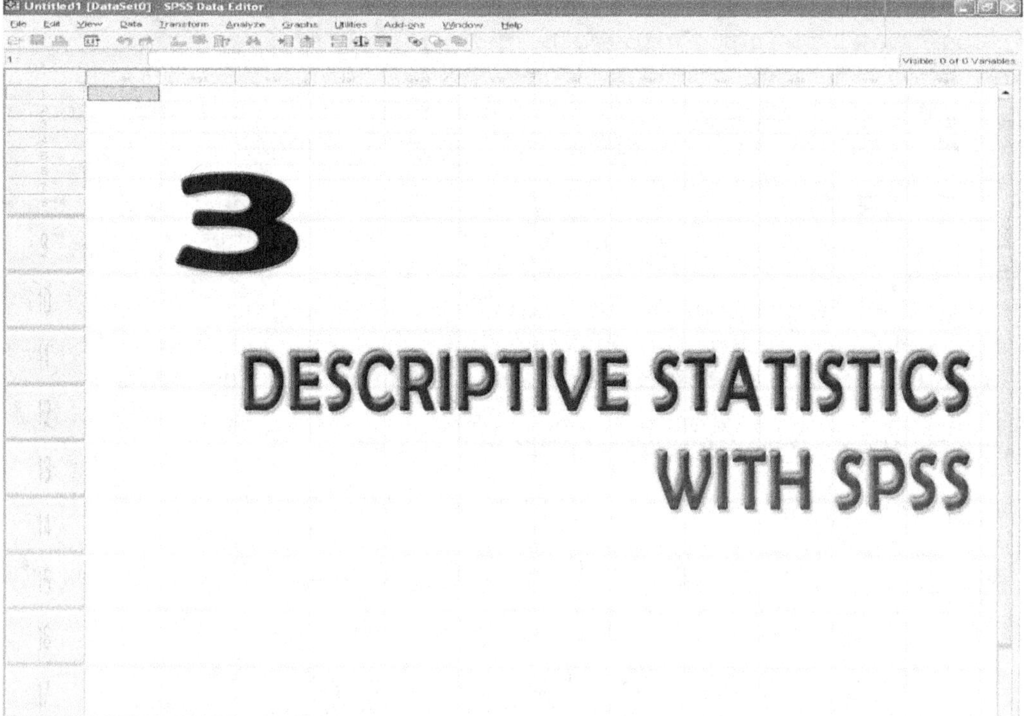

DESCRIPTIVE STATISTICS

The data collected by an investigator can be presented in the form of a table, diagram or graph. In addition, it is possible to describe the data based on numerical measures. When the statistical data is described in numerical measures it is called descriptive statistics. There are several measures to describe a data set. They are generally classified into two types: (i) measures of central tendency and (ii) measures of dispersion.

The measures of central tendency or, generally, averages, describe the central theme of the data and summarise the characteristics of an entire mass of data. Since these values locate a distribution at some value of the variable, they are sometimes, referred to as measures of location. The most common and useful measure of central tendency is the arithmetic mean. There are other measures, which have limited usage in different fields. These are median, mode, geometric mean, harmonic mean and weighted mean.

The measures of dispersion describe the extent of scatter of the values around a measure of central tendency, i. e. , how far or how near are the values to the average. Standard deviation is the most important and common measure of dispersion. The other measures of dispersion with limited usage are the range, quartile deviation and mean deviation.

In addition, there are certain other measures useful in describing the aspects of data which are not illustrated by the measures of central tendency and dispersion. These are measures of skewness and kurtosis. Skewness describes the nature of symmetry of a distribution and kurtosis describes the extent of concentration of values around the mean of a distribution.

A simple way to describe any data is to find out the measures of central tendency, dispersion, skewness and kurtosis. All these measures are collectively known as descriptive statistics. When the reader starts to use SPSS, he is supposed to have a sound knowledge on statistics. Anyhow a brief description on the theoretical aspects of mean, median, mode, standard deviation, skewness and kurtosis are presented to enable the reader to refresh before interpreting the results.

MEASURES OF CENTRAL TENDENCY

Arithmetic Mean

Mean is defined as the sum of all the items of a variable divided by the total number of items in the sample.

$$\text{Mean} = \frac{\text{Sum of all the items in a sample}}{\text{Total number items in the sample}}$$

The definition of mean is expressed in algebraic equation as

$$\bar{X} = \bar{X} = \frac{\sum x}{n}$$

where,

$\bar{X}$—arithmetic mean of the variable X

$\sum X$—sum of all the items of the variable X

n—total number of items in the sample

i—variates of X from 1 to n.

The above formula is used when individual values are given. But when the data is classified, a different formula is used based on whether the series is discrete or continuous.

Discrete series   In the case of discrete series, where the frequencies are given, the arithmetic mean can be calculated by applying the following formula

$$X = \frac{\Sigma f_i x_i}{\Sigma f_i}$$

where,

f —frequency

x—variable

i—variate of x taking the value of 1 to n.

Continuous series   In the case of continuous series, where the frequencies are given against class interval, the arithmetic mean can be calculated by applying the following formula

$$\overline{X} = \frac{\Sigma f_i x_i}{\Sigma f_i}$$

where,

f —frequency

m—mid point of the interval of the classes of the variable

$$\left(\text{Mid} - \text{point} = \frac{\text{lower limit} + \text{upper limit}}{2} \right)$$

Median

Median is defind as the middle value or item of a given data set arranged in ascending or descending order of magnitude. It divides the series into two equal parts, one part consisting of all the values greater than the median and the other part consisting of all the values less than the median value. It is considered as the positional average.

Individual series

$$M = \frac{N+1}{2} \text{ th item}$$

where,

N—total number of items

M—Median

Discrete series

$$M = \frac{N+1}{2} \text{ th item}$$

where,

N—total frequency

Continuous series

$$M = l + \frac{h}{f}\left(\frac{N}{2} - C\right)$$

where,

l— lower limit of the median class

h—magnitude of the median class

f—frequency of the median class

N—is the total frequency

C—cumulative frequency of the class preceding (before) the median class

Mode

Mode is the point of maximum concentration. It is the value in the data that is repeated maximum number of times. It is defined as the value of the variable which occurs most frequently in a sample.

Continuous series

$$Z = l + \frac{f - f_1}{2f - f_1 - f_2} \times C$$

where,

Z—mode

l—lower limit of the modal class

f—frequency of the modal class

f_1—frequency of the class preceding (before) the modal class

f_2—frequency of the class succeeding (after) the modal class

c—class interval

A frequency distribution can be unimodal. If only one number is repeated maximum number of times, then the sample has a single mode. If a sample has two modes, it is called bimodal. Multimodal or polymodal samples also occur.

MEASURES OF DISPERSION

The measures of central tendency describe one aspect of the data viz. its central position. However, this measure alone is not enough to describe the data fully. The difference between the value of an item from the mean (any measure of central tendency) is called deviation. An average of the deviations of the values of various items from a measure of central tendency is called a measure of dispersion.

Standard Deviation

Standard deviation is defined as the square root of the arithmetic mean of the squared deviations of the various items from arithmetic mean. In short, it is called the root-mean-square-deviation. The mean of square deviations is called the variance. Therefore, the square root of *variance* is the standard deviation.

$$\text{Standard Deviation, } \sigma = \sqrt{\frac{\Sigma d^2}{N}}$$

where,

X—variable

σ—standard deviation

$\overline{X}$—mean of the variable $X = \dfrac{X_i}{n}$

d_i—deviation $= X - \overline{X}$

d_i^2—squared deviation $= (X - \overline{X})^2$

Discrete series

$$\sigma = \sqrt{\frac{\Sigma fd^2}{N} - \frac{\left(\Sigma fd^2\right)}{N}}$$

where,

f—frequency

N—total

Skewness

Measures of central tendency and dispersion like mean and standard deviation (σ) respectively, describe two important aspects of the distribution of the data, the central value and extent of scatter of the values around this central value. However, these do not describe all the aspects of the distribution. For example, two distributions may have the same mean and σ and still be different. One of the two distributions may be a symmetrical distribution and the other may be asymmetrical. An asymmetrical distribution is said to be a skewed distribution i. e. , the distribution is skew. Skewness describes the extent of asymmetry in a distribution.

Positively skewed distribution A positively skewed distribution has the following properties:

    i.   More items on the right of the highest ordinate (a vertical line drawn from the X-axis to the curve), i. e. , the mode.

    ii.   Arithmetic mean > Median > Mode.

    iii.   The frequency curve has a steep rise and a slow fall with a long tail at the right.

Negatively skewed distribution A negatively skewed distribution has the following properties:

    i.   More items on the left of the highest ordinate.

    ii.   Arithmetic mean < Median < Mode.

    iii.   The frequency curve has a slow rise and deep fall with a long tail at the left.

Values equidistant from mode do not have equal frequencies. A numerical measure is developed to evaluate the skewness of a distribution. It is called the Karl Pearson's coefficient of skewness.

$$\text{Karl Pearson's coefficient of skewness} = \frac{(\text{Mean} - \text{Mode})}{\text{s}\tan\text{dard deviation}}$$

$$= -1 \text{ to } +1$$

When the mode is not well defined or when the distribution has more than one mode, then

$$\text{Karl Pearson's coefficient of skewness} = \frac{3(\text{Mean} - \text{Median})}{\text{s}\tan\text{dard deviation}}$$

$$= -3 \text{ to } +3$$

If the value is negative, the distribution is negatively skew and the frequency curve is negatively skewed with a long tail towards left. If positive, the distribution is positively skew and the frequency curve is positively skewed with a long tail towards right. If the value is 0, the distribution is symmetrical. Any value, + or –, between 0 and 1 or 0 and 3, reflects the extent of skewness.

Kurtosis

The flatness or peakedness of frequency curve is described by a measure called kurtosis. A frequency distribution that is normal gives a bell-shaped curve. It is called mesokurtic. A curve that is flat is called platykurtic. When the frequencies are more or less evenly distributed i.e. , the frequencies are less concentrated around the mean it gives a flat curve. When the items are concentrated more close to the mean values, i.e. , the frequencies are higher in the middle, it gives a peaked curve. A peaked curve is called leptokurtic.

The kurtosis of a random variable is the ratio of its fourth central moment μ_4 to the fourth power of its standard deviation (σ).

$$\text{Co-efficient of kurtosis } \beta_2 = \frac{\mu^4}{s^4}$$

If the coefficient of Kurtosis is 3, then the frequency curve is mesokurtic; if >3, then it is leptokurtic; if <3 then it is platykurtic.

DESCRIPTIVE STATISTICS WITH SPSS

Quantitative Data

Example 3. 1

Weight of babies (kg) below 6 months taken from a hospital record is given below. Calculate mean, median, mode, standard deviation and coefficient of skewness and kurtosis.

3.0	4.5	4.3	2.5	3.5	2.5	4.0	4.5	6.5	5.0
4.0	5.0	4.1	4.2	4.3	4.5	3.3	3.5	3.6	5.3
5.4	5.5	5.5	5.7	5.8	5.6	5.8	5.9	6.0	3.4
6.1	6.2	6.3	5.5	6.3	6.3	7.0	4.0	3.4	5.0

Step 1 Open the **SPSS Data Editor.**

Step 2 Click **Variable View** and name the variable as "babywt". Choose **Type** as Numeric. Let the default column **Width** remain as such, select "3" under **Decimals** and type "Weight of babies (kg) below six months" under **Label**. No need to give values under **Value** column as the data is numeric (Figure 3. 1).

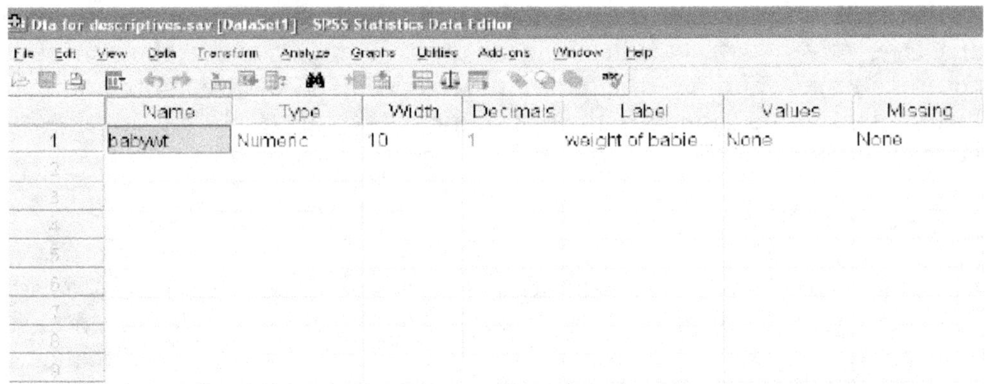

Figure 3.1   Naming the variable (babyweight) in **Variable View**

Step 3 Now click **Data View** and type the values under the first column where the name appears as given in Figure 3.2.

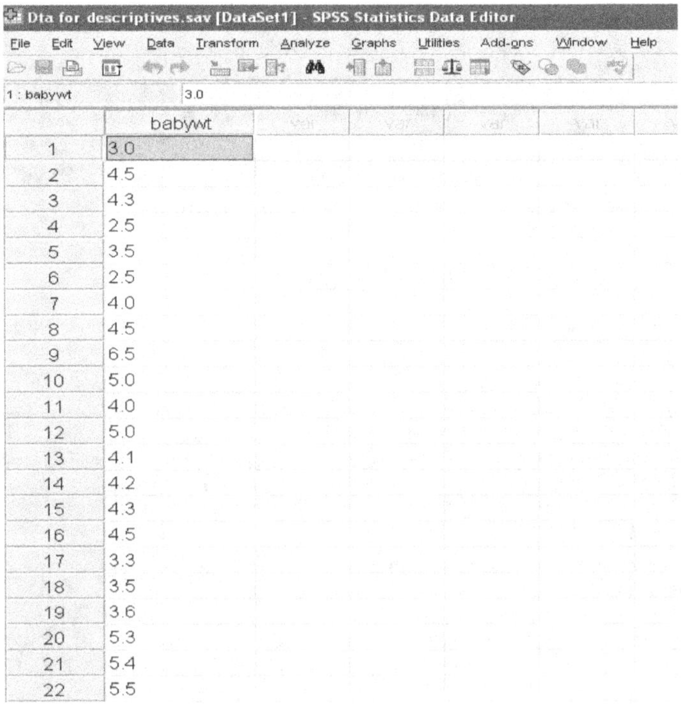

Figure 3.2   Entering data (weight) in **Data Editor**

Step 4 Choose **Analyze** from the main menu, click **Descriptive Statistics**, then select Frequencies. The drop down menu appears as given in Figure 3.3.

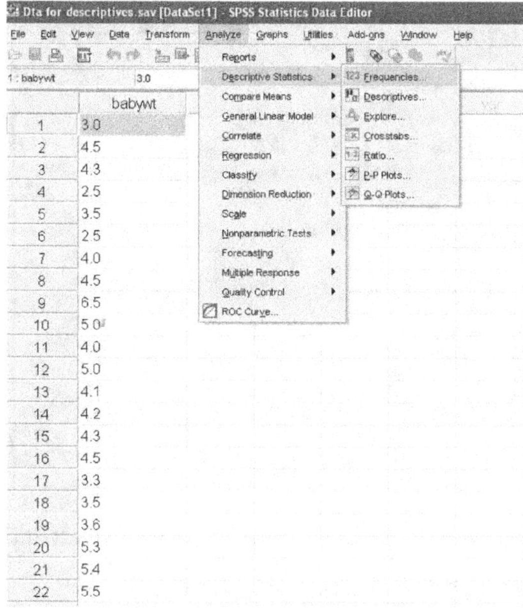

Figure 3.3   Selecting descriptive statistics from main menu

The Frequencies dialog box appears as given in Figure 3.4. Transfer the variable **Weight of babies (kg)** into the **Variable(s)**: box. Check the display **Weight of baby (kg)** under the Variable(s): box

Step 5 Click **OK** to continue.

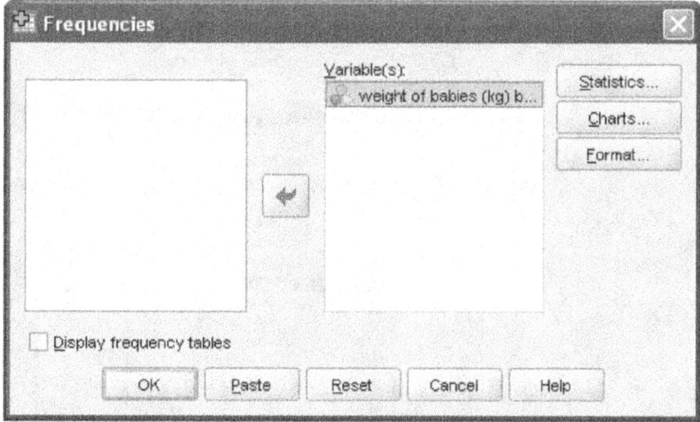

Figure 3.4   **Frequencies** dialog box with variable transferred

Step 6 Click Statistics to open **Frequencies**: **Statistics** dialog box and select mean, median and Mode under **Central Tendency**. Std. deviation and variance under **Dispersion**, Skewness and Kurtosis under **Distribution** (Figure 3.5).

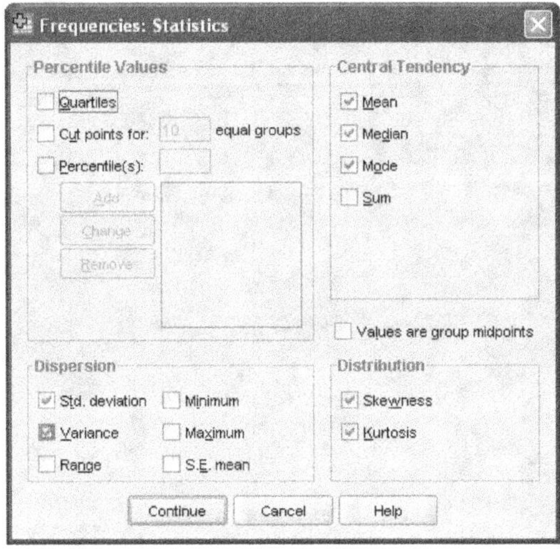

Figure 3.5   The **frequencies: Statistics** dialog box with selected descriptive statistics

Step 7 The statistical output appears in the screen as given below (Output 1).

Output 1

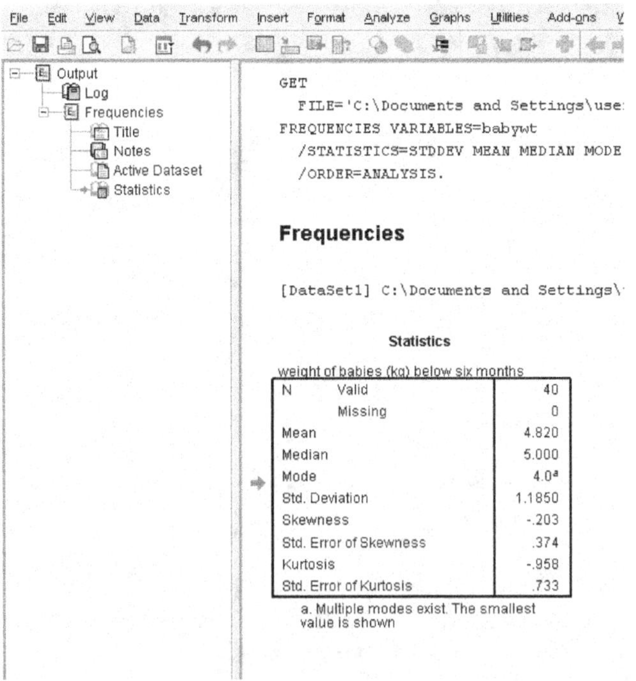

Note   You can use the same procedure both for descriptive as well as for charts. If you want to draw a histogram for the above data, go to the main menu, select **Descriptives** and then **Frequencies** to get the dialog box. Now click **Charts…** to open **Frequencies**: **Charts**. In the **Chart Type** box, click **Histogram** radio button and mark the normal curve by clicking it (Figure 3.6). Click **Continue** to return to the **Frequencies** dialog box. Click **OK** to run the analysis. The output appears as shown in Output 2.

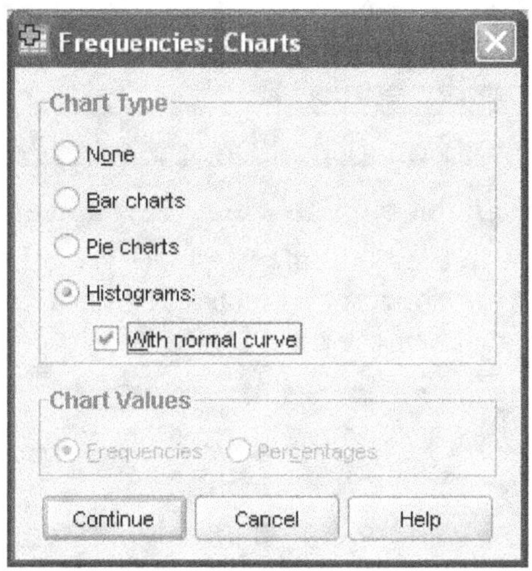

Figure 3.6   The **Frequencies: Charts** dialog box with histogram with normal curve selected

Output 2

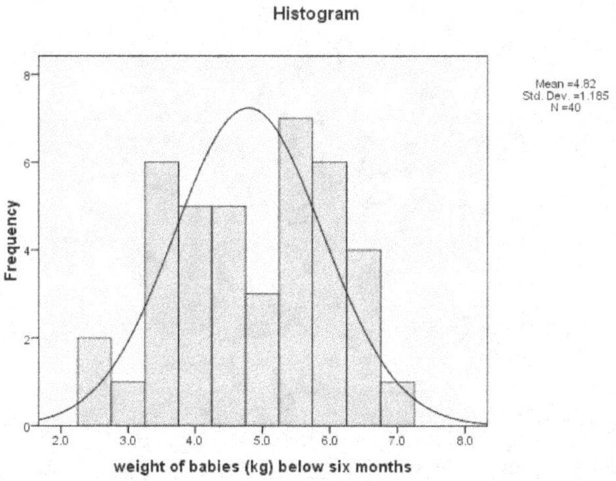

Histogram with normal curve

The procedure described above deals with raw data, sometimes there is a need to work with classified data, in such cases we need to follow a different procedure.

Example 3.2

The following table gives the number of working hours and the number of persons to complete a particular task. Calculate mean, median, mode, standard deviation, skewness and kurtosis.

Number of working hours	5	6	7	8	9	10	11
Number of persons		10	12	21	15	10	7	4

Step 1 Name the variables in **Variable View** and enter data in **Data View**.

Step 2 Click **Data** in the main menu, select **Weight Cases (Figure 3.7)** (This step is important for classified data, as it gives weightage for the frequencies of the class).

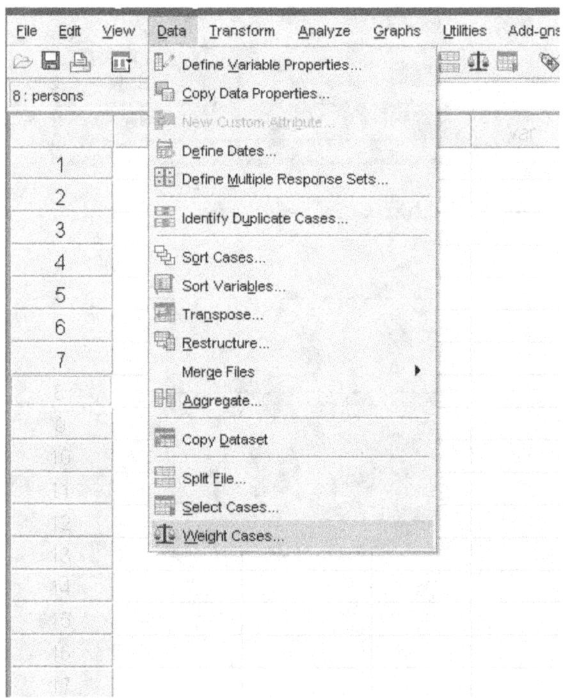

Figure 3.7   Selecting **Weight Cases** from main menu

Step 3 Select **Weight** cases by radio button under **Weight** cases.

Step 4 Transfer **Number of persons** (i.e., the frequency of the data) to

Frequency Variable, then click **OK** (Figure 3.8). Now the display disappears from the screen.

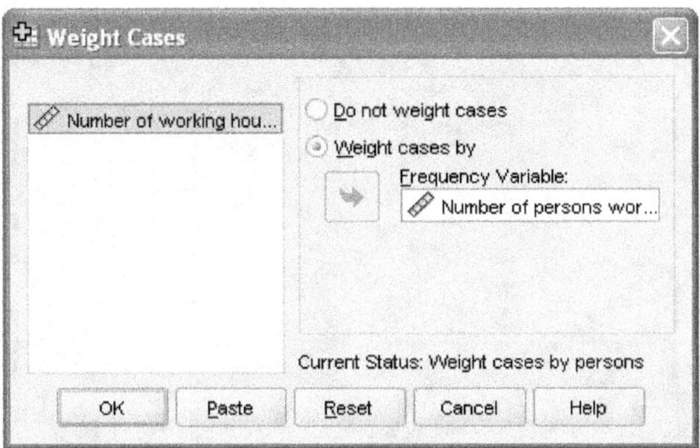

Figure 3.8 The **Weight cases** dialog box with number of persons transferred to **Frequency Variable**

Step 5 Choose **Analyze** from the main menu. Click **Descriptive Statistics** and select **Frequencies**.

Step 6 The **Frequencies** dialog box appears. Transfer the variable **Number of hours** into the **Variable(s):** box. Check the display **Number of hours** under the **Variable(s):** box (Figure 3. 9a).

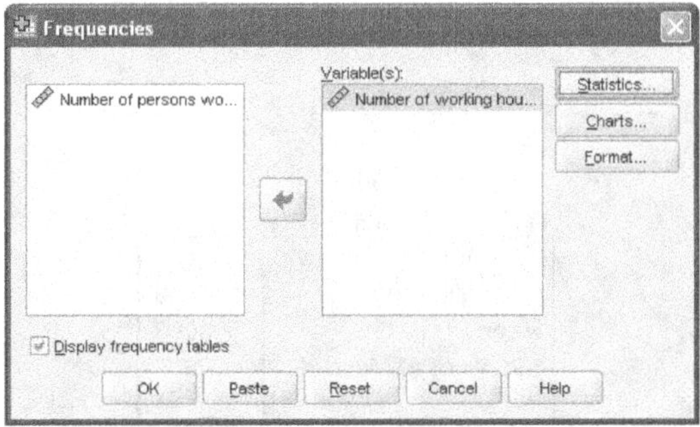

Figure 3.9a **Frequencies** dialog box with Number of working hours transferred to **Variable (s):** box

Step 7 Click Statistics to open **Frequencies: Statistics** dialog box and select mean, median and mode under **Central Tendency**. Standard deviation and SE mean under **Dispersion** Skewness and kurtosis under Distribution (Figure 3. 9b).

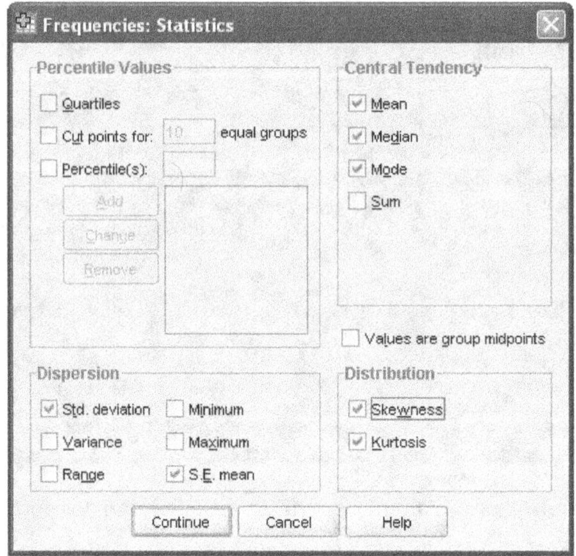

Figure 3.9b   **Frequencies: Statistics** dialog box with **Descriptives** selected under different heads

Step 8   Then click **Continue** and then click **OK** to run the analysis.

Step 9   The output appears with descriptive statistics like mean, median and mode, standard deviation and *SE* mean, skewness and kurtosis as shown in the output.

Output 3

Statistics

Number of working hours

N	Valid	79
	Missing	0
Mean		7.5063
Std. Error of Mean		.18625
Median		7.0000
Mode		7.00
Std. Deviation		1.65540
Skewness		0.33
Std. Error of Skewness		0.27
Kurtosis		-0.58
Std. Error of Kurtosis		0.53

Descriptive statistics table

Note   A similar procedure is adopted to workout problems in continuous series.

Nominal and Ordinal Data or Qualitative Data

The frequencies of the nominal or categorical variable are represented in rows and columns in the form of a table. This could be obtained by several ways. **Tables of frequencies** (from **Table** menu) and **Crosstabs** (from **Descriptive Statistics**) provide a two way contingency table. In addition **Crosstabs** from **Descriptive Statistics** also gives the frequencies with row and column totals (this procedure also provides statistics such as Chi-square and Correlation coefficient). **Frequencies** in **Descriptive Statistics** gives frequency distributions for both nominal and ordinal variables. It also provides percentages and cumulative frequencies. There are also options for selecting graphics like bar charts, pie charts and histogram.

Nominal data: formulating frequency table

Example 3. 3

Formulate a frequency table and draw a pie diagram for the following data on the blood group of 45 students in a class.

AB	B	O	A	O	O	A
O	B	AB	B	A	B	A
B	O	B	AB	A	O	O
A	O	AB	O	O	A	
A	B	A	A	AB	O	
A	A	O	A	O	A	
A	O	A	O	O	B	

Step 1 Name the variable as **bloodgp** and click on the cell named **Type** select **String**, label under the column **Label** as **Blood group of students in a class** (Figure 3.10).

	Name	Type	Width	Decimals	Label	Values	Missing	Columns	Align	Measure
1	Bbloodgp	String	8	0	Blood group of ...	None	None	8	Left	Nominal
2										
3										

Figure 3.10   Naming the variable blood group under **Variable View**

Step 2 Enter the blood group case by case in Data Editor as in Figure 3.11.

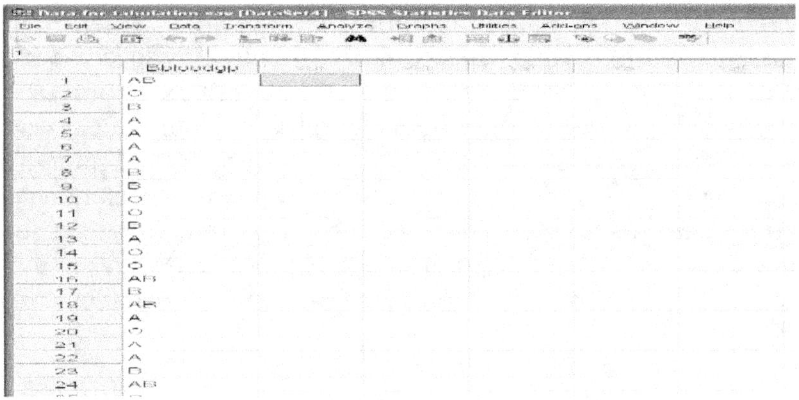

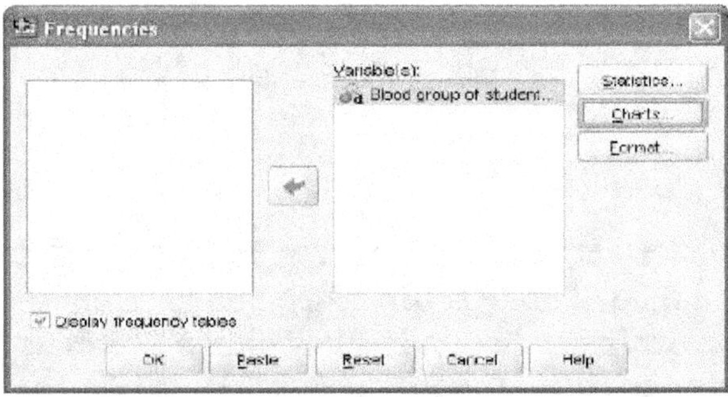

Figure 3.11   Data on blood group entered in **Data View**

The following steps offers both frequencies and charts.

Step 3 Choose Analyze from main menu, select **Descriptive Statistics** and then select **Frequencies** to open **Frequencies** dialog box (Figure 3. 12a) and transfer **blood group** to variable box. Click **Charts** to open **Frequencies**: **Charts dialog box** and select **Pie chart** option and click continue (Figure 3.12b).

Figure 3.12a   **Frequencies** dialog box with variable transferred

Step 4 Click **Charts** to obtain **Frequencies: Charts** dialog box and select **Chart(s)** radio button. There are also Chart Values options. If you want to have display of values on the chart, select **Frequencies** or **Percentages** under **Chart Values**.

Step 5 The output appears as shown below (Output 1).

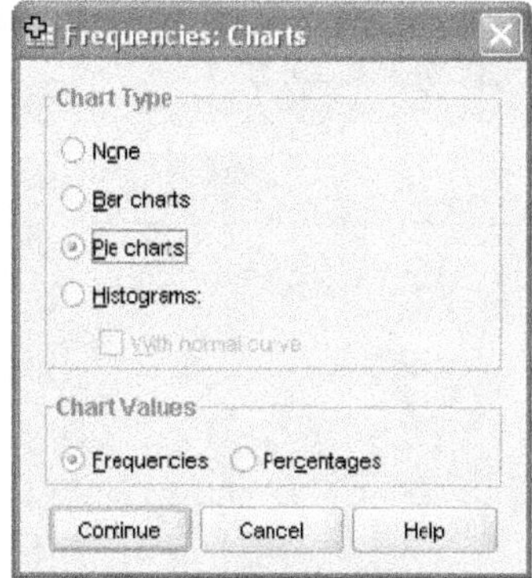

Figure 3.12b   Frequencies: charts dialog box with **Pie charts** option selected

Output 1

	Frequency	Percent	Valid Percent	Cumulative Percent
Blood group of students in a class				
Valid A	16	35.6	35.6	35.6
AB	5	11.1	11.1	46.7
B	8	17.8	17.8	64.4
O	16	35.6	35.6	100.0
Total	**45**	**100.0**	**100.0**	

Frequency table showing blood group of students in a class

Output 2

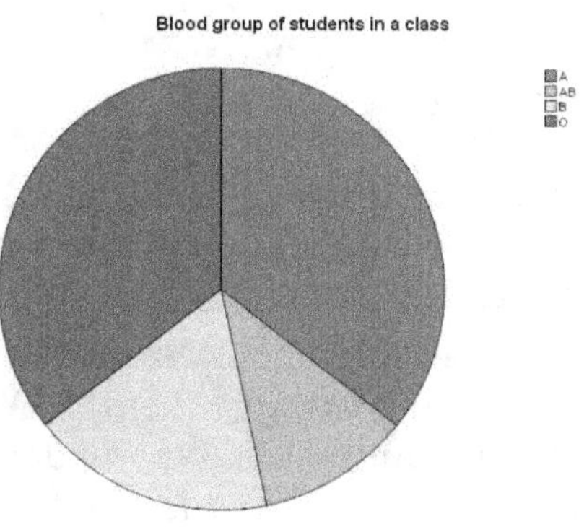

Pie chart

Note: If you select Bar Charts under Frequencies Chart then barchart appears in the output as in Output 3.

Output 3

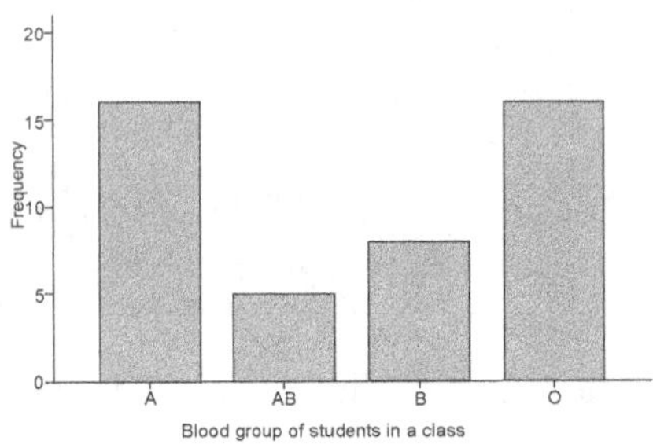

Simple bar chart

Categorical data: formulating frequency table

Example 3.4

Formulate a frequency table and draw a clustered and a stacked/subdivided bar diagram for the following data on the blood group of 90 students in a class.

Male							Female						
AB	B	O	A	A	O	A	O	B	O	A	O	O	O
O	B	AB	O	B	B	A	B	B	AB	B	A	B	B
B	O	B	A	AB	O	O	O	O	B	AB	A	O	O
A	O	AB	O	O	A		A	O	AB	O	O	A	
A	B	A	A	AB	O		O	B	A	A	AB	O	
A	A	O	A	O	A		A	A	O	A	O	A	
A	O	A	O	O	B		A	O	A	O	O	B	

Step 1 Name the variable as **bloodgp** and click on the cell named **Type**, select **String**. Type under the column **Label** as Blood group of students in a class.

Step 2 Type the second variable under **Name** as "Gender", in the second column **Type**, retain **Numeric**. Let the **Width** remain as default, **Decimal** column could be 0. Type under **Label** as "**Gender of students in a class**" as given in Figure 3.13.

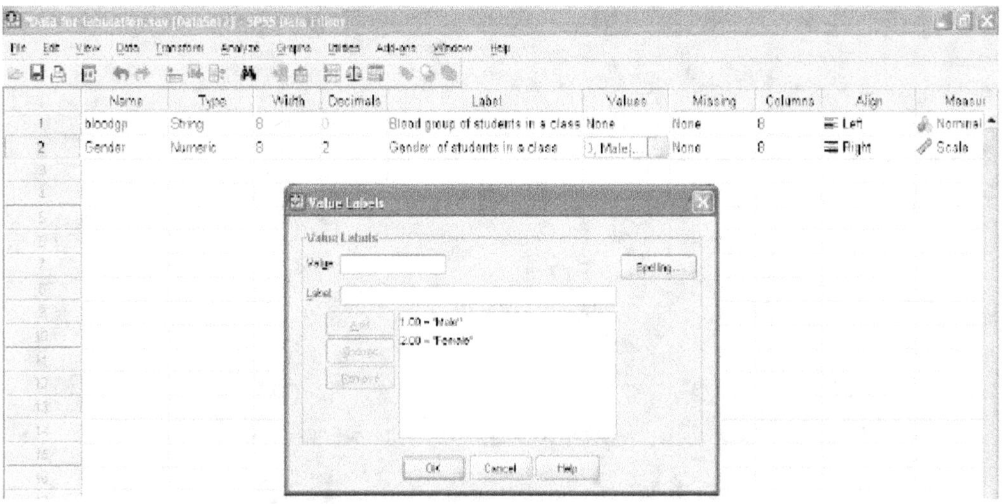

Figure 3.13   **Variable View** with **Value Labels** dialog box with values labelled

Step 3 Enter data in **Data View**.

Step 4 Choose **Analyze** then click **Descriptive Statistics** and then select **Frequencies** .... to open the **Frequencies** dialog box and then select **Crosstabs** (Figure 3.14).

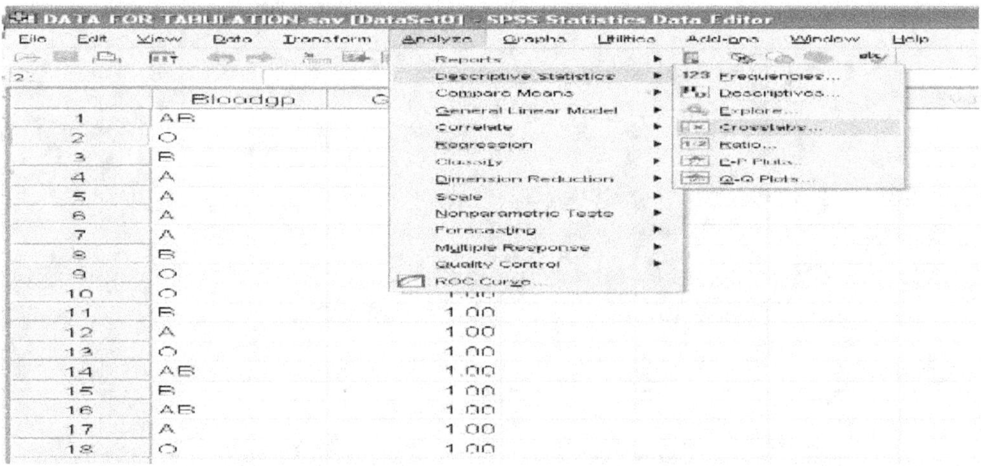

Figure 3.14   Selecting **Crosstabs** option from main menu

Step 5 Transfer the variables in the **Crosstabs** to **Row(s)** and **Column(s)** (Figure 3.15) and select **Display clustered bar charts** (Figure 3.16).

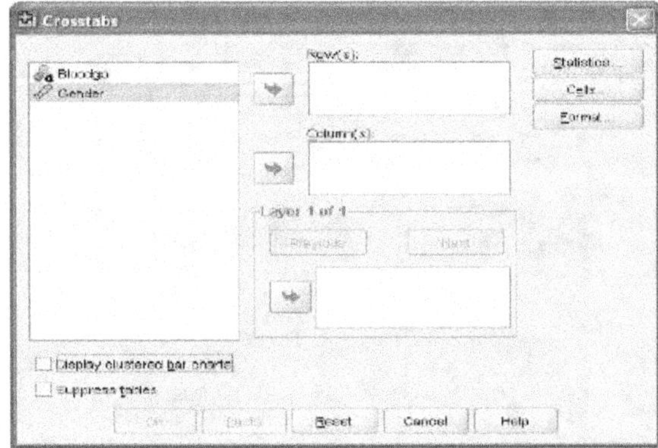

Figure 3.15   Crosstabs dialog box with variables displayed

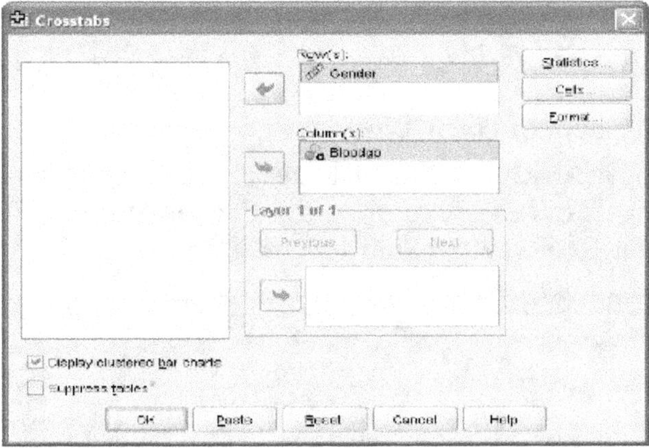

Figure 3.16   **Crosstabs** dialog box with variables selected in **Row(s)** and **Column(s)** and **Display clustered bar charts**

Step 6 Click OK, the Output appears as in Output 1. The row and column headings could be edited (Refer Chapter 2).

Output 1

Gender of students in a class * Blood group of students in a class Cross tabulation

Count		A	AB	B	O	Total
		Blood group of students in a class				
Gender of students in a class	Male	16	5	8	16	45
	Female	15	4	9	17	45
Total		31	9	17	33	90

Output 2

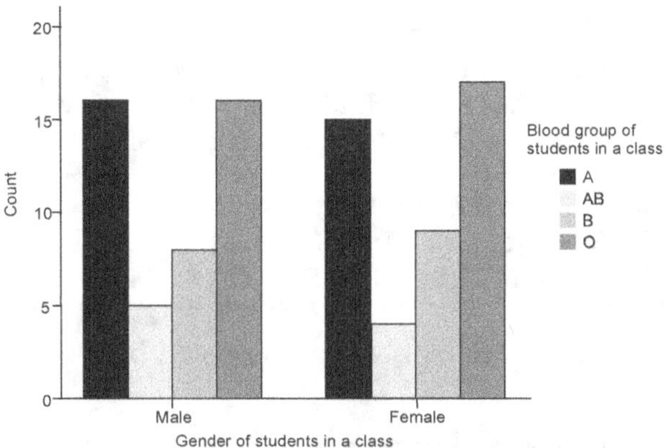

Clustered bar chart showing blood group of students with respect to gender in a class

Review Exercises

1. Data on length of leaves (cm) for two groups of trees are given below. Calculate the mean, median, mode, standard deviation, standard error, skewness and kurtosis. Interpret your results.

Group I	50	65	63	50	54	60	66	68	71	64
Group II	62	72	68	58	65	70	72	70	71	70

2. Calculate the mean, standard deviation, skewness and kurtosis for the following data on the height (cm) of 40 students and describe the distribution.

151	152	156	175	151	164	174
185	168	160	155	153	165	163
170	167	165	157	164	167	170
174	163	158	165	168	183	172
155	180	159	169	171	155	
164	175	174	159	172	177	
185	168	160	155	153	165	

3. Calculate mean, median, mode, standard deviation, standard error, skewness and kurtosis for the following distribution.

Number of flowers (x)	1	2	3	4	5	6	7
Number of plants (y)	8	4	12	9	2	2	1

4. Marital status of men in 2 different streets in a particular city is given below. Formulate a frequency table.

Street 1	M, M, M, S, M, M, S, M, S, M, M, M, M, M, S, M, M, M, S, M, S, M, M, M, M, S, M, M, M, M, M, M, M, M, M, S,M, M, M, M, M, M, M, M, M, M, M, S, S, S, M, M, M, M, M, M, M, M
Street 2	M,M, M, M, M, M, M, M, S, M, M, S, M, S M,S, M, M, M, M, M, M, S, M, M, S, M, M, M, M, M, M, M, M, S, M, M, S, M, M,M, M, M, M, M, M,M, M, M, S, S, M, M, M, M

5. The blood group of students in a class is given below formulate frequency table.

Day scholars							Hostellers					
AB	B	O	A	A	O	A	O	B	O	A	O	O
O	B	AB	O	B	B	A	B	B	AB	B	A	B
B	O	B	A	AB	O	O	O	O	B	AB	A	O
A	O	AB	O	O	A	A	A	O	AB	O	O	A
A	B	A	A	AB	O	A	O	B	A	A	AB	O
A	A	O	A	O	A	O	A	A	O	A	O	A
A	O	A	O	O	B	B	A	O	A	O	O	B

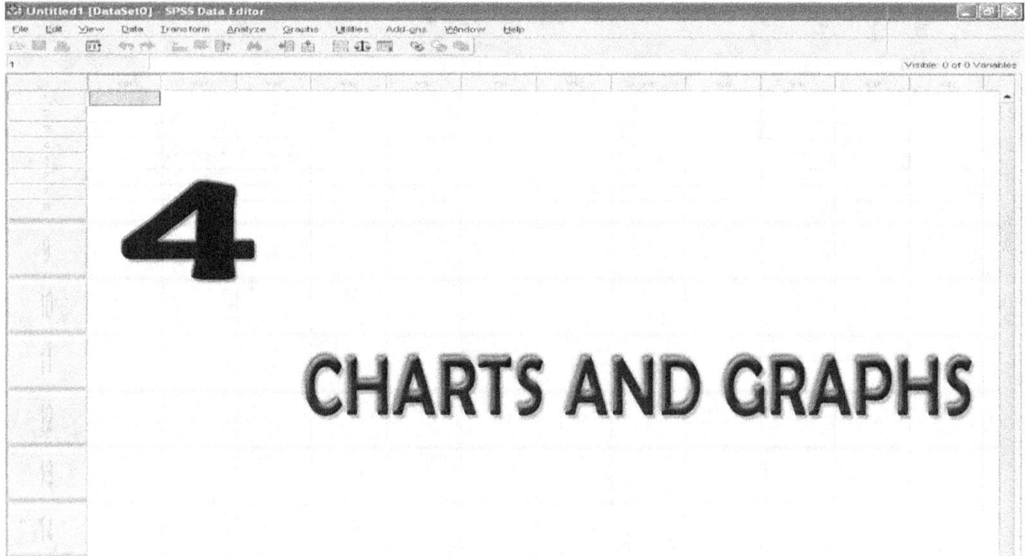

4

CHARTS AND GRAPHS

SPSS provides a wide range of options for graphs and charts. There is an option for **Graphs** in the main menu, and there is also an option for the same in the analytical procedure. For example there is **Charts** option in the **Frequencies** procedure and a **Profile plot** option in **ANOVA** procedure. The graphs could be made to appear attractive by using **Chart Builder** or **Interactive** from sub menu. By clicking on the **Chart Builder** item in the **Graph** menu, the **Gallery of Charts and Graphs** is obtained. The **Gallery** is useful in selecting a desirable graph or chart.

BAR CHARTS

Bar Charts are desirable for discrete variables, both qualitative and quantitative. There are simple bar charts, clustered bar charts and stacked bar charts. Bar charts are one-dimensional diagrams in which the height of the bar is equal to the frequency or the mean of the variable. One has the option to choose any one depending upon the suitability of the data. For a quantitative variable, bar charts with error bars can be drawn, whereas for the enumeration variables or qualitative variables only bar charts can be drawn and not error bars.

Simple Bar Charts

Simple bar charts are desirable to compare the mean of groups of observations (height of students in a class) or the simple frequency of qualitative variable (blood group of students in a class).

Simple bar charts for qualitative variables

Example 4.1

Formulate a frequency table and draw a bar diagram for the following data on the blood group of 45 students in a class.

AB	B	O	A	O	O	A
O	B	AB	B	A	B	A
B	O	B	AB	A	O	O
A	O	AB	O	O	A	
A	B	A	A	AB	O	
A	A	O	A	O	A	
A	O	A	O	O	B	

Step 1 Name the variable in Variable View and enter data in data editor.

Step 2 Choose **Graphs** from the main menu and click **Bar** (Figure 4.1) to open **Bar charts** dialog box (Figure 4.2).

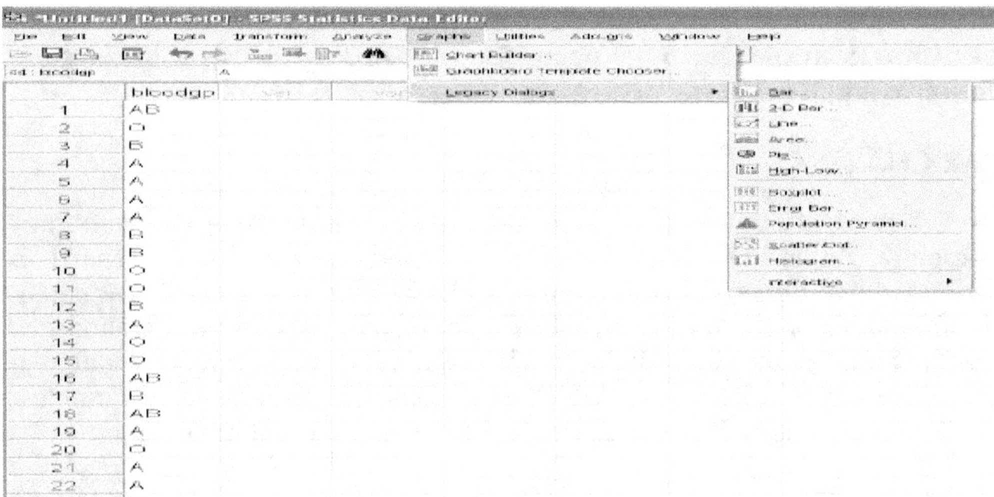

Figure 4.1   Selecting Bar chart option from main menu

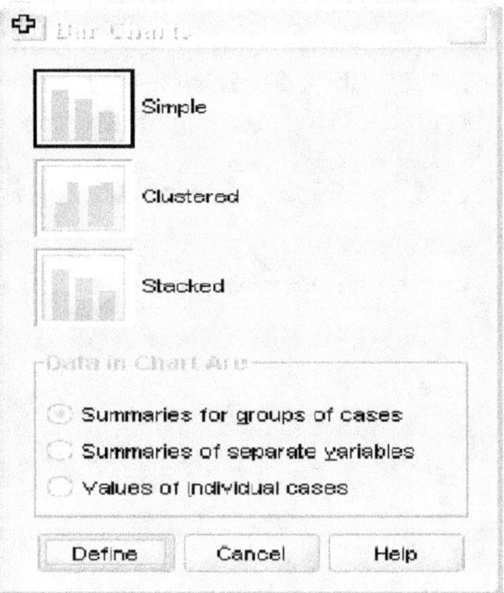

Figure 4.2   Bar Charts dialog box to select Simple Bar

Step 3   Select **Simple** and click **Define** to open the **Define Simple Bar: Summaries for Groups of Cases** dialog box (Figure 4.3).

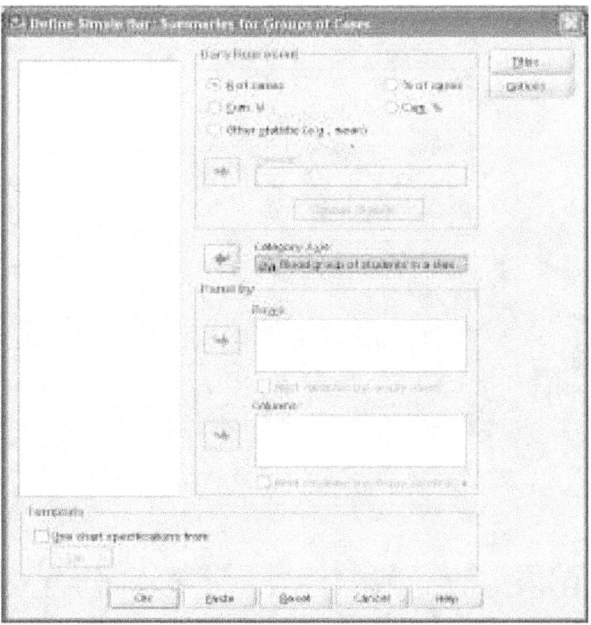

Figure 4.3   Define Simple Bar: Summaries for Group of Cases dialog box with blood group of students selected in Category Axis

Step 4 Transfer the variable name to category Axis.

Step 5 Click **Titles** to open the dialog box and enter the title in the text box (Figure 4.4). Click **Continue** to return to **Bar charts** dialog box and then click **OK** to get the chart.

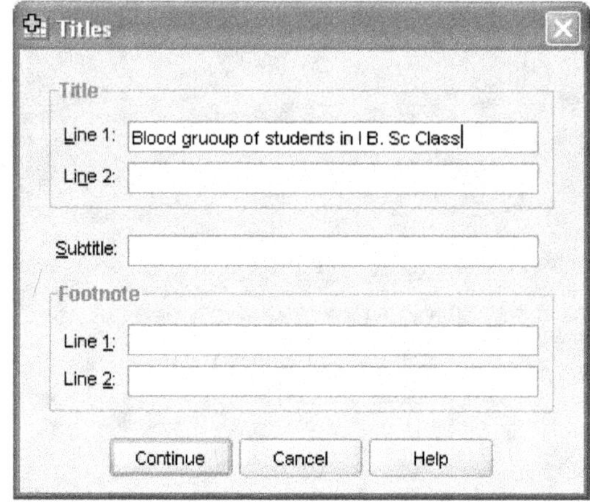

Figure 4.4   Titles dialog box with title typed under Line 1 as "Blood group of students in I B. Sc. Class"

Step 6 The chart appears in output.

Output

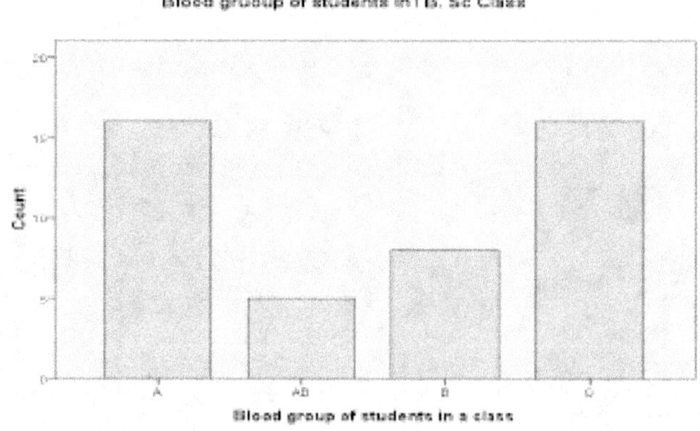

Simple Bar Chart for Blood group of students in I B.Sc. class

Simple bar chart with error bars for quantitative variables   Bar charts with error Bars are suitable for **discrete quantitative variables** where the height of the bar represents the mean of a group of observations and a vertical line with horizontal bar erected on top of the bar represents the standard error of the mean.

Therefore, in a bar chart with error bars both mean and standard error values are represented.

Example 4.2

Four groups of children are fed on four different diets and their haemoglobin levels are estimated. The data are given in the following table. Represent the data in the form of bar diagram with standard error.

Diet 1	11.2, 12.0, 11.0, 12.0, 13.0, 10.0, 11.0, 9.0, 10.0, 10.0
Diet 2	12.0, 12.0, 12.5, 12.0, 13.0, 11.5, 10.5, 11.0, 11.5, 12.0
Diet 3	13.0, 12.5, 13.0, 13.0, 12.0, 12.5, 11.0, 12.0, 11.5, 13.0
Diet 4	9.5, 9.6, 10.0, 12.0, 11.0, 9.8, 10.0, 10.0, 9.8, 9.9

Step 1 Name the variable (as categorical) in **Variable View** and enter data in **Data Editor**.

Step 2 Choose **Graphs** from main menu then click **Legacy Dialogs** and then select **Bar…** to open **Bar charts** dialog box (Figure 4.5).

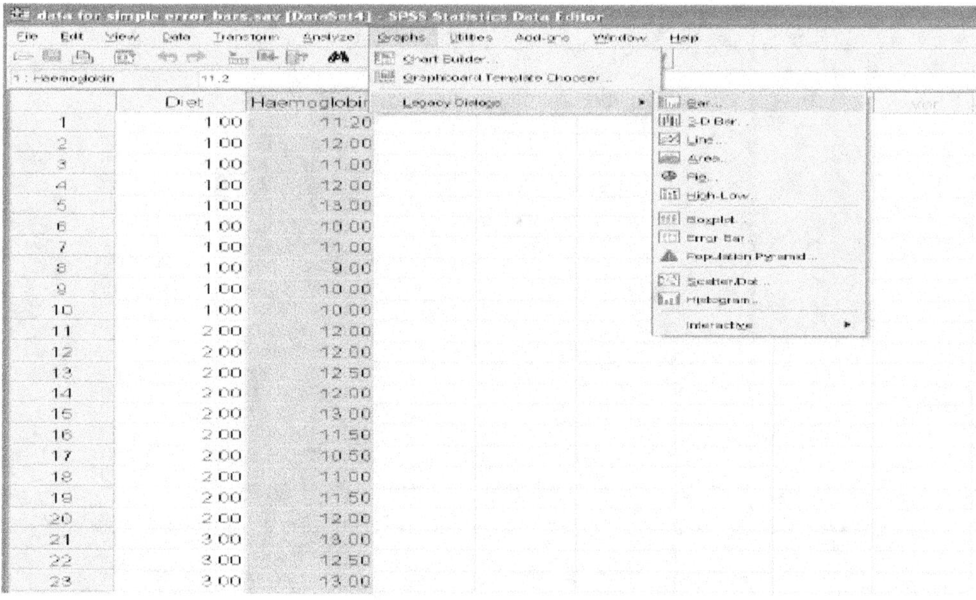

Figure 4.5 Selecting Bar Chart option from main menu

Step 3 Select **Simple** and click **Define** to open the **Define Simple Bar: Summaries for Groups of Cases** dialog box.

Step 4 Transfer the variable names as shown in Figure 4.6. "Haemoglobin" into **Variable** and "Group of children fed on different diet" into Category Axis.

Step 5 Select the radio button **Other statistic** (e.g. mean) under **Bars Represent**. This step is important to display mean, in the bar chart otherwise number of cases will be represented in the bar chart.

Figure 4.6 **Define Simple Bar: Summaries for Group of Cases** dialog box with "MEAN Haemoglobin in gm%" selected under **Variable** and "Group of children fed on different diet" in **Category Axis.**

Step 6 Click **Options** to open the **Options** dialog box, select **Display error bars** box as shown in Figure 4.7. Click **Continue** to return to **Define Simple Bar**.

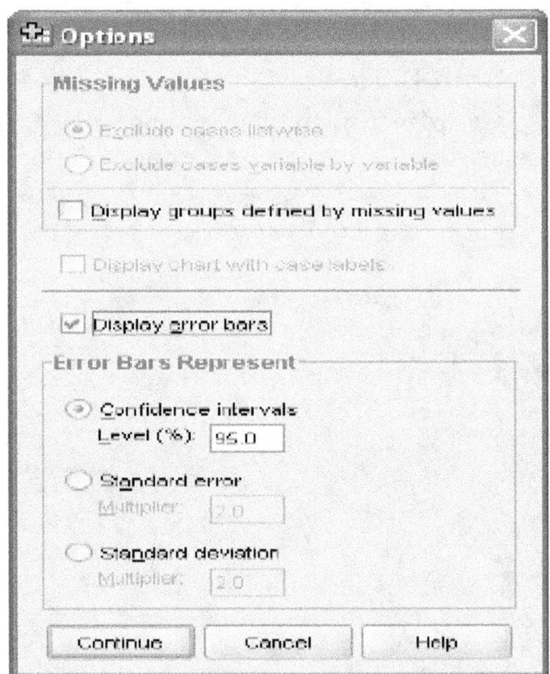

Figure 4.7 Options dialog box with Display error bars selected

Step 7 Click **Titles** to open **Titles** dialog box (Figure 4.8) and enter the Title in the text box.

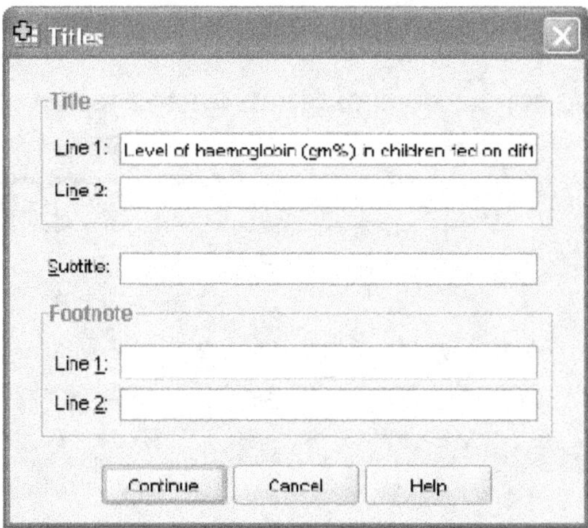

Figure 4.8 Titles dialog box with title "Level of haemoglobin (gm%) in children fed on different diet"

> **Step 8** Click **Continue** to return to **Bar charts** dialog box and then click **OK** to get the chart. The output summarising the mean values with standard error on levels of haemoglobin among children fed on different diets appears as given in the output.

Output

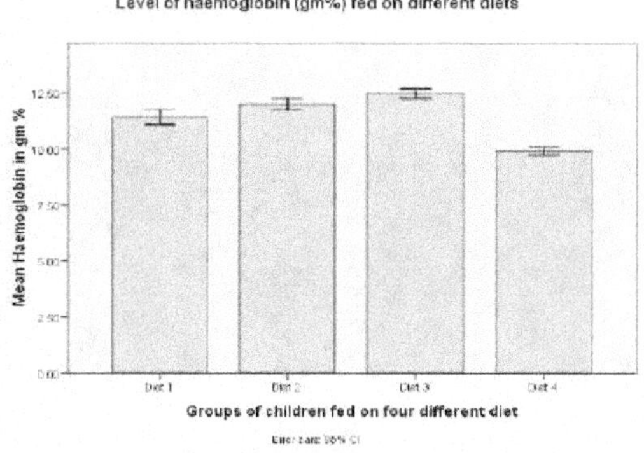

Simple bar diagram with error bars

Clustered Bar Charts

This chart shows two or more categories of variables in the same graph. The clustered chart could be plotted for the following data on blood group and gender. The second variable defines the clusters.

Example 4.3

Draw a clustered and stacked bar diagram for the following data on the blood group of 90 students in a class.

Male								Female					
AB	B	O	A	A	O	A	O	B	O	A	O	O	O
O	B	AB	O	B	B	A	B	B	AB	B	A	B	B
B	O	B	A	AB	O	O	O	O	B	AB	A	O	O
A	O	AB	O	O	A		A	O	AB	O	O	A	
A	B	A	A	AB	O		O	B	A	A	AB	O	
A	A	O	A	O	A		A	A	O	A	O	A	
A	O	A	O	O	B		A	O	A	O	O	B	

Step 1 Name the variable in **Variable View**. Enter data in **data editor**.

Step 2 Choose **Graphs** from the main menu click **Legacy Dialogs** and then click **Bar** to open **Bar charts** dialog box (Figure 4.9).

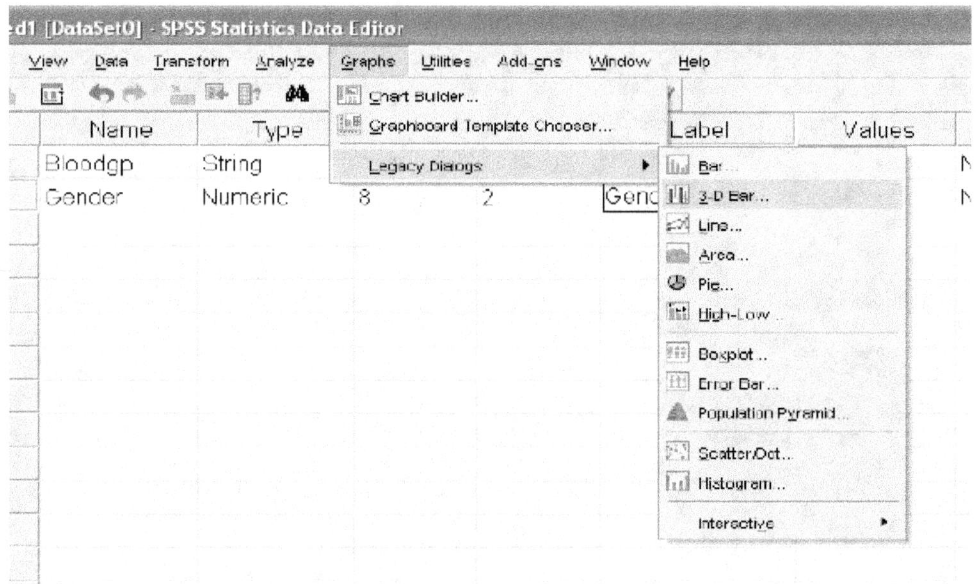

Figure 4.9   Selecting Bar chart option from main menu

Step 3 Select **Clustered** and click **Define** to open the **Define Simple Bar: Summaries for Groups of Cases** dialog box (Figure 4.10).

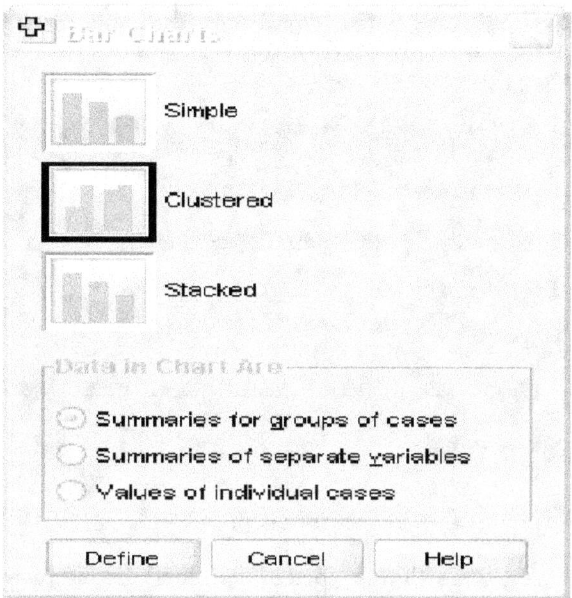

Figure 4.10 Bar charts dialog box to select clustered bar chart

Step 4 Transfer the variable names namely "Gender" to **Category Axis** and "Blood group" to **Define Clusters** by (Figure 4.11). For enumeration data of this kind select radio button **N of cases** under **Bars Represent**.

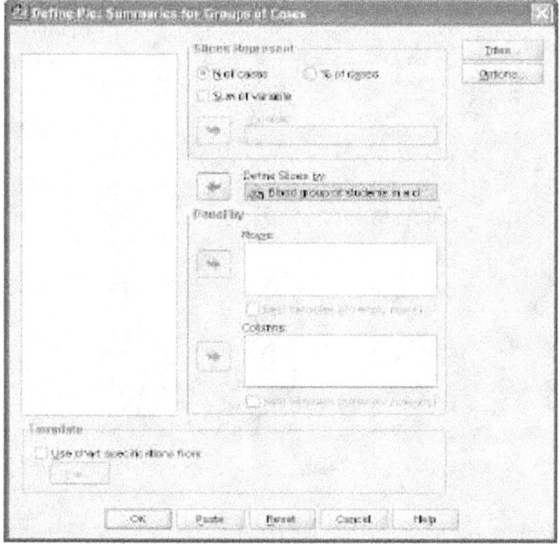

Figure 4.11 Define Clustered Bar: Summaries for Group of Cases dialog box to transfer bloodgp to Define Cluster by and gender to Category Axis

Step 5 Click Options to open Options dialog box and click Titles to open the Titles dialog box (Figure 4.12) and enter the title in line 1 in the text box.

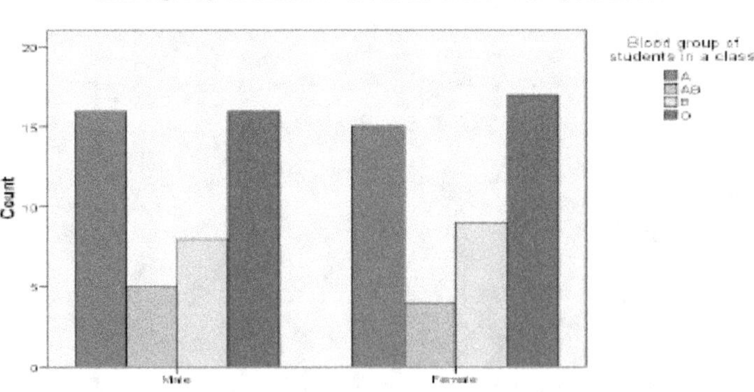

Figure 4.12   Titles dialog box with title typed under Line 1 as "Blood group of students in I B. Sc. Class"

Step 6 Click **Continue** to return to **Bar charts** dialog box and then click **OK** to get the chart.

Step 7 The chart appears as in output (Output 1).

Output 1

Clustered bar chart

If you select stacked in bar charts dialog box (Figure 4.10) a stacked bar diagram appears as an Output 2.

Output 2

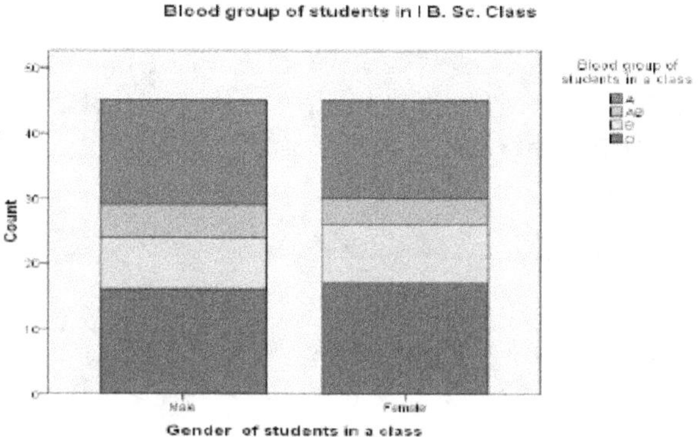

Clustered bar chart with error bars   Clustered or panneled bar chart is drawn for a data set consisting of a variable measured for 2 or 3 factors with different levels each. In the example 4.2 the level of haemoglobin in children fed on four different diets were given. Four different diets are levels of the factor namely diet. If such data are collected from three primary health centres (PHC) then primary health centre becomes a second variable and the three PHCs become the levels. We can represent this kind of data with clustered or panneled bar charts with error bars.

Example 4.4

Draw a paneled or custrered bar chart with error bars for a similar data given in Example 4.2, for children belonging to two primary health centres.

	healthcentre	Diet	Haemoglobin			
1	1.00	1.00	11.20			
2	1.00	1.00	12.00			
3	1.00	1.00	11.00			
4	1.00	1.00	12.00			
5	1.00	1.00	13.00			
6	1.00	1.00	10.00			
7	1.00	1.00	11.00			
8	1.00	1.00	9.00			
9	1.00	1.00	10.00			
10	1.00	1.00	10.00			
11	1.00	2.00	12.00			
12	1.00	2.00	12.00			
13	1.00	2.00	12.50			
14	1.00	2.00	12.00			
15	1.00	2.00	13.00			
16	1.00	2.00	11.50			
17	1.00	2.00	10.50			
18	1.00	2.00	11.00			
19	1.00	2.00	11.50			
20	1.00	2.00	12.00			
21	1.00	3.00	13.00			
22	1.00	3.00	12.50			
23	1.00	3.00	13.00			

Figure 4.13   Data editor with 23 cases (a portion) entered for three different variables

Step 1 Enter data as in example 4.2. Include the new variable Primary Health Centre **(PHC)** in **Variable View**, **Label** the variable and give the **Value** by coding 1 as PHC1, 2 as PHC2 and 3 as PHC3 (Figure 4.13).

Step 2 Follow the steps as given for clustered bar chart and transfer the variables i.e., "Haemoglobin" into **Variables**, "Primary Health Centre into **Category Axis** and "Group of children" into **Define Clusters by** (Figure 4.14).

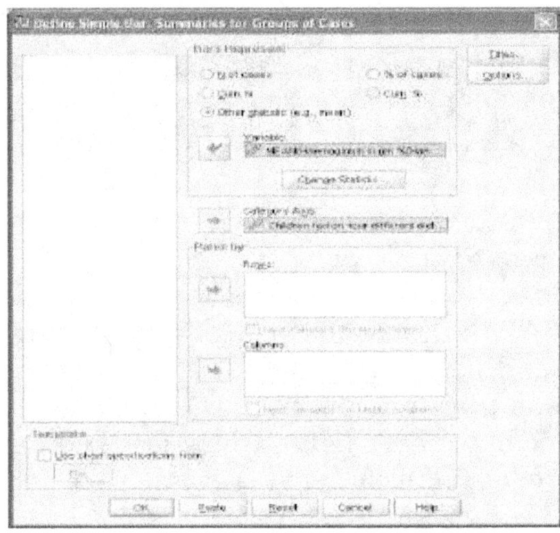

Figure 4.14 **Define Clustered Bar: Summaries for Group of Cases** dialog box with "MEAN Heamoglobin in gm%" selected under **Variable**, "Primary heath Centers"in **Category Axis** and "Group of children fed on different diet" in "**Define Clusters by**" box.

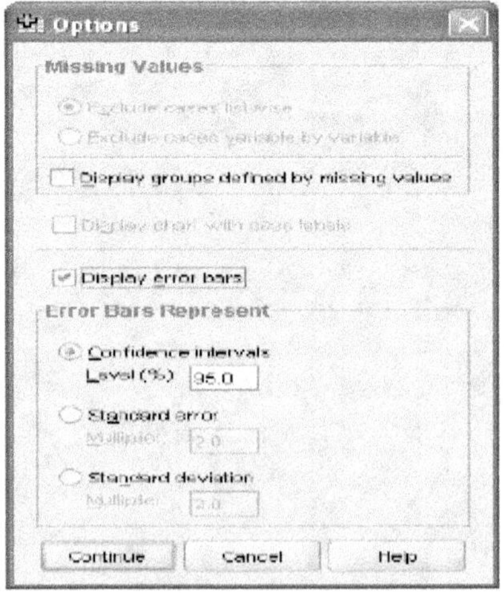

Figure 4.15 **Options** dialog box with **Display error bars** selected

Step 3 Click **Options** to open the **Options** dialog box, select **Display error bars** box as shown in Figure 4.15. Click **Continue** to return to **Define Simple Bar**.

Step 4 Click Titles to open Titles dialog box and enter the Title in the text box (Figure 4.16).

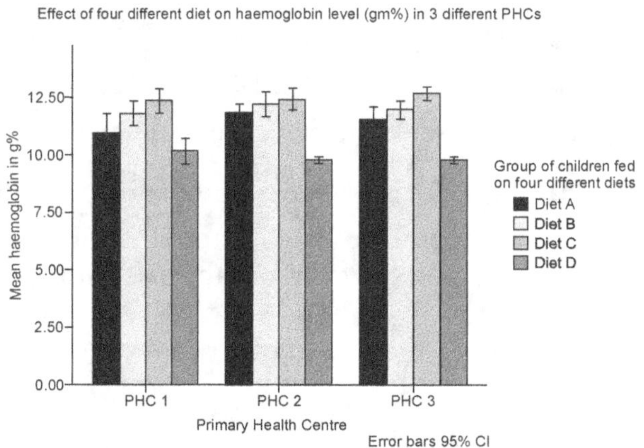

Figure 4.16   **Titles** dialog box with title "Effect of four different diet on haemoglobin (gm%) in children in 3 PHCs"

Step 5 Click **Continue** to return to **Bar charts** dialog box and then click **OK** to get the chart. The output summarizing the mean values with standard error on levels of haemoglobin among children fed on different diets appears in clusters for three different PHCs as given in the output.

Output

Clustered bar charts with error bars

Error Bar Charts

Error bar chart is an alternative to bar chart, in which the mean of the sample is represented by a single point and the spread of the variable, the standard error is represented by a vertical line or like a letter T or whiskers passing through the point.

Example 4.5

Draw an **Error bar chart** for the data given in Example 4.4.

> **Step 1** Choose **Graphs** from the main menu click **Legacy Dialogs** and then select **Error Bar**…to open the **Error Bar** dialog box (Figure 4.17).

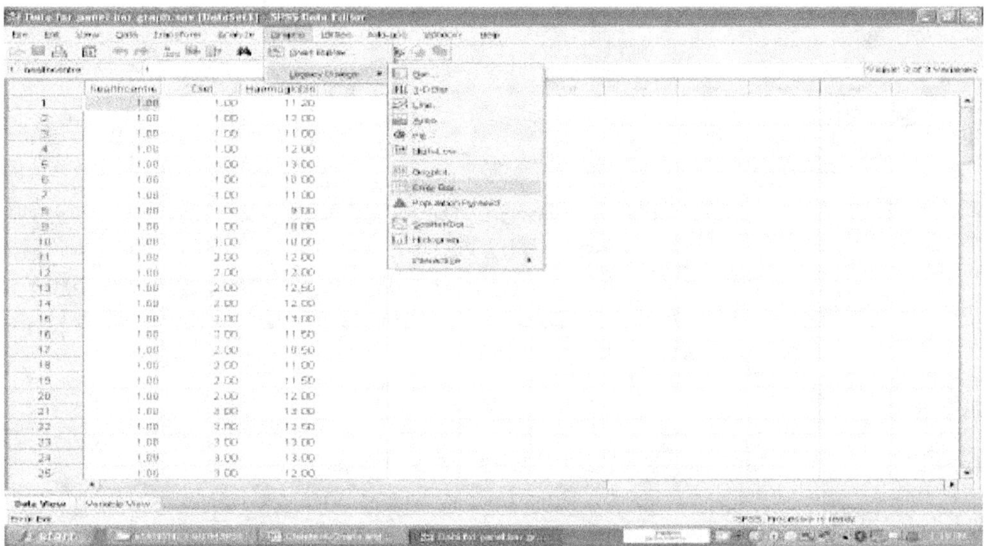

Figure 4.17   Selecting error bar from main menu

> **Step 2** Select **Clustered** from **Error Bar** dialog box **(Figure 4.18)**.
>
> **Step 3** Click Define to open Define Clustered Error Bars: Summaries for groups of cases and transfer variables as shown in a Figure 4.19.

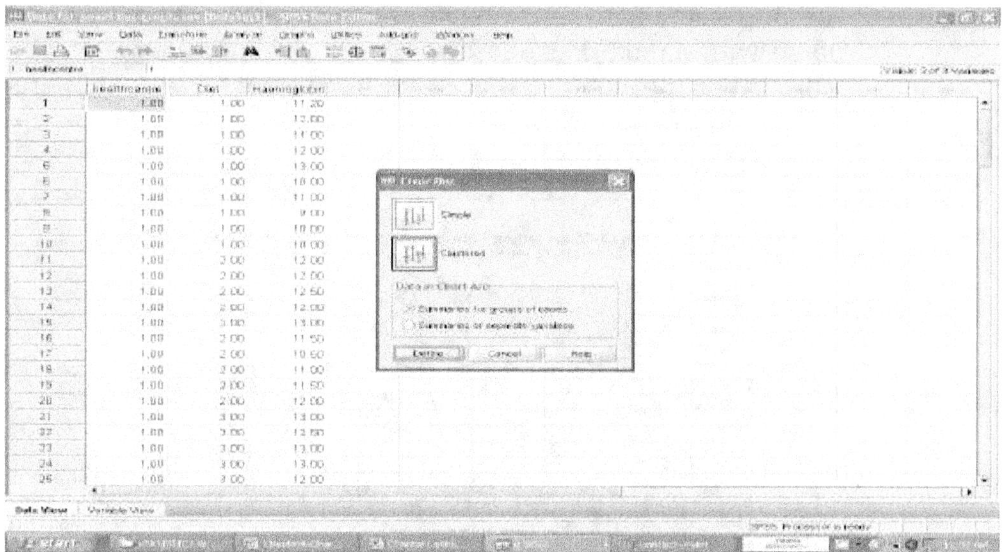

Figure 4.18 **Error Bar** dialog box with **Clustered** selected

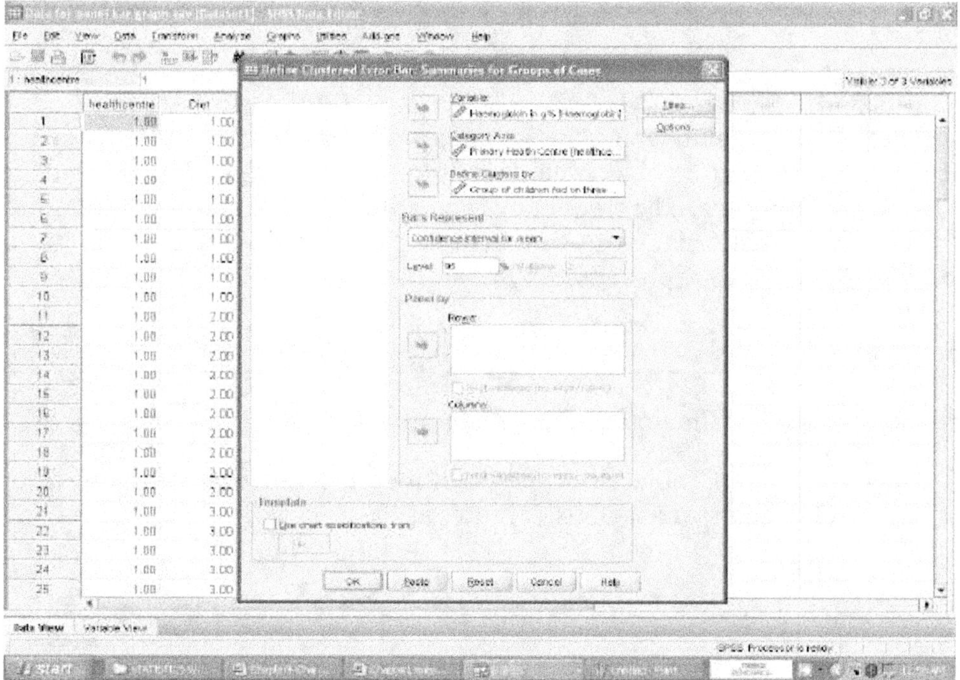

Figure 4.19 Define Clustered Error Bars: Summaries for groups of cases dialog box

Step 4 Click **Title** and type title as in Example 4.4.

Step 5 Click **Continue** and then click **OK**.

Step 6 The output summarising the mean values on levels of haemoglobin as points with standard error as the letter T on either side for children fed on four different diets appears in clusters for three different PHCs as in the output.

Output

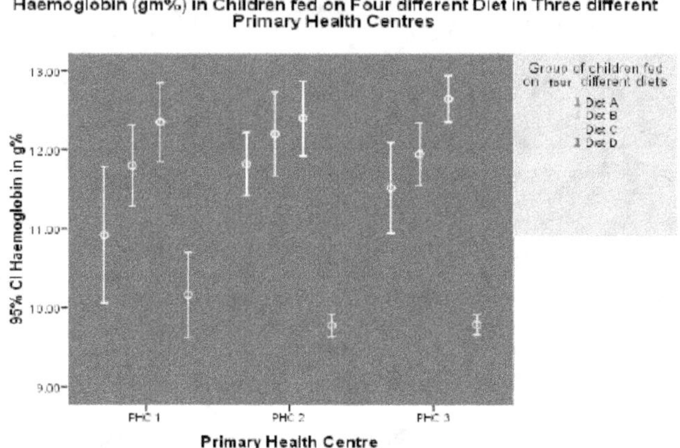

PIE CHART

It is a circular diagram in which the frequency of different **classes** is equal to the angle of different sectors of a circle. It is used to display the relative frequencies of the same set of data. The frequency of qualitative variables is represented by Pie chart. It is an alternative to **bar chart**. The data on blood group given in Example 4.1 could be represented by a pie chart.

Example 4.6

Draw a Pie chart for the data given in Example 4.1.

Step 1 Choose Graphs from the main menu, click Legacy Dialogs to open Pie charts dialog box (Figure 4.20).

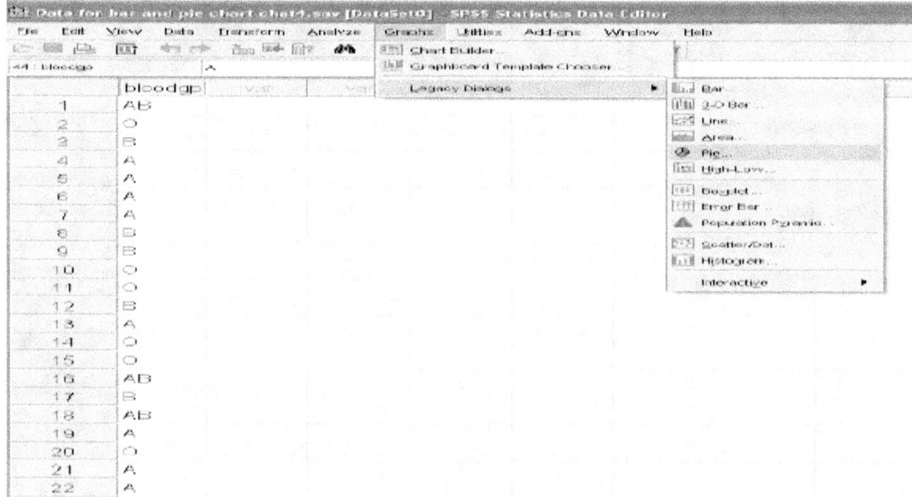

Figure 4.20   Selecting Pie Chart option from main menu

Step 2 Click **Define** to open the **Define Pie: Summaries for Groups of Cases** dialog box (Figure 4.21).

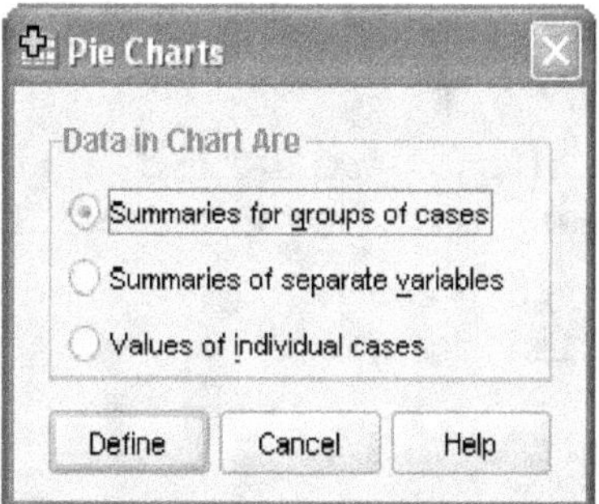

Figure 4.21   **Pie Charts** dialog box to select **Summaries for groups of cases**

Step 3 Click the variable (blood group) and transfer it into the **Define Slices** by box. If you want to represent %, select **% of cases**, otherwise **N of cases** (Figure 4.22).

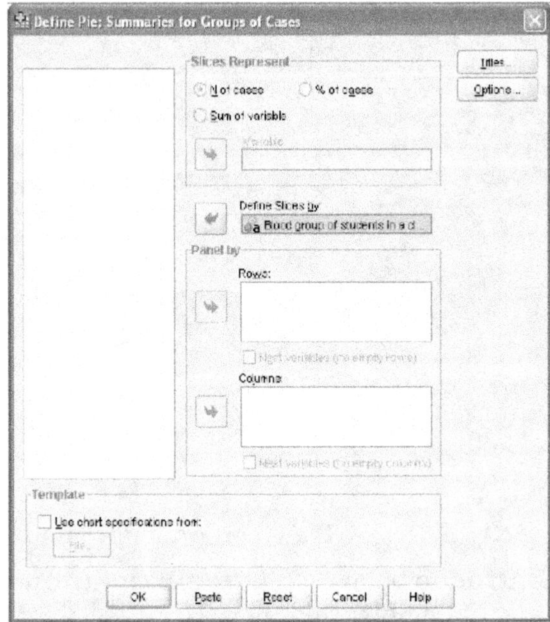

Figure 4.22   Define Pie: Summaries for Group of Cases dialog box with "Blood group of students" selected in Define Slice by

Step 4   Finally click **Title** to open the **Title** dialog box. Type the title, then click **Continue** to return to the **Define Pie** box.

Step 5   Click **OK** to get the pie chart. The output summarising the blood groups in sectors of the circle appears as given in Output 1.

Output 1

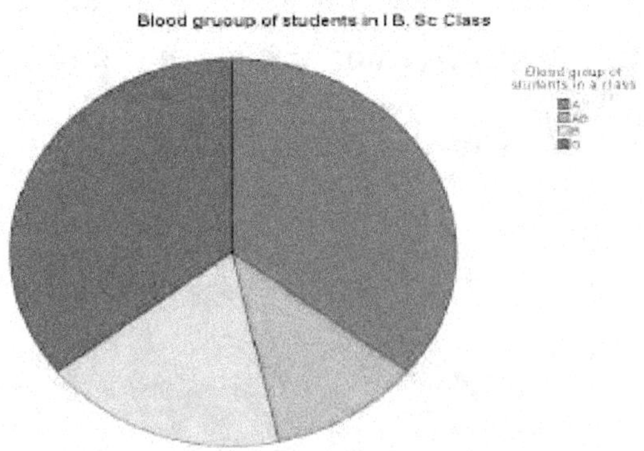

Pie chart showing Blood group of students in I B.Sc. Class

Step 6 From the output, any slice can be labelled within or can be exploded from the circle, if needed to emphasise a particular category. It is done by highlighting the slice and selecting Explode Slice. The output presenting the slice exploded for blood group AB appears as in Output 2.

Output 2

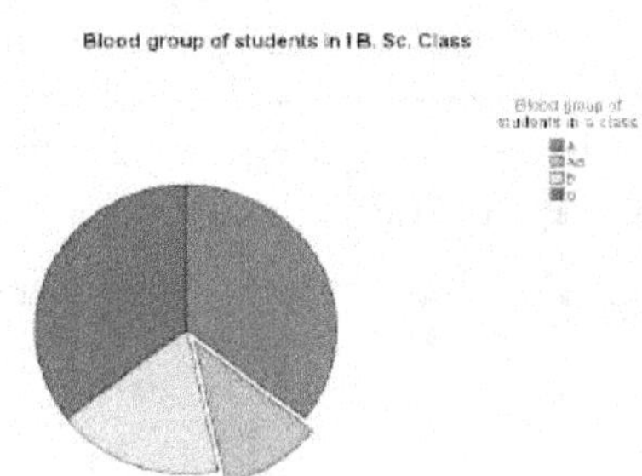

Pie chart showing Blood group with slice exploded for blood group AB

SCATTER PLOTS AND DOT PLOTS

Scatter Plots

The relationship between two quantitative variables can be represented in the form of scatter plot. The scale of values of two variables such as age of the person and his systolic blood pressure are set on horizontal (X-axis) and vertical axes (Y-axis) respectively, each person is represented by a point and each point in turn represents his age and blood pressure. The scatter plot should be always plotted and examined for the extent of scatter before the calculation of correlation coefficient or analysis of regression.

Example 4.7

Draw a scatter plot for the following data on age (years) versus systolic blood pressure (mm Hg.)

Age	BP	Age	BP
56	160	40	126
42	130	53	145
60	125	35	118

Age	BP	Age	BP
50	135	38	120
54	145	39	123
49	115	37	138
39	140	70	160
62	120	75	163
65	140	65	146
70	160	64	146

Step 1 Choose **Graphs** from the main menu to open the **Scatter/Dot** dialog box (Figure 4.23).

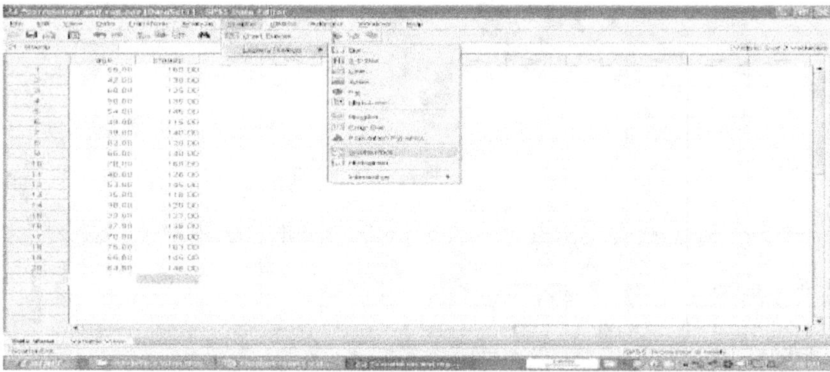

Figure 4.23   Selecting Scatter/Dot from main menu

Step 2 Click **Define** to open the **Simple Scatter** plot dialog box (Figure 4.24).

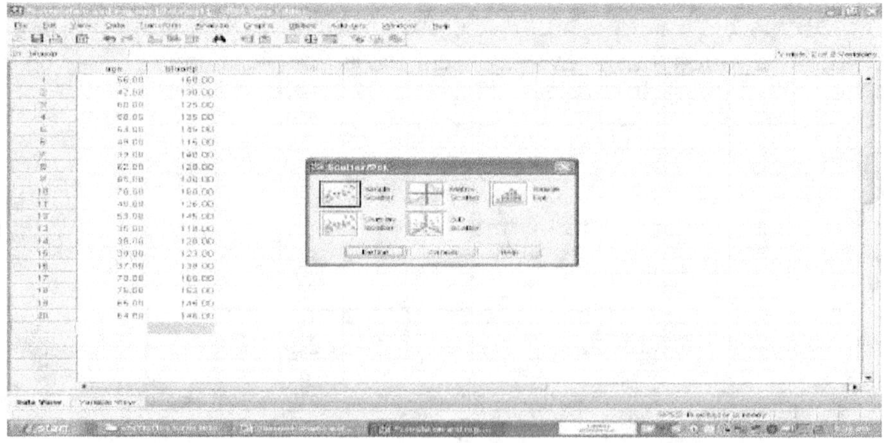

Figure 4.24   Scatter/Dot dialog box with **Simple Scatter** selected

Step 3 Transfer the variable names as shown in Figure 4.25.

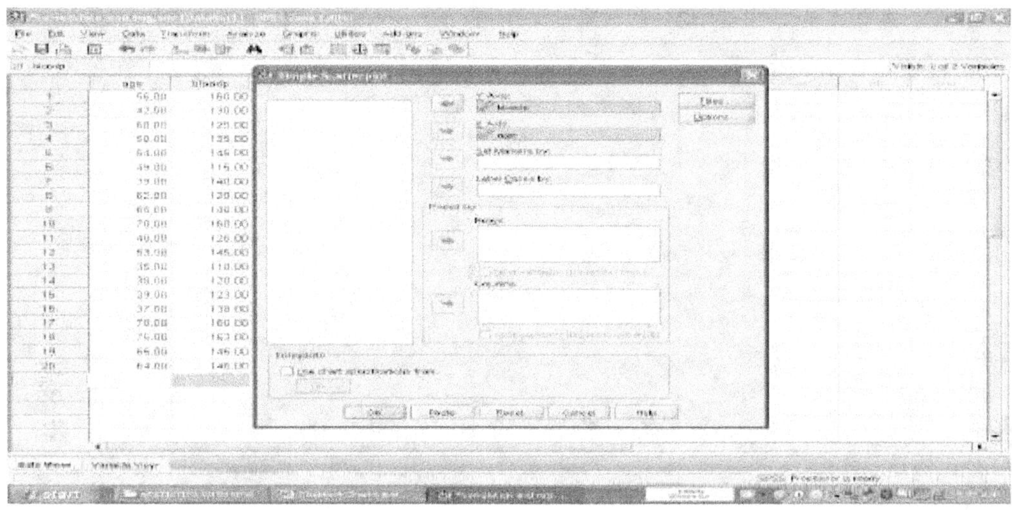

Figure 4.25 **Simple Scatter Plot** dialog box with variables blood pressure and age selected in y and x axis respectively

Step 4 Click Titles to get Titles box and type the title as shown in Figure 4.26.

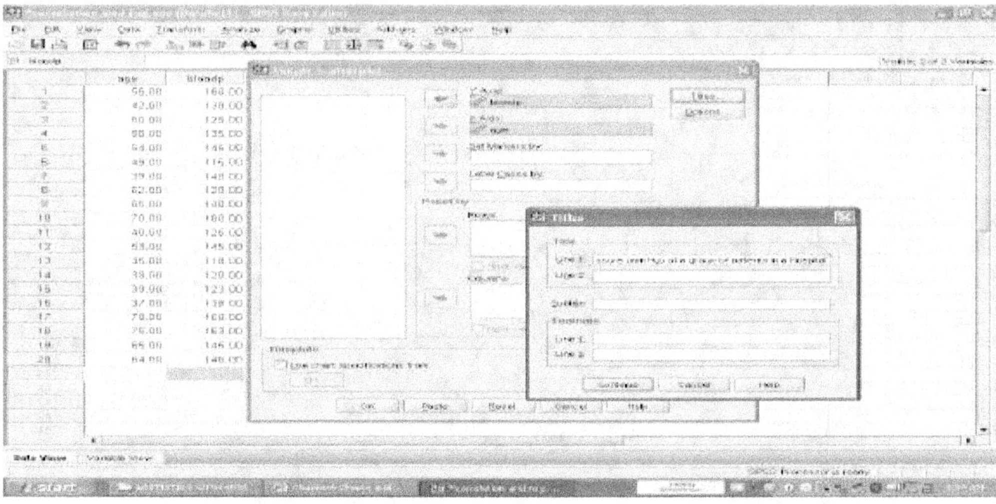

Figure 4.26 Titles box with title typed in Line 1

Step 5 Click **Continue** and then **OK** to get the scatter plot.

Step 6 The output appears with "**Age of the patients** in x-axis and Systolic pressure in mm Hg in y-axis with a dot for each person as in the output.

Output

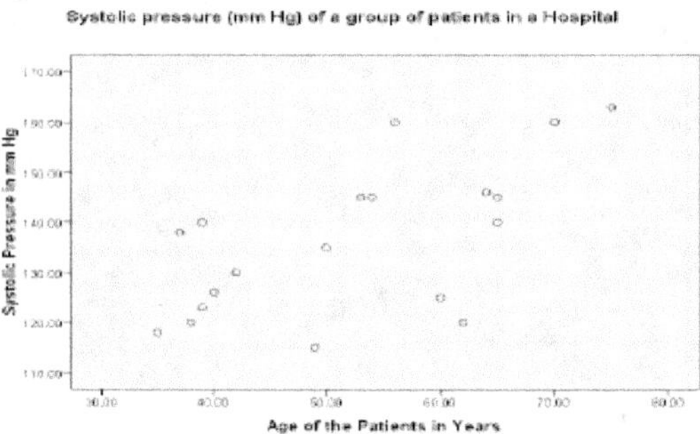

Scatter plots or Dot plots

LINE GRAPHS

Line graphs are drawn for two variables or more than two variables. Line graphs can be drawn with just one line or more than one line in the graph. The above example on blood pressure (mm Hg) of the individuals in relation to age can be represented in the form of a line graph; the total range of blood pressure is divided into fixed intervals.

Example 4.8

Draw a line graph for age versus systolic blood pressure for the data given in Example 4.6.

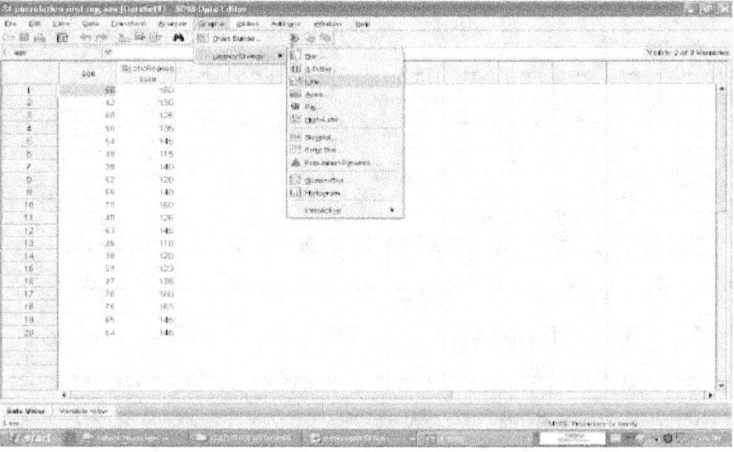

Figure 4.27   Selecting Line option from main menu

Step 1 Enter data, choose **Graphs** from the main menu, select **Legacy Dialog** and click **Line** to open **Line Chart** dialog box (Figure 4.27).

Step 2 Select **Simple** under **Line Charts** and then **Define** (Figure 4.28).

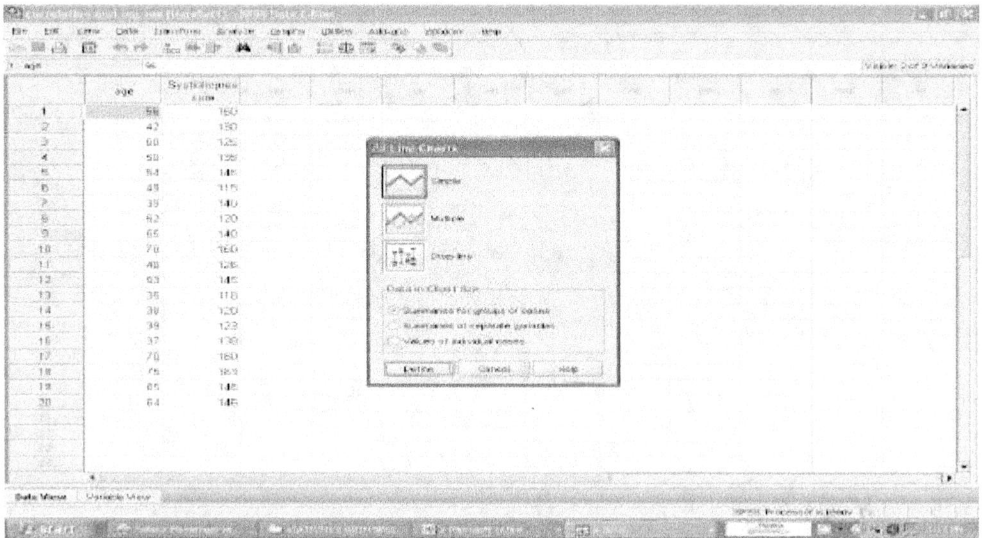

Figure 4.28   Selecting Simple from Line charts dialog box

Step 3 Transfer the variables, then click **Titles** and type the title (Figure 4.29).

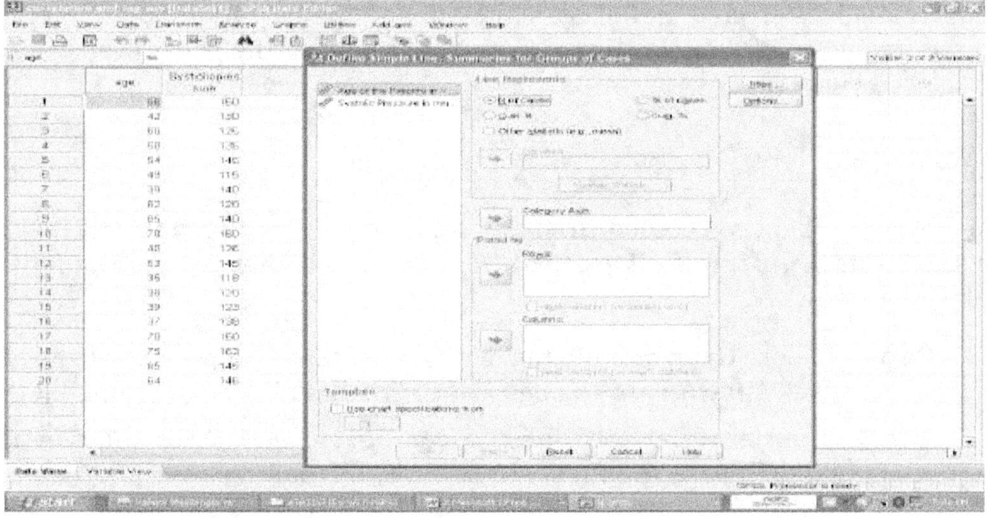

Figure 4.29   **Define Simple Line: Summaries for groups of cases** dialog box with variables to be selected

Step 4 Click **Continue** and then **OK** to get the output. The output appears with a title and a line representing blood pressure (mm Hg) of the individuals in y-axis and age of the person in x-axis.

Output

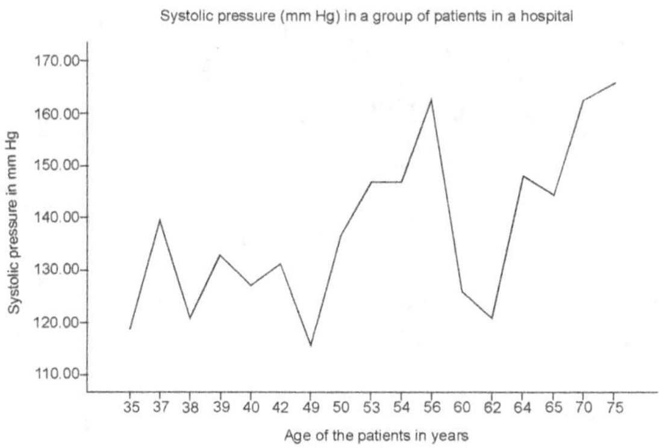

Simple Line Chart

HISTOGRAM

Histogram is a two-dimensional diagram to represent a measurement variable which is continuous. There are a number of such variables like marks obtained by students, weight and height of animals, length of leaves, etc. In this the variable is taken in the X-axis and the frequency of the variable in Y-axis. A bar or a rectangle is erected on the class interval and the height of the bar is equal to the frequency of that class interval and the width of the bar is proportional to the class interval.

Example 4.9

Weights of 40 babies recorded from a hospital are entered in **Data Editor** as described in **Chapter 3 (Page 56)**. A histogram is drawn by adopting the following steps.

Step 1 Choose **Graphs** from the main menu, select **Legacy Dialogs** and click **Histogram** to open **Histogram** dialog box (Figure 4.30).

Step 2 Transfer weight of babies to **Variables**, click **Title** and type the title (**Figure 4.31**).

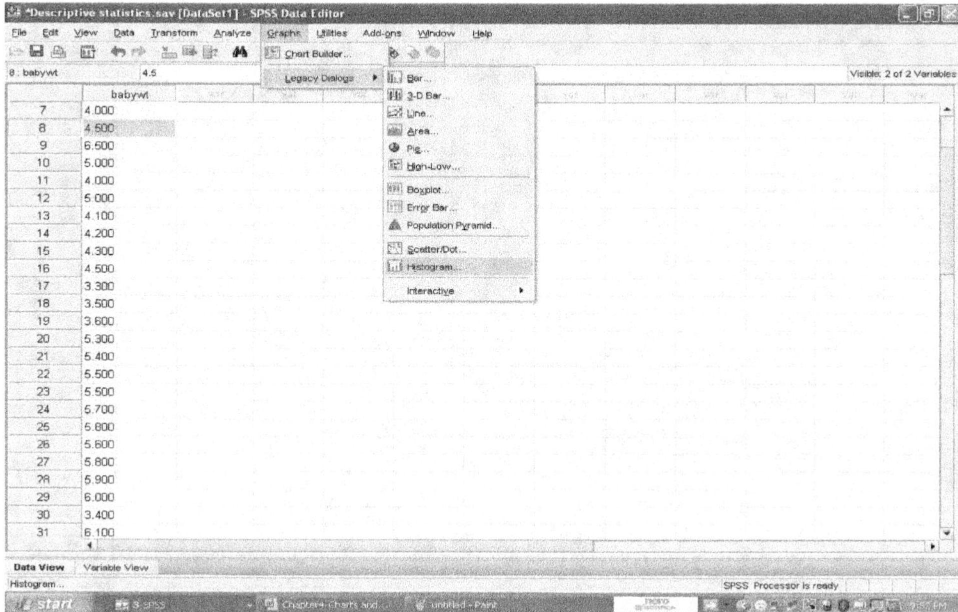

Figure 4.30 Selecting Histogram from main menu

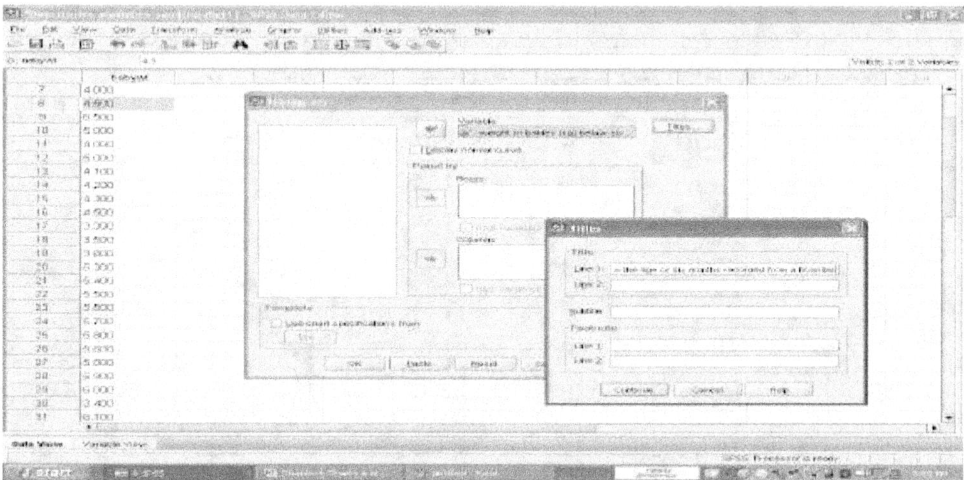

Figure 4.31 Histogram dialog box with variable transfered and Title dialog box with title typed

Step 3 Click **Continue**, then click **OK** to get the output. The output appears with a title and rectangular bars erected on class intervals in X-axis ranging from 2.00 to 8.00, representing the weight (kg) of babies. The height of the bar is equal to the frequency in Y-axis.

Output

Weight (kg) of the baby below the age of six months recorded from a hospital

Mean = 4.82
Std. Dev. = 1.185
N = 40

Weight of babies (kg) below six months

Histogram

Review Exercises

1. The calcium carbonate (mg/L) levels of four different ponds are given below; **draw bar charts with error bars.**

Pond 1	Pond 2	Pond 3	Pond 4
95.5	130	124	165
100	135	125	180
12	123	130	175
112	124	124	180
115	130	135	176
112	135	124	156
113	145	142	175

2. Draw box plot for the data given in exercise 1.

3. Draw a histogram with frequency curve for the following data on height in cm.

155	171	170	169	167	180	158
153	172	172	175	152	163	164

177	164	165	174	164	160	165
174	169	168	165	151	175	150
164	165	163	170	167	159	
163	162	168	154	170	157	

4. Draw a scatter plot and a line graph for the following data on height (cm) and weight (kg) of 10 individuals.

Height (cm)	165	160	157	158	168	170	171	169	165	163
Weight (kg)	55	57	54	54	60	65	76	66	59	52

5. The expenditure of a family on different items is given below. Represent the data in the form of a pie diagram.

Item	Expenditure in Rs.
Rent	2000
Food	4000
Clothing	1000
Education	900
Saving	1000
Others	1600

6. The following data represent the expenditure of three families on different items, draw subdivided bar diagram.

Item	Expenditure in Rs		
	Family A	**Family B**	**Family C**
Rent	2000	1000	3000
Food	4000	2000	4000
Clothing	1000	1000	2000
Education	900	600	2500
Saving	1000	100	500
Others	1600	600	1600

7. Marital status of men in two different streets in a particular city is given below. Represent the data by bar chart (M—Married, S—Single).

Street 1	M, M, M, S, M, M, S, M, S, M, M, M, M, M, S, M, M, M, S, M, S, M, M, M, M, S, M, M, M, M, M, M, M, M, M, M, S, M, M, M, M, M, M, M, M, M, M, M, M, M, S, S, S, M, M, M, M, M, M, M, M,
Street 2	M, M, M, M, M, M, M, S, M, M, S, M, S M, S, M, M, M, M, M, M, S, M, M, S, M, M, M, M, M, M, M, M, S, M, M, S, M, M, M, M, M, M, M, M, M, M, M, M, S, S, M, M, M, M,

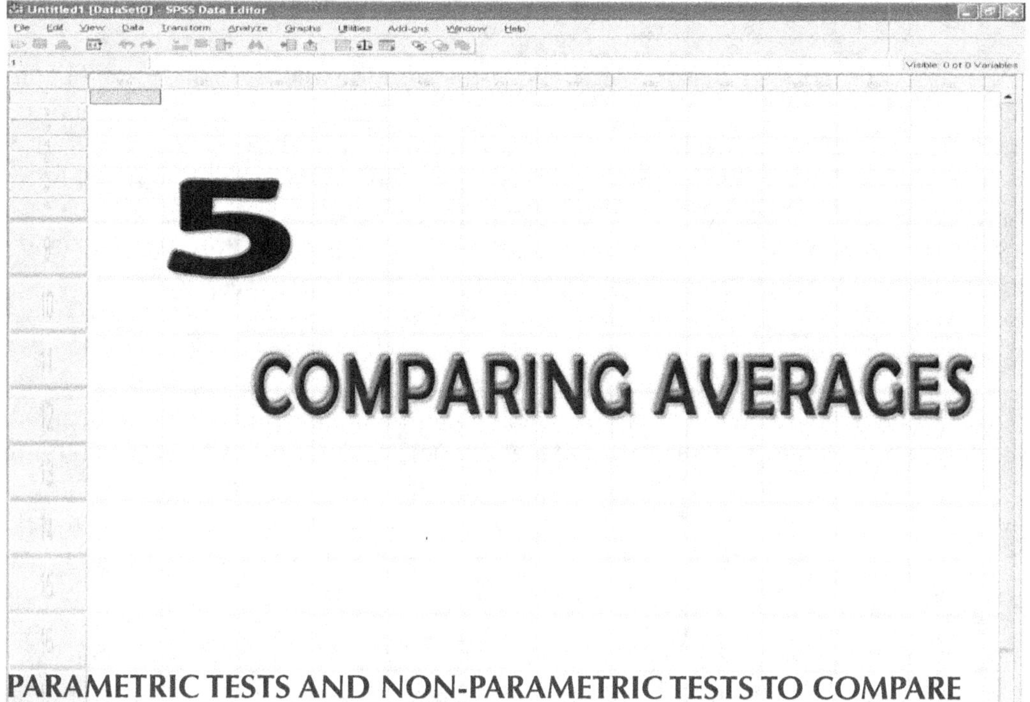

5

COMPARING AVERAGES

PARAMETRIC TESTS AND NON-PARAMETRIC TESTS TO COMPARE AVERAGES

This chapter deals with the statistical procedures for testing the significance of averages. The objective of any statistical enquiry is to infer the characteristics of a population by analysing the characteristics of a small sampling group. In carrying out these analyses we come across different situations. In some studies, we assume that the sample/samples have come from population which are normally distributed and have equal mean and variance, for example, the height of individuals in a population. To test the significance of difference, the hypothesis is proposed on population parameters. Such testing procedures are called parametric tests. Many other common statistical procedures like regression and analysis of variance have similar assumptions.

However, there are statistical methods/tests that comprise procedures not requiring estimations of population mean or/and not stating hypotheses about parameter, for example, increase in pulse rate in doing some adventurous activity. In this case we do not have any existing population and so we do not assume mean and variance (population parameters) in proposing a hypothesis.

The procedures that do not state hypotheses about parameter are called non-parametric tests. The following explanations and examples deal with Student's t-test and its non-parametric equivalents like Mann–Whitney test and Wilcoxon test.

STUDENTS *t*-TEST

W.S. Gosset described a distribution called *t*-distribution and the test of significance based on it is called *t*-test. The *t*-distribution is based on degrees of freedom. Degrees of freedom is defined as the number of variates that can be entered in that distribution before the value of the remainder of the variates are fixed to produce a certain value ($df = n - 1$). The *t*-test enables us to test the significance of difference between two sample means or significance of a single mean. These procedures are called two-sample test and one-sample test respectively.

Two-sample Test

Independent sample t-test A safe decision making depends on careful understanding of data. There are different experimental and quasi-experimental researches where the observations of the same variables are compared under different conditions. In such situations two-sample test is the most appropriate test. When we go ahead with two-sample test, we have to decide whether the two groups are independent or related. What do we mean by independent samples? A sample of 100 individuals is drawn from the population and randomly divided into two groups and one group is subjected to some experimental conditions and the rest to control conditions. In this set up the individuals in one group have no effect on the other group. The two groups are independent, i.e., the two groups are independent samples of data, each consisting of 50 observations. The most appropriate test for this situation is the independent sample *t*-test.

The independent samples *t*-test procedure compares means for two groups of cases. Ideally, for this test, the subjects should be randomly assigned to two groups, so that any difference in response is due to treatment (or lack of treatment) and not due to other factors. This is not the case if you compare average income for males and females. A person is not randomly assigned to be a male or female. If you want to apply independent samples *t*-test, you should ensure that differences in other factors are not masking or enhancing a significant difference in means. Differences in average income may be influenced by factors such as education (and not by sex alone).

For example, patients with high blood pressure are randomly assigned to a placebo group and a treatment group. The placebo subjects receive an inactive pill and the treatment subjects receive a new drug that is expected to lower blood pressure. After the subjects are treated for two months, the two-sample *t*-test is used to compare the average blood pressures for the placebo group and the treatment group. Each patient belongs to one group and is tested once.

There are many situations in which an investigator must decide whether an observed difference between two sample means is attributed to chance or whether the two samples have come from two populations with unequal means. For instance, he may want to know whether there is a real difference in the performance of men and women in completing a task with respect to time. One may be interested to know whether the average diet in one country is more nutritious than that in another country. A biologist may be willing to know whether the difference in the wing length of a particular variety of bird, at two different geographical areas, is large enough to suggest speciation. A healthcare provider may be interested in recommending a particular diet to increase haemoglobin level in children. In all these situations, we have two sets of data from two different populations, either hypothetical or existing. Here the null hypothesis is that there is no difference in the means of two samples.

The formula for manual calculation is as follows:

$$t = \frac{\left|\overline{X} - \overline{X}_2\right|}{\sqrt{SE_1^2 + SE_2^2}}$$

where,

$\overline{X}_1$ —mean of sample 1

$\overline{X}_2$ —mean of sample 2

SE_1—standard error of sample 1

SE_2—standard error of sample 2

Standard error is calculated by applying the following formula, where SD is the standard deviation and n_1 and n_2 are the size of sample 1 and 2.

$$SE_1 = \frac{SD_1}{n_1}; \qquad\qquad SE_2 = \frac{SD_1}{n_2}$$

Standard deviation is calculated as

$$SD_1 = \sqrt{\frac{\sum\left(X_i - \overline{X}_1\right)^2}{n_1 - 1}}; \qquad\qquad SD_2 = \sqrt{\frac{\sum\left(X_i - \overline{X}_2\right)^2}{n_2 - 1}}$$

where,

n_1—size of sample 1

n_2—size of sample 2

t value calculated follows $n_1 + n_2 - 2$ degrees of freedom.

The null hypothesis is $\overline{X}_1 = \overline{X}_2$.

The t-values calculated may be positive or negative.

The significance level is set either as 0.05 or 0.01. It is up to the investigator to set either of these levels. In the former case we reject the null hypothesis if t is either greater than the 97.5th percentile or less than the 2.5th percentile of t-distribution with specified degrees of freedom. When we say the significance level is 0.05, the confidence level is 95% and if the significance level is 0.01, the confidence level is 99%.

Independent sample t-test with SPSS

Example 5.1

Two groups of children were fed on two different diets namely, diet A and diet B. The level of haemoglobin in blood were estimated and presented in the table below. Test the superiority of diet B over diet A in increasing the haemoglobin level.

Diet	Haemoglobin (gm%)													
A	10	11	12	11	10	9	10	9.5	12	13	11	11	12	10
B	11	11	12	13	11	9	12	10	11	12	12	12	13	10

Null hypothesis The diet B is not superior to diet A in increasing the haemoglobin level.

Step 1 Open **Data Editor**, click **Variable View**, name the variable as "Diet" under **Name**, select **Numeric** under **Type**, label as **Diet** under Label (Figure 5.1).

Step 2 Click on the grey area under **Value**. A popup window opens as in Figure 5.2, type 1 in the **Value** box and "**Diet A**" in **Label** box and click Add to transfer it to the box below. Type "2" in the **Value** box and "Diet B" in **Label** box and click **Add** to transfer it to the box below and click **OK**.

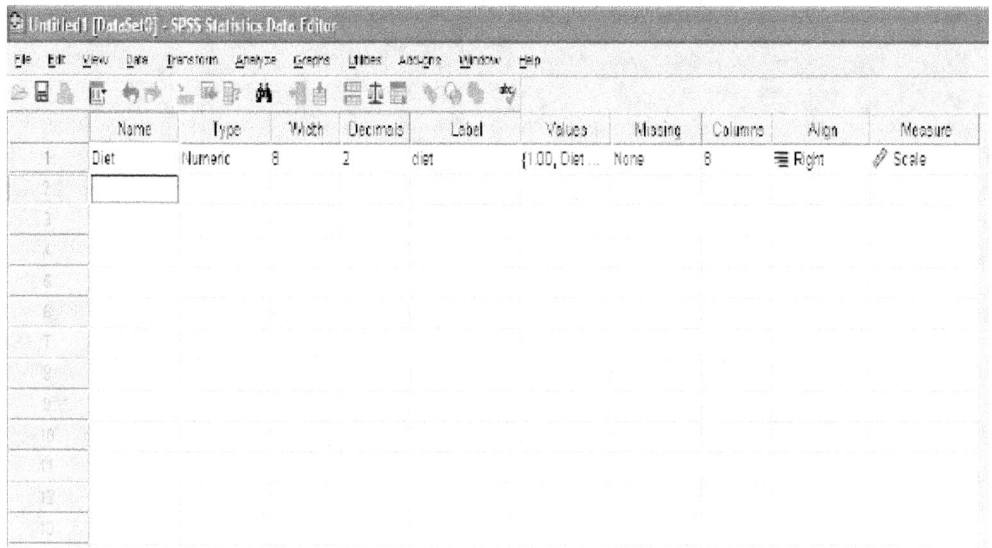

Figure 5.1   **Variable View** with name of the variable **Diet** typed under **Name**

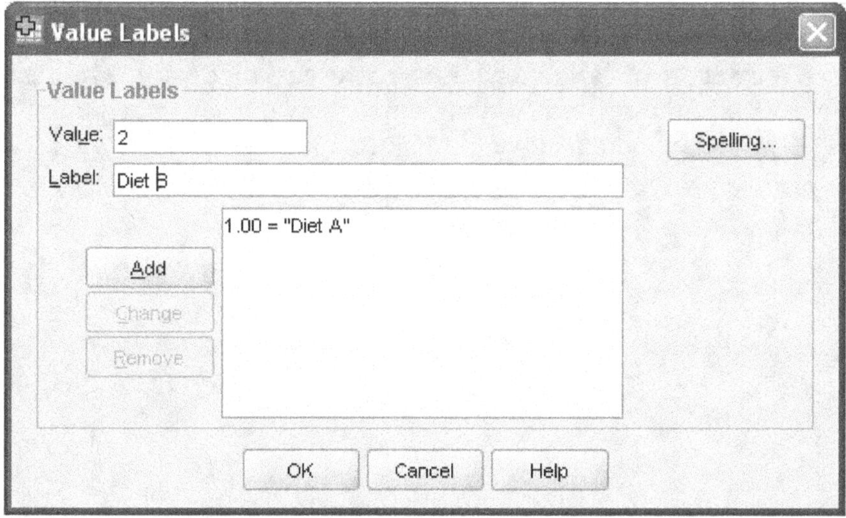

Figure 5.2   **Value Labels** box to enter code numbers for grouping variable

Step 3 Go to the second row and type "Haemoglobin" under **Name** select **Numeric** under **Type**, type as "Level of haemoglobin (gm%)" under **Label** (Figure 5.3).

	Name	Type	Width	Decimals	Label	Values	Missing	Columns	Align	Measure
1	Diet	Numeric	8	2	diet	{1.00, Diet...	None	8	Right	Scale
2	Haemoglobin	Numeric	8	2	Haemoglobin (gm%)	None	None	8	Right	Scale

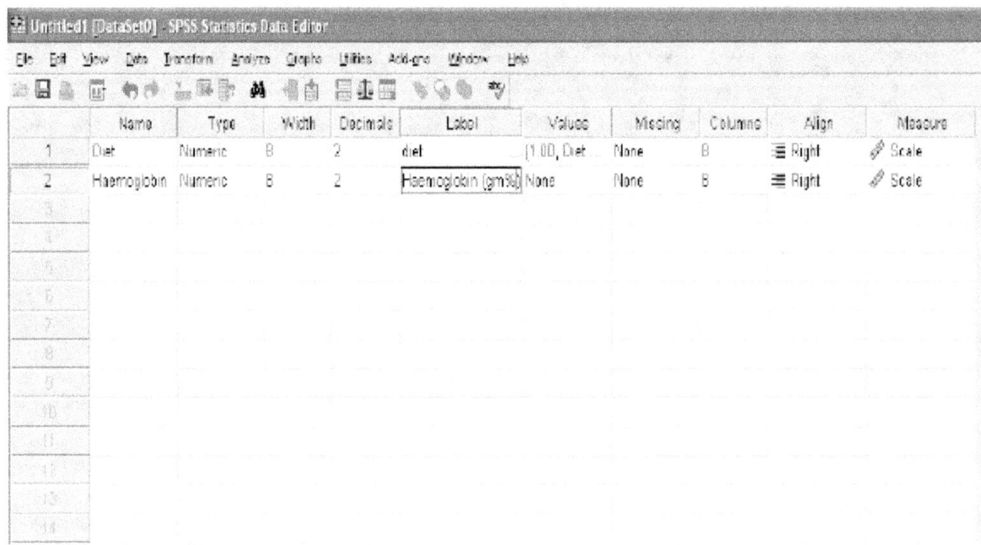

Figure 5.3 Variable View with two variables named under **Name**

Step 4 Click **Data View** and enter data in the column under **Diet** as "1" for 1 to 14 cases and "2" from 15 to 28 cases (here diet is entered as categorical variable where 1 represents diet A and 2 represents diet *B).* In the second column, enter the values for haemoglobin under Haemoglobin as given in Figure 5.4.

	Diet	Haemoglobin
1	1.00	10.00
2	1.00	11.00
3	1.00	12.00
4	1.00	11.00
5	1.00	10.00
6	1.00	9.00
7	1.00	10.00
8	1.00	9.50
9	1.00	12.00
10	1.00	13.00
11	1.00	11.00
12	1.00	11.00
13	1.00	12.00
14	1.00	10.00
15	2.00	11.00
16	2.00	11.00
17	2.00	12.00
18	2.00	13.00
19	2.00	11.00
20	2.00	9.00
21	2.00	12.00
22	2.00	10.00
23	2.00	11.00
24	2.00	12.00
25	2.00	12.00
26	2.00	12.00
27	2.00	13.00
28	2.00	10.00

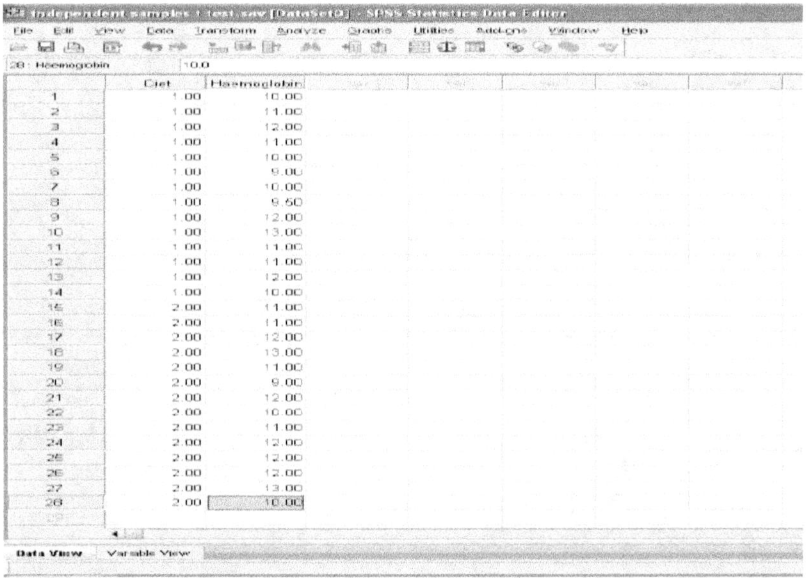

Figure 5.4 Data View with data entered for two variables

Step 5 Choose **Analyze**, select **Compare Means** and then select **Independent samples T-Test** (Figure 5.5).

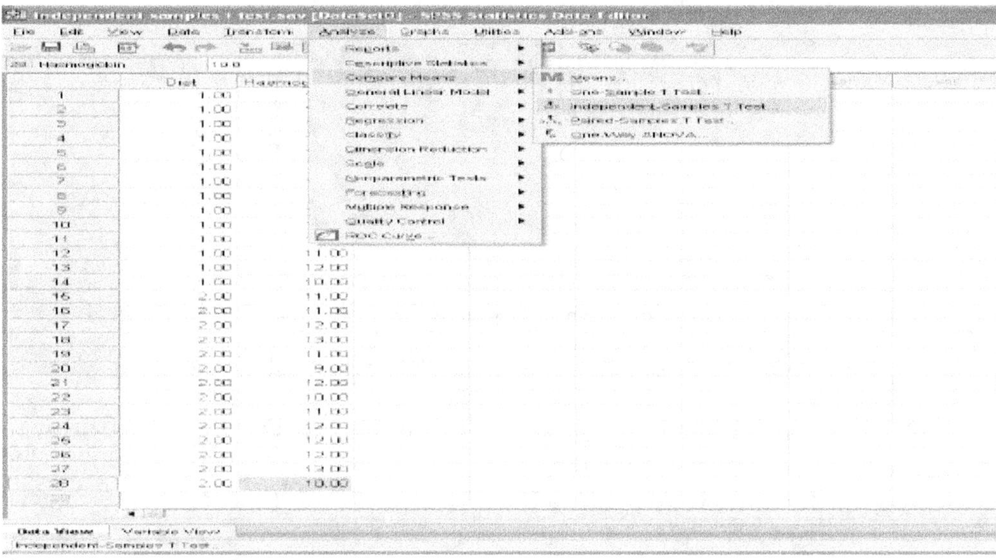

Figure 5.5   Selecting **Independant-samples T-Test** from main menu

Step 6 Independent-Samples T-Test window **opens**, transfer **Haemoglobin** to **Test Variable(s):** and **Diet** to **Grouping Variable:** (Figure 5.6).

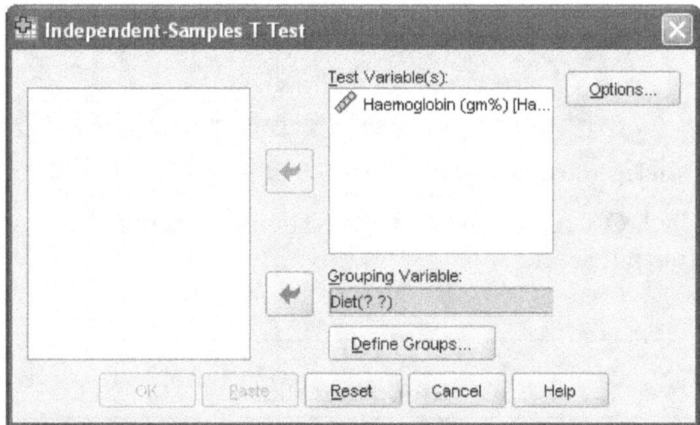

Figure 5.6   **Independent-Sample T-Test** dialog box with the variables transferred into **Test Variable(s);** and **Grouping Variable** boxes

Step 7 Click on **Define Groups**, a pop up window with **Define Groups** opens. Type **1** under Group **1** and "**2**" under **Group 2** (here we are giving the values as 1 and 2 since we have specified these values for two groups to be compared, Diet A and Diet B respectively), click **Continue** (Figure 5.7).

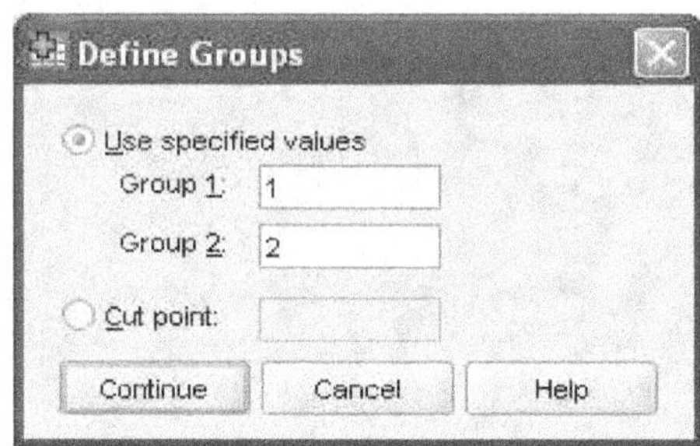

Figure 5.7 Define Groups dialog box with values specified

Step 8 Click **Options**. A popup window opens (Figure 5.8). Check the **Confidence interval** box. It has the default value as 95%. Click Continue (If you want to increase the confidence level to 99, type there as "99").

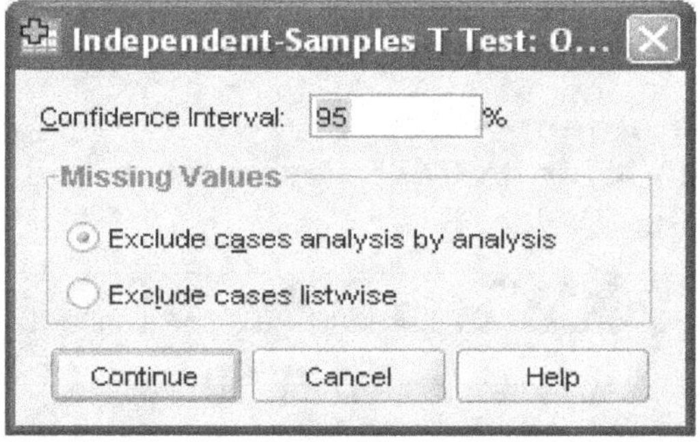

Figure 5.8 Independent-samples T-Test: box with 95% confidence Interval selected

Step 9 Click **OK** to run the analysis. The output appears as given in below (output 1 and 2).

Output 1

Group Statistics

	diet	N	Mean	Std. Deviation	Std. Error Mean
Haemoglobin (gm%)	Diet A	14	10.8214	1.14	0.3
	Diet B	14	11.3571	1.15	0.31

Output 2

Independent Samples Test

		Levene's Test for Equality of Variances		t-test for Equality of Means						
									95% Confidence Interval of the Difference	
		F	Sig.	t	df	Sig. (2-tailed)	Mean Difference	Std. Error Difference	Lower	Upper
Haemoglobin (gm%)	Equal variances assumed	.002	.966	-1.239	26	.226	-0.54	0.43	-1.42	0.35
	Equal variances not assumed			-1.239	25.996	.226	-0.54	0.43	-1.42	0.35

Interpretation

Output 1 gives the mean haemoglobin level in the individuals fed with Diet A is 10.82 with a standard deviation of 1.136 (gm %) and for Diet B, the mean level is 11.357 with a standard deviation of 1.15 (gm %).

Output 2 gives the t-value, degrees of freedom, significance level and 95% confidence interval for the mean. The t-value of -1.239 for 26 ($14 + 14 - 2$ as each group has 14 values) degrees of freedom (df) is not significant as significance value (for two-tailed test) is 0.226 which is >0.05. Therefore, we accept the null hypothesis, i.e., diet B is not superior to diet A in increasing the haemoglobin level.

Paired sample t-test

In independent samples t-test we have tested the significance of difference between means of two independent samples. In that case the observation or value of each item is completely independent. But in a situation where the observations are not completely independent but dependent, they are given as pairs of observations (each pair is from same subject). At times, we have a set of data, where the observations or measurements are made on the same individual, for example, a physician wants to test the efficiency of a particular drug for reducing blood pressure. In this case he may take a group of 50 individuals who are hypertensive and measure the blood pressure and have it as a set of data. These 50 individuals are given the particular drug and the blood pressure is measured and the values are written against each case. Now we have a set of paired data, i.e., blood pressure before and after giving the drug. In this case also we have two sets of observations but a pair for each case (Though there are 100 observations in two groups they are based on only 50 individuals). The most appropriate test is a two-sample test but here it is a paired sample t-test and not independent samples *t*-test.

The paired-sample *t*-test procedure compares the means of two variables for a single group. The procedure computes the differences between values of the two variables for each case and tests whether the average differs from 0.

Formula for manual calculation is given by

$$t = \frac{\bar{D}}{s/\sqrt{n}}$$

where,

$\bar{D}$ —mean differece

S—standard deviation

n—size of sample

$$\bar{D} = \frac{\Sigma D}{n}$$

$$D = X_i - Y_i$$

where,

D—difference between pair of observations

X_i—Value before

Y_i—Value after

$$s = \sqrt{\frac{\left(\Sigma D - \bar{D}\right)^2}{n}}$$

Paired sample t-test with SPSS

Example 5.2

An investigator wants to evaluate the effect of a particular supplementary diet in increasing the level of haemoglobin in man. He selected a group of 15 individuals, the level of haemoglobin in these persons were estimated and then these individuals were fed on the supplementary diet. After feeding for a sufficient period of time, the level of haemoglobin in these persons were estimated. The data obtained in this study is given in the form of a table. Evaluate the efficiency of the supplementary diet in increasing haemoglobin (gm %) level.

Before	10	12	11	10	9.5	10.5	11.5	10	9.8	10.5	12	11	11.5	10.5	9.9
After	11	12	12	11	10	11.5	12	10	10	11	13	12	12	11	10

Null hypothesis The supplementary diet is not effective in increasing haemoglobin level in human.

Step 1 Open **Data Editor**, click **Variable View**, name the variable as "**HBbefore**" under **Name**, select **Numeric** under **Type**, label as "Before- Haemoglobin level (gm%)" under **Label**, then go to the second row and type under **Name** as "**HBafter**", select **Numeric** under **Type**, label as "After-Haemoglobin level (gm%)" under **Label** (Figure 5.9).

Step 2 Click **Data View** and enter data under **Before** and **After**.

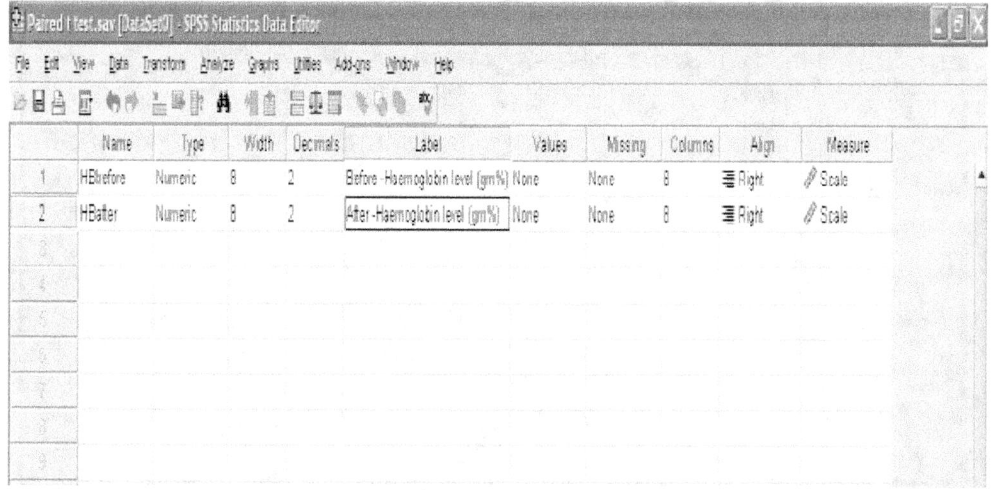

Figure 5.9 **Variable View** with two variables entered

Step 3 Choose **Analyze**, then select **Compare Means** and then select **Paired-Samples T Test** (Figure 5.10).

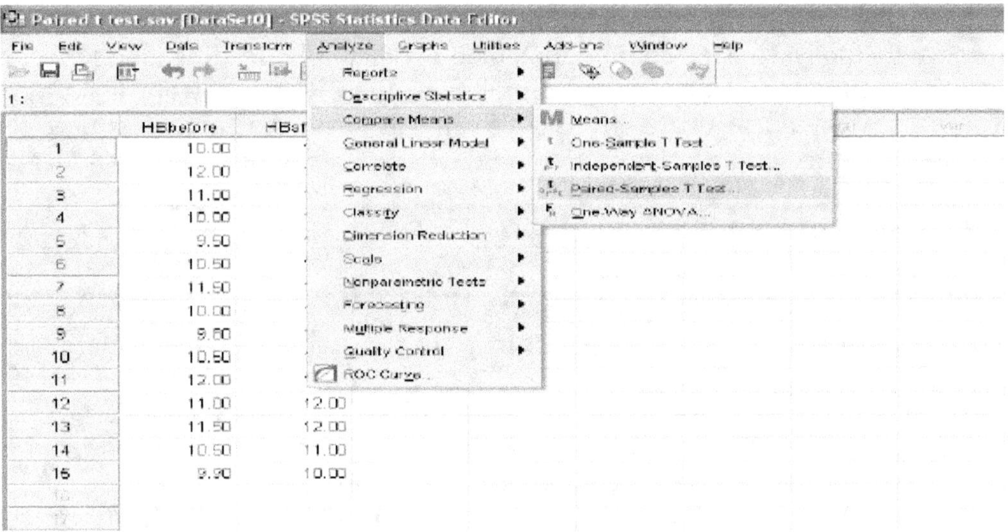

Figure 5.10 Selecting **Paired-Samples T Test** from main menu

Step 4 A pop up window appears as **Paired-Sample T Test** as in Figure 5.11.

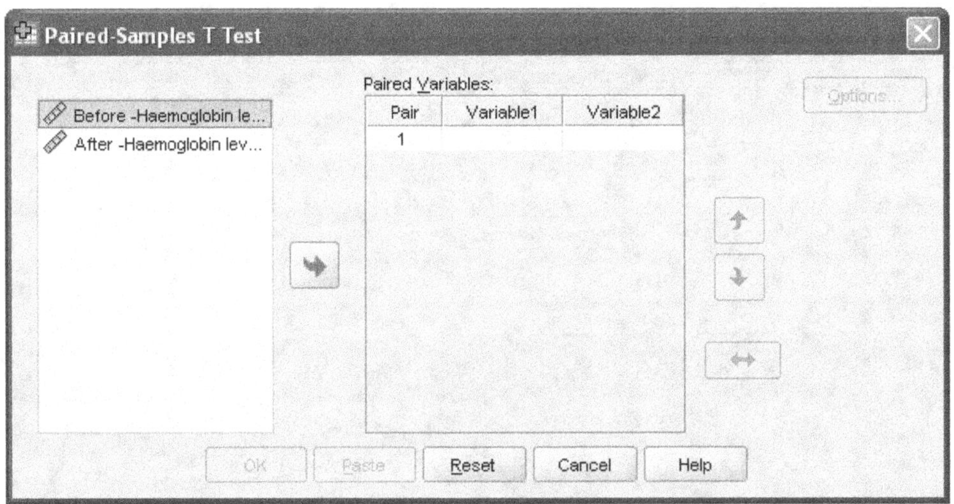

Figure 5.11 **Paired-Samples T Test** dialog box

Step 5 Transfer the variable **Before–Haemoglobin** to **Variable 1** and **After–Haemoglobin** to **Variable 2** as in Figure 5.12.

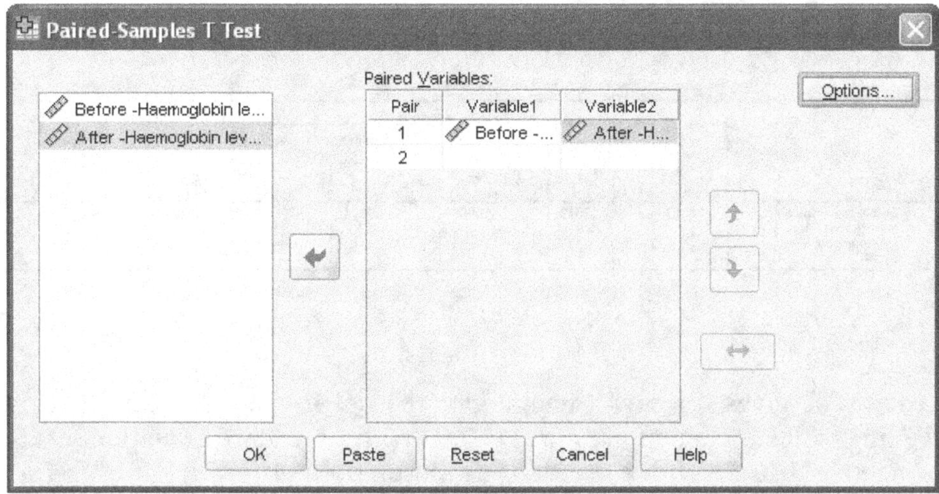

Figure 5.12   **Paired-Samples T Test** dialog box with paired variables transferred

Step 6 Click **Options** and check the **Confidence Interval box** (Figure 5.13). It has the default value as 95% (If you want increase the confidence level to 99 type as "99"), click **Continue**.

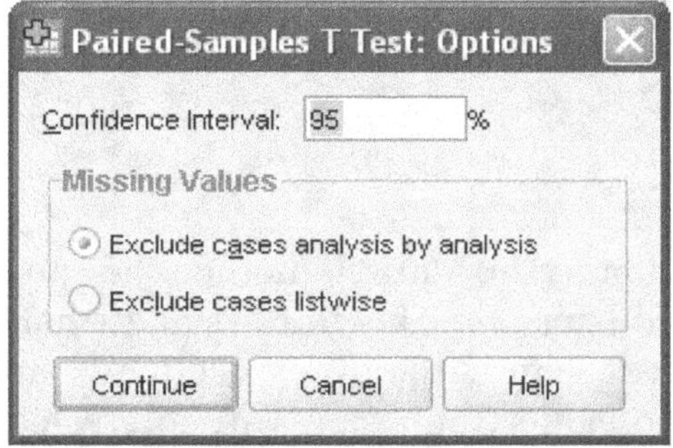

Figure 5.13   **Paired-Samples T Test: Options** with Confidence Interval 95% selected

Step 7 Click **OK** to run the analysis. The outputs appear as shown here.

Output 1

Paired Samples Statistics

		Mean	N	Std. Deviation	Std. Error Mean
Pair 1	Before -Haemoglobin level (gm%)	10.6467	15	.81404	.21019
	After -Haemoglobin level (gm%)	11.2333	15	.94239	.24332

Output 2

Paired Samples Test

		Paired Differences							
					95% Confidence Interval of the Difference				
		Mean	Std. Deviation	Std. Error Mean	Lower	Upper	t	df	Sig. (2-tailed)
Pair 1	Before -Haemoglobin level (gm%) - After - Haemoglobin level (gm%)	-.58667	.39073	.10088	-.80304	-.37029	-5.815	14	.000

Interpretation

Output 1 gives the mean haemoglobin level in the individuals before feeding with supplementary diet as 10.64 with a standard deviation of 0.81 (gm %) and 11.23 with a standard deviation of 0.94 (gm %) after feeding with the supplementary diet.

Output 2 gives the t-value, degrees of freedom, significance level and 95% confidence interval for the mean difference. The t-value of -5.815 for 14 degrees of freedom (df) is highly significant as significant value for two-tailed test is 0.000 (Output 2). Therefore, we reject the null hypothesis. Hence, supplementary diet is effective in increasing haemoglobin level in human.

One-Sample *t*-Test

The one-sample t-test procedure tests whether the mean of a single variable differs from a specified constant. This test assumes that the data are normally distributed. This procedure tests the difference between a sample mean and a known or hypothesized value. Suppose we are interested in testing

1. if the sample mean $\overline{X}$ differs significantly from specified value of population mean μ_0
2. if the given population has a specified value of the population mean say, μ_0.
3. if the given random sample $x_1, x_2 \ldots x_n$ of size n has been drawn from a normal population with a specified mean μ_0.

Basically, all these three situations call for the same procedure. In these conditions the null hypothesis is set up as follows:

i. H_0: There is no significant difference between the sample mean and population mean, i.e., in other words $\overline{X} = \mu_0$.

ii. $H_0: \mu = \mu_0$ i.e., the population mean is μ_0.

iii. H_0: The given random sample is drawn from the normal population with mean μ_0.

$$t = \frac{\left|\overline{X} - \mu_0\right|}{S/\sqrt{n}}$$

where,

S—standard deviation of the sample

n—sample size

$$S = \sqrt{\frac{1}{n-1}\Sigma\left(X_i - \overline{X}_i\right)^2}$$

where,

X_i—the value of the variable X, and

$\overline{X}$—mean

Applications of one-sample t-test   Several variables like height, weight, leaf length, respiratory output, pulse rate, blood pressure, blood sugar, haemoglobin level, weight of grapes, fruits in a garden, etc. are variables which can be classified and given on an interval scale. When these values are plotted on a graph the resulting graph is most frequently bell shaped with a single mode and is called as a normal curve. The values of different measures of central tendency like mean, median and mode tend to occur in the centre of the distribution. The values of the variable on either side of the measure of central tendency, namely mean are distributed equally. The sum of deviations of different values from the mean on either side is equal to zero. This kind of distribution is called normal distribution. One-sample *t*-test is applicable to any data on a continuous scale and the researcher collects data on only one-sample and the sample size is large. This test is not applicable for small samples. One sample *t*-test allows us to test whether a sample mean (of a normally distributed interval variable) significantly differs from a hypothesized value.

In all the above examples, based on the sample data, a single value is assigned to a population parameter. The population parameter, thus assigned is accepted or rejected by hypothesis testing and inferences are drawn on population mean and standard deviation. The application of one-sample *t*-test is explained with the following examples.

One-sample t-test with SPSS

Example 5.3

The following data gives the haemoglobin level (gm%) in a group of 15 women students studying in a college. Test whether the haemoglobin level in the young women is significantly lower than the average level of 13 gm% expected for women population. Infer whether the women in the age group are having the tendency towards anaemia.

Case	1	2	3	4	5	6	7	8	9	10	11	12	13	14	15
Haemoglobin (gm%)	10	12	11	10	9	8	12	10	11	9	10	12	11	9	10

Null hypothesis The haemoglobin level in women studying in a college do not differ significantly from the haemoglobin level of 13 gm% of women population.

Step 1 Open **Data Editor**, click **Variable View**, name the variable as "**Haemoglobin**", select **Numeric** under **Type**, label as "Haemoglobin (gm%)" under **Label**, click **Data View** and enter data in **Data View** under **Haemoglobin** as given in Figure 5.14.

	Haemoglobin
1	10
2	12
3	10
4	11
5	9
6	8
7	12
8	10
9	11
10	9
11	10
12	12
13	11
14	9
15	10

Figure 5.14   Data View with values entered for haemoglobin

Step 2 Choose **Analyze**, select **Compare Means** and than select **One-sample T Test** (Figure 5.15).

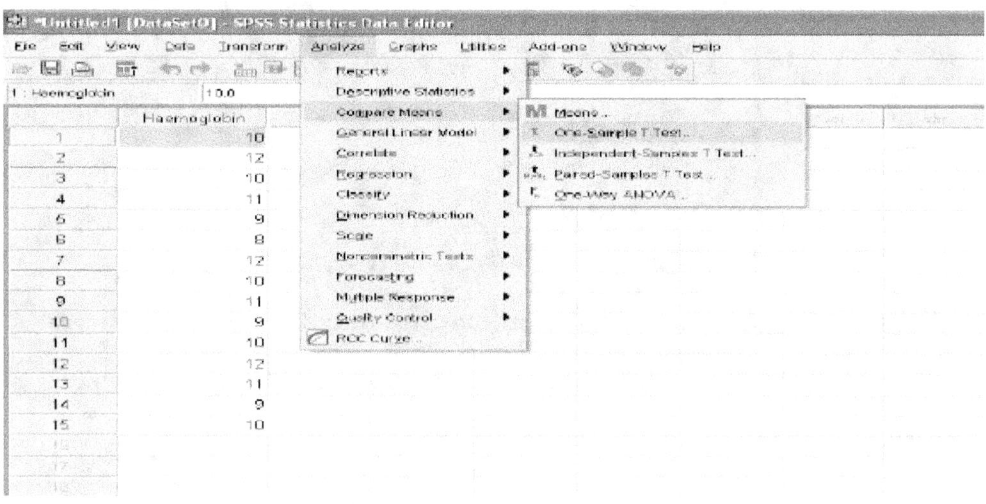

Figure 5.15   Selection of **One-Sample T Test** from main menu

Step 3 Transfer the variable under study "Haemoglobin (gm %)" to **Test variable(s)**: box (Figure 5.16). Type in the **Test Value** box as 13 (Here we are testing whether the mean level of haemoglobin of this sample differs significantly from the normal level of 13 gm % expected for women in the population).

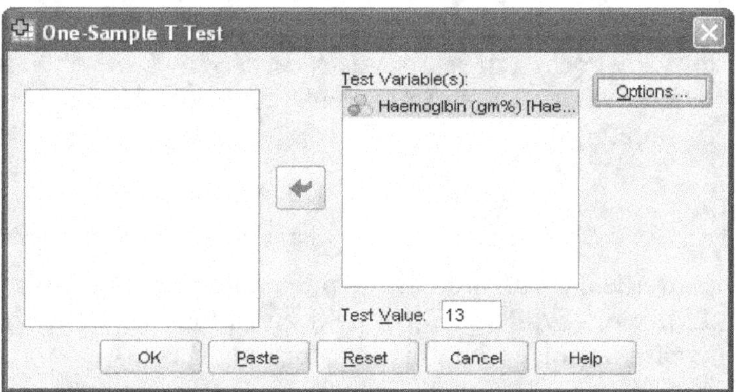

Figure 5.16   **One-sample T Test** with variable transferred in Test variable(s) box

Step 4 Click **Options** and check the **Confidence Interval** box (Figure 5.17). It has the default value as 95%. Click **Continue** (If you want increase the confidence level to 99% type as "99").

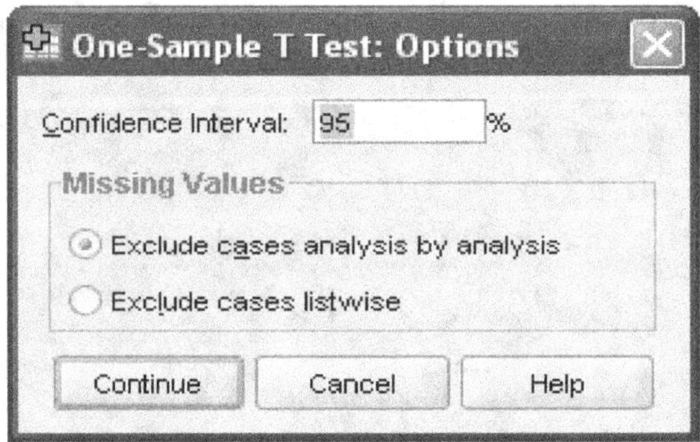

Figure 5.17   One-Sample T Test: Options to type confidence Interval

Step 5 Click OK to run the analysis. The outputs appear as given below.

Output 1

Interpretation

Output 1 gives the mean haemoglobin level as 10.27 (gm %) and standard deviation of 1.22.

Output 2 gives the *t*-value, degrees of freedom, significance level and 95% confidence interval for the mean. *t*-value of -8.657 for 14 degrees of freedom (*df*) is highly significant as significant value is 0.000. Therefore, we reject the null hypothesis. Thus, haemoglobin level in the young women is significantly lower than the average level of 13gm% expected for women in the population. The women in that age group are having the tendency towards anaemia.

Example 5.4

The following are the data on increase in pulse rate (beats/minute) recorded by a doctor on 32 persons while performing a given task. Find whether there is a significant increase in pulse rate while performing this task.

Null hypothesis   There is no increase in pulse rate while performing a given task.

Step 1 Open **Data Editor**, Click **Variable View**, name the variable as Pulse, select **Numeric** under **Type**, label as "Pulse rate in beats/minute" under **Label**. Click **Data View** and enter data in **Data view** under **Pulse** as given in Figure 5.18.

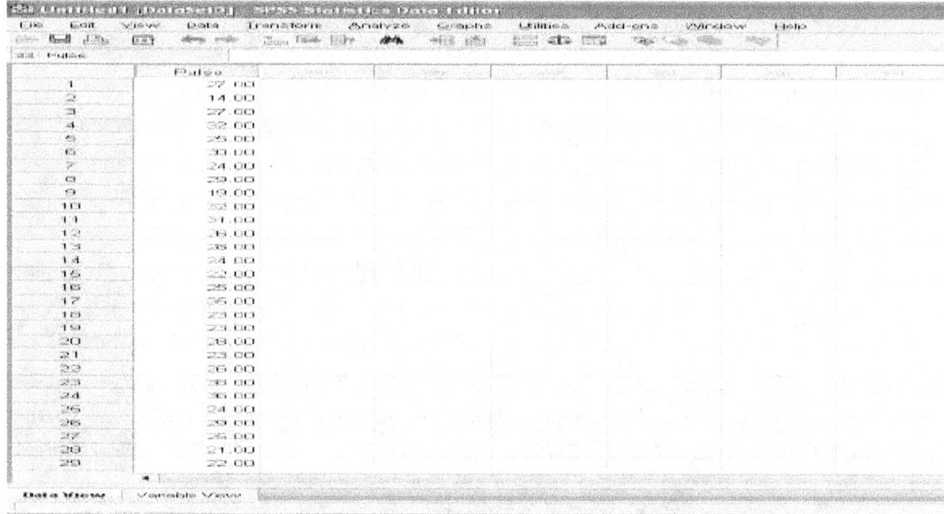

Figure 5.18   **Data Editor** with values entered

Step 2 Choose Analyze, Compare Means and than select One-Sample T Test (Figure 5.19).

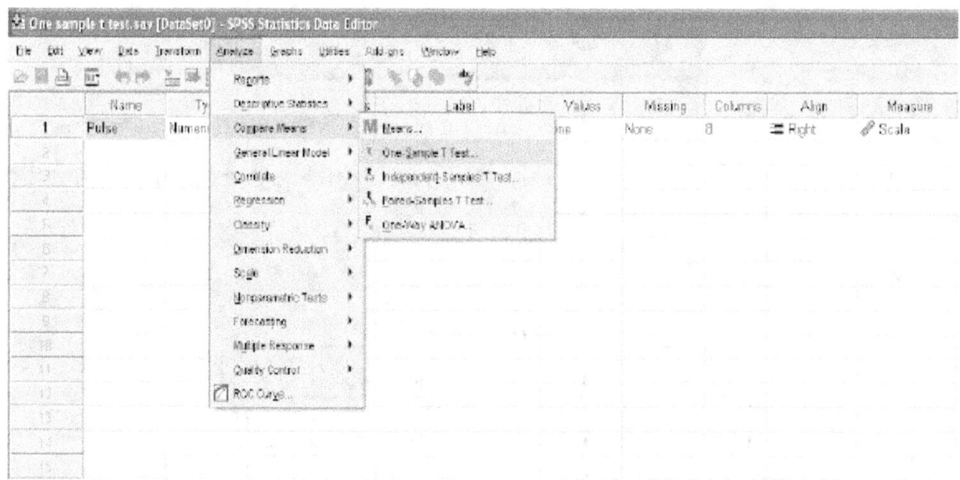

Figure 5.19   Selecting **One-Sample T Test** from main menu

Step 3 Transfer the variable under study (Haemoglobin) to **Test variable(s):** box (Figure 5.20). In the **Test Value** box you will see 0 as default, do not alter it (Here we are not having any of the expected increase in pulse rate. This is in contrast to the situation in the previous example of haemoglobin level, where we had the expected level for women in the population).

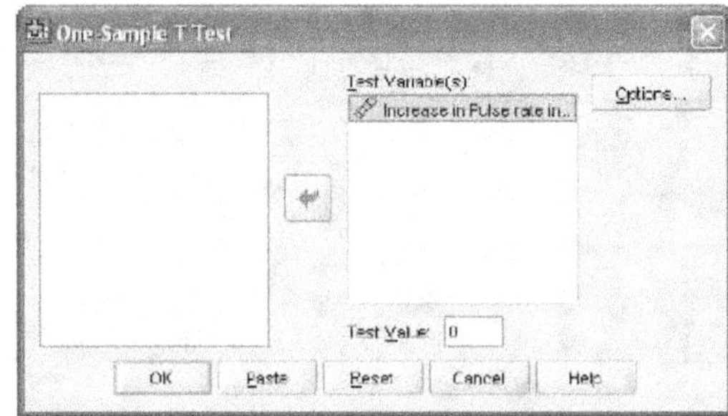

Figure 5.20   **One-Sample T Test** with variable transferred in test variable(s): box

Step 4 Click Options in One-Sample T-Test: Options dialog box, Confidence Interval has 95% as default (otherwise type 95 in than) and then click Continue (Figure 5.21).

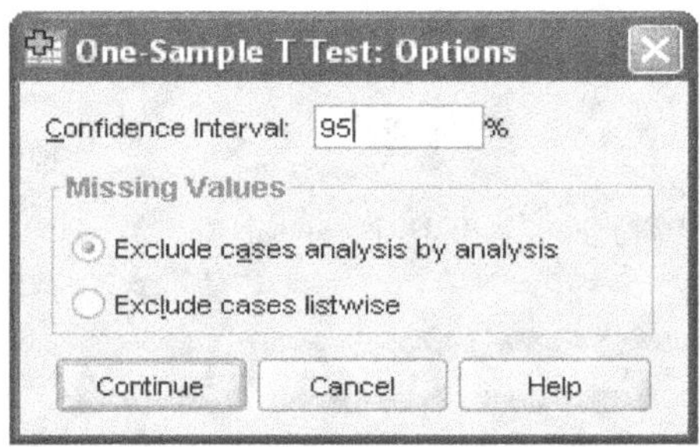

Figure 5.21   Selecting confidence Interval from **One-Sample T Test: Options**

Step 5 Click OK to run the analysis. The outputs appear as in Output 1 and 2.

Output 1

One-Sample Statistics

	N	Mean	Std. Deviation	Std. Error Mean
Increase in Pulse rate in beats / minutes	32	26.5313	5.43	0.96

Output 2

One-Sample Test

	Test Value = 0					
					95% Confidence Interval of the Difference	
	t	df	Sig. (2-tailed)	Mean Difference	Lower	Upper
Increase in Pulse rate in beats / minutes	27.64	31	2.1E-23	26.53125	24.5736	28.4889

Interpretation

Output 1 gives the average increase in pulse rate of 26.5 beats/minute and standard deviation of 5.43.

Output 2 gives the *t*-value, degrees of freedom, significance level and 95% confidence interval for the mean. *t*-value of 27.64 for 31 degrees of freedom (*df*) is highly significant as significance values for two-tailed test is 0.000. **Therefore, there is an increase in pulse rate of persons performing the given task**. The average increase in pulse rate (namely population mean μ) lies in the interval from 24.57 to 28.489 beats/minute. To make it simple the average increase in pulse rate of the population in performing the given task may lie between 24.57 and 28.049 beats/minute. In making such a statement we are 95% confident.

OTHER TESTS FOR COMPARING AVERAGES

Non-parametric tests such as two-sample testing procedures are sometimes stated as applicable to data on ordinal scale, but this is not so. It is applicable to data on either interval or ratio scale.

Mann-Whitney's Test for Independent Samples

Mann–Whitney test is a **non-parametric analog** to the independent samples *t*-test. It is one of the best known non-parametric significance tests. It was proposed initially by Frank Wilcoxon in 1945, for equal sample sizes, and extended to arbitrary sample sizes ways by Mann and Whitney (1947). This, like many non-parametric tests, uses the ranks of data rather than their raw values to calculate the statistic. When we workout the problem manually, the ranks are assigned for the entire data, the ranks are summed up and Mann–Whitney statistics (U) is calculated by applying the formula

$$U = n_1 n_2 + \frac{n_1 (n_1 + 1)}{2} - R_1$$

where, n_1 and n_2 are the number of observations in samples 1 and 2 respectively, R_1 is the sum of the ranks of observations in sample 1 and 2.

In this test the calculated U is interpreted based on the table values as in other tests. Since we use SPSS, the details are not furnished here. Mann–Whitney test is one of the most powerful non-parametric tests, however, when either Mann-Whitney test or two-sample *t*-test is applicable; the former is about 95% as powerful as the latter.

The Mann–Whitney U test requires four conditions:

1.   The dependent variable must be on interval or ratio scale or at least on ordinal scale.
2.   The independent variable has only two levels.
3.   Design of study is between-subject.
4.   The subjects are not matched across conditions.

Application of Mann–Whitney test   Mann–Whitney test is used in different fields, but it is used frequently in fields like Psychology, Medicine, Nursing and Business. For example, in Psychology, Mann–Whitney test is used to compare attitude, behavior etc. In medicine, it is used to know the effect of two medicines. It is also used to know whether or not a particular medicine cures an ailment. In Business, it can be used to know the preferences of different people.

Mann-Whitney with SPSS   Independent samples on interval scale.

Example 5.5

The pulse rate (pulse/min) of two independent random samples, one from male population and the other from female population sitting inside a fast moving coach are given below. Find out whether there is a difference in the mean pulse rate of two (male and female) populations.

Male	72	69	72	68	68	70	70	68	68	69	69	75	74
Female	73	72	75	70	68	73	74	74	70	72	71	71	63

Null hypothesis   The pulse rate of both male and female sitting inside a fast moving coach is equal.

Step 1 Open Data Editor, click **Variable View**, name the variable as "Gender", select **Numeric** under **Type**, label as "Gender" under **Label** (Figure 5.22). Click on the grey area under **Value** and type "1" in the **Value** box and "male" in **Label** box and click **Add** to transfer it to the box below, type "2" in the **Value box** and "female" in **Label box**, click **Add** to transfer and click **OK**. Go to the second row and type as "Pulse" under **Name**, select **Numeric** under **Type**, type as "Pulse rate (counts/minute)" under **Label**.

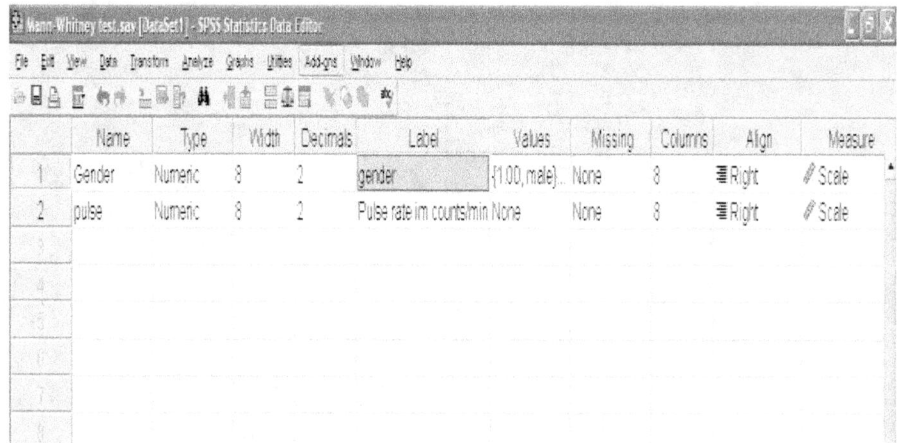

Figure 5.22   Variable View with variables entered

Step 2 Click on **Data View** and enter data as in Figure 5.23.

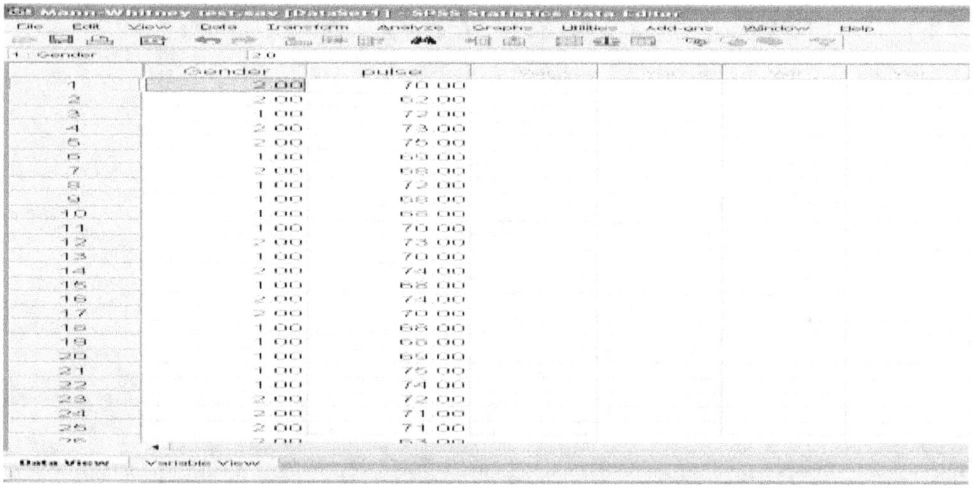

Figure 5.23   Data Editor with data

Step 3 Choose **Analyze**, click **Non-parametric** and then select **2 Independent Samples** (Figure 5.24).

Step 4 In the **Two-Independent-Samples Tests** dialog box (Figure 5.23), transfer **Pulse rate** in counts/min to **Test Variable List** box and **Gender** to **Grouping Variable** box (this step is similar to Independent sample *t*-test). Now click on **Define Groups** and type "1" (for male) in the **Group 1** box and "2" (for female) in **Group 2** box (Figure 5. 25) and click **Continue**.

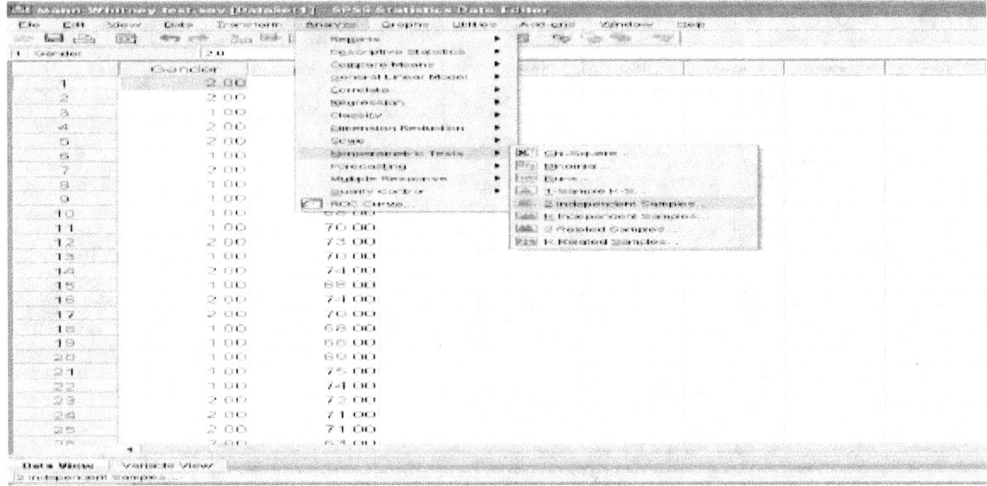

Figure 5.24   Selecting **2 Independent Samples** from main menu

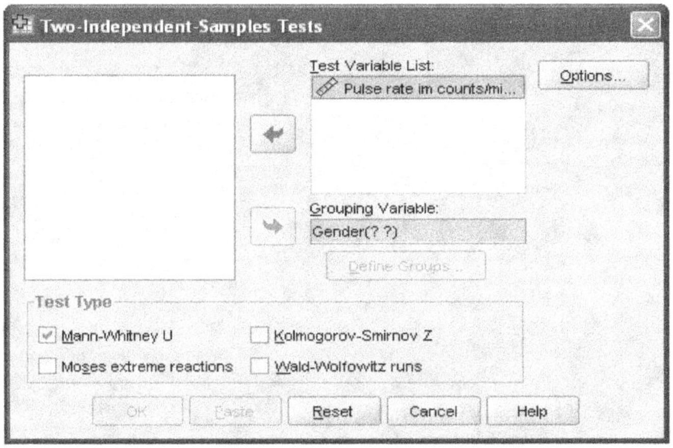

Figure 5.25   **Selecting Mann-Whitney U** from **Two-Independent Samples** tests dialog box

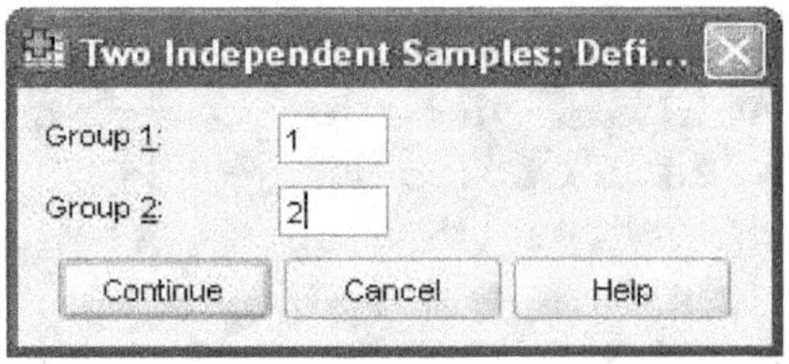

Figure 5.26   Defining group 1 and 2 in **Two-Independent Samples** dialog box

Step 5   The previous step will bring you back to Two-Independent-Samples Tests pop up window, now select Mann-Whitney U under Test Type (Figure 5.27).

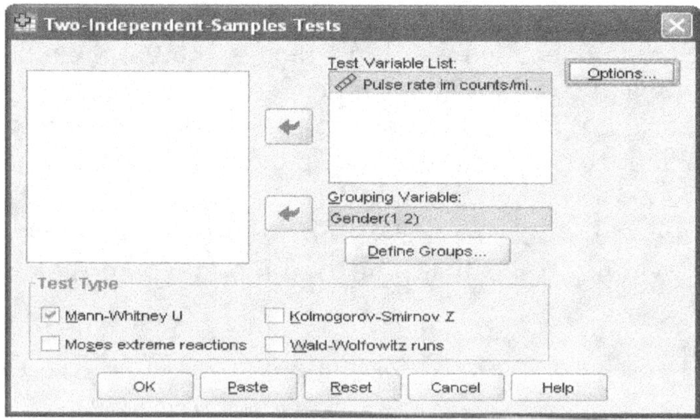

Figure 5.27   **Two-Independent–Samples Tests** dialog box with Mann–Whitney U selected

Step 6   Click **OK** to run the analysis. The outputs appear as to heads **Ranks** and **Test Statistics**.

Output 1

Ranks

	gender	N	Mean Rank	Sum of Ranks
Pulse rate in counts/min	male	13	12	156
	female	13	15	195
	Total	26		

Output 2

Test Statistics[b]

	Pulse rate in counts/min
Mann-Whitney U	65.000
Wilcoxon W	156.000
Z	-1.010
Asymp. Sig. (2-tailed)	.313
Exact Sig. [2*(1-tailed Sig.)]	.336[a]

a. Not corrected for ties.

b. Grouping Variable: gender

Interpretation

In Mann–Whitney U test we need to report the test statistics and its significance. Since Mann–Whitney's U value is 65.00 and exact p-value for 2 tailed including one tailed is 0.336 which is > 0.05, the null hypothesis can be accepted at 0.05 level of significance. There is enough evidence to conclude that there is no difference in the mean pulse rate of male and female populations sitting inside a fast moving coach in the given study.

Mann-Whitney test for independent sample (ordinal scale) with SPSS Mann-Whitney test can also be used for data on ordinal scale.

Example 5.6

Twenty five undergraduate students were guided by two different lab technicians separately. On the basis of final grades, test the null hypotheis that the students perform equally well in the course.

Technician A	A	A	A	A–	B	B	C+	C+	C	C	C–			
Technician B	A	A	B+	B+	B	B–	C	C	C–	D	D	D	D	D–

Null hypothesis The performance of the students is the same (equal) under two lab technicians.

Step 1 Open Data Editor, click **Variable View**, name the variable as "Technician", select **Numeric** under **Type**, label as "Technician" under **Label** (Figure 5.28). Click on the grey area under **Value** and type "**1**" in the **Value** box and "**Technician A**" in **Label** box and click **Add** to transfer it to the box below and type "**2**" in the **Value** box and "Technician B" in **Label** box and click **Add** to transfer it to the box and click **OK**. Go to the second row and type as **Grade** under **Name**, "select **Numeric**" under **Type**, type as "**Grade**" under **Label**. In the "**Value column type 1** in the **Value** box and **grade A** in **Label** box and click **Add** to transfer it to the box. Give the values in a similar way like 2, 3, 4, 5, 6, 7, 8, 9and 10 for A-, B+, B, B-, C+, C, C-, D and D- respectively by clicking **Add** each time.

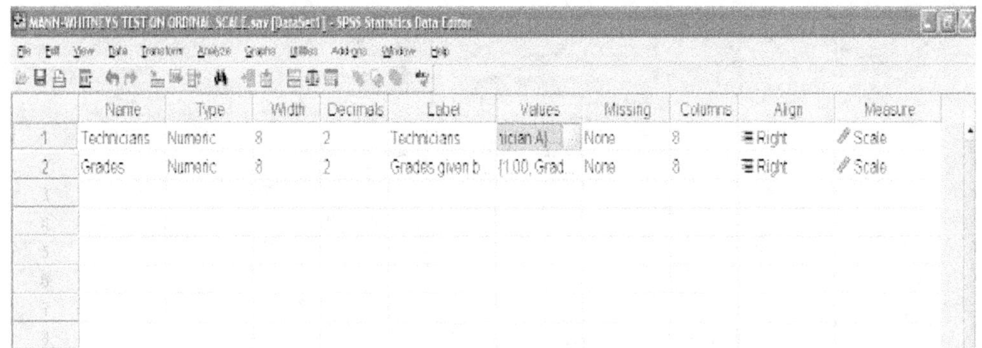

Figure 5.28   Variable View with 2 variables entered

Step 2 Click on data editor and enter data in **Data Editor** as in Figure 5.29.

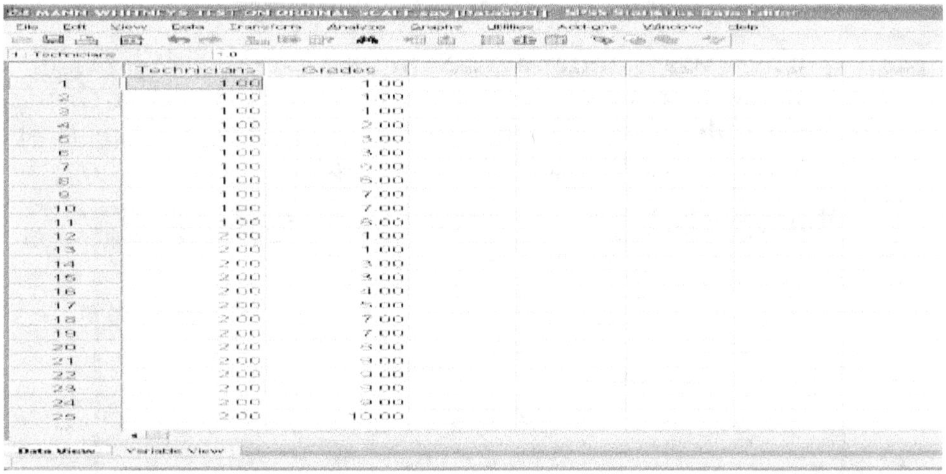

Figure 5.29   Data View with data entered

Step 3 Choose **Analyze**, click **Non-parametric** and then select **2 Independent Samples** (Figure 5.30).

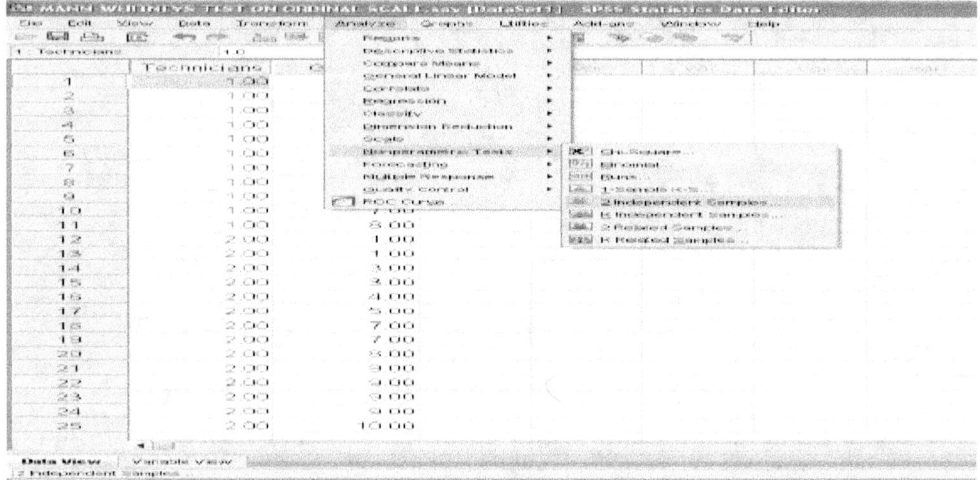

Figure 5.30 Selecting **Two Independent Samples** from main menu

Step 4 In the **Two-Independent-Sample Tests** (Figure 5.31), transfer **Grade** to **Test variable List box** and **Technicians** to **Grouping Variable** box (this step is similar to Independent sample *t*-test). Select **Mann–Whitney U** under **Test Type**.

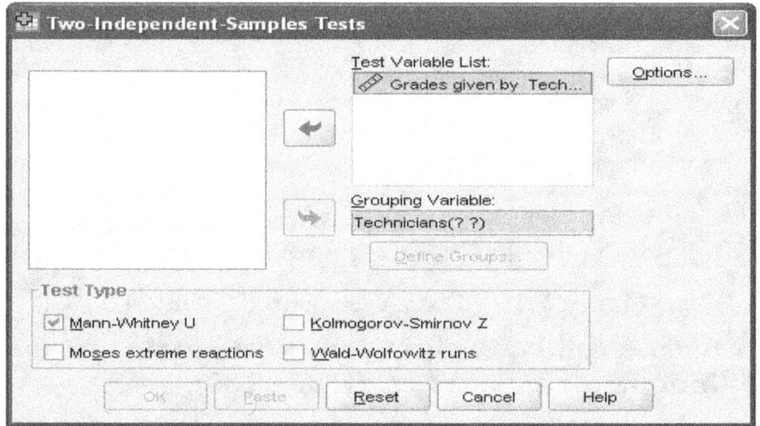

Figure 5.31 Mann–Whiney U Selected in **Two Independent Samples** tests box

Step 5 Click on **Define Groups** and type 1 (Technicians A) in the **Group 1** box and "2" (Technicians B) in **Group 2** box (Figure 5.32) and click **Continue**.

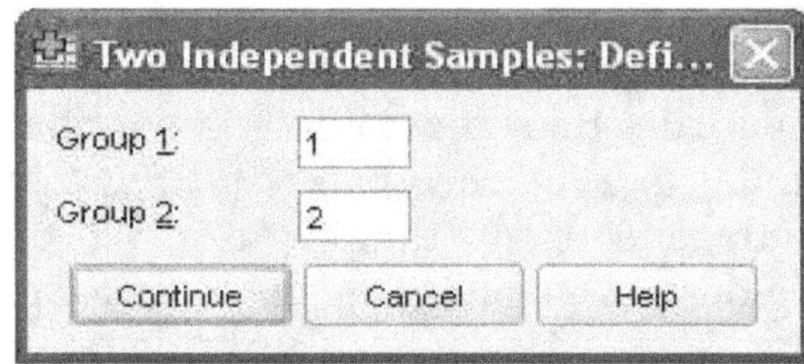

Figure 5.32   Defining groups in **Two-Independent Samples** dialog box

Step 6 Click **OK** to run the analysis. The outputs appear as given below.

Output 1

Ranks

	Technicians	N	Mean Rank	Sum of Ranks
Grades given by Technicians	Technician A	11	10.14	111.50
	Technician B	14	15.25	213.50
	Total	25		

Output 2

Test Statistics[b]

	Grades given by Technicians
Mann-Whitney U	45.500
Wilcoxon W	111.500
Z	-1.742
Asymp. Sig. (2-tailed)	.082
Exact Sig. [2*(1-tailed Sig.)]	.085[a]

a. Not corrected for ties.

b. Grouping Variable: Technicians

Interpretation

Output 1 gives the number of cases, mean rank and sum of ranks. Mann–Whitney U statistics is 45.5 and *p*-value for two tailed including one tailed is 0.085 which is >0.05, therefore the null hypothesis can be accepted at 0.05 level of significance. The performance of the students guided by the two lab technicians is the same.

Wilcoxon Matched-Pairs Sample Test

The Wilcoxon Matched-Pairs Ranks test is a non-parametric test that is often regarded as being similar to a matched pairs t-test, just as Mann–Whitney test is the analog to the independent two-sample t-test. Wilcoxon signed-ranks test applies to two-sample designs involving repeated measures, matched pairs, or "before" and "after" measures. It is applicable to data on ratio scale and ordinal scale as well. The Wilcoxon test is used to determine the magnitude of difference between matched groups.

The matched-pair (or paired-sample) version (observation pairs (x_1, y_1), (x_2, y_2), ...) is concerned with the differences $(x_1 - y_1)$, $(x_2 - y_2)$, ... With the assumption that these differences are independent observations from a symmetric distribution, the null hypothesis is that this distribution has median zero. The testing procedure involves the calculation of the difference between each set of pairs. Then one ranks the absolute values of difference from low to high and then gives the sign of each difference to the corresponding rank. Then the rank with + sign and rank with – are summed up separately. For a two-tailed test we reject the hypothesis if either T+ or T– is less than or equal to the critical value (given in the table). The p-value answers this question: If the median difference in the entire population is zero (the treatment is ineffective).

Wilcoxon matched-pairs signed-rank test with SPSS

Example 5.7

The table below shows the hours of relief provided by two analgesic drugs in 15 patients suffering from arthritis. Is there any evidence that one drug provides longer relief than the other?

Drug A	3.0	2	3.6	2.6	7.4	3	16	7	3.3	2	6.8	8.5	7	8	5.6
Drug B	3.5	3.5	5.7	2.4	9.9	4	18.7	6.6	4.5	4	9.1	1.8	8.5	7.5	2.9

Null hypothesis   Drug A and Drug B provides similar relief.

> **Step 1** Open **data Editor**, click **Variable View**, name the variable as **Drug A** select numeric under **Type**, label as **Relief in hours after taking drug A** under **Label**, then come to the second row and type under **Name** as **Drug B** select numeric under **Type**, label as **Relief in hours after taking drug B** under **Label** (Figure 5.33).

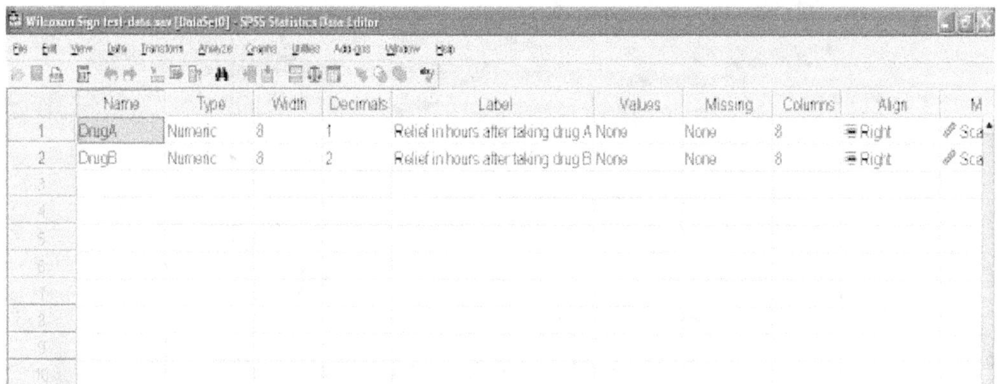

Figure 5.33   **Variable View** wtih two variables named

Step 2 Click **Data View** and enter data under **Drug A** and **Drug B**.

Step 3 Choose **Analyze**, click **Non-parametric** and select **2 Related Samples** (Figure 5.34).

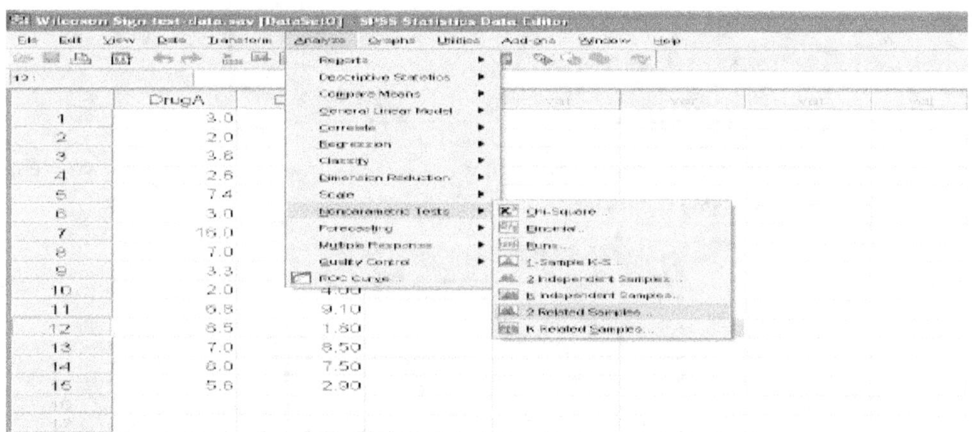

Figure 5.34   **Selecting 2 Related Samples** from main menu

Step 4 A pop up window appears as **Two-Related samples Test** as given in Figure 5.35.

Step 5 Transfer **Drug A-Relief in hours** . . . to the right hand side under **Variable 1** and **Drug B-Relief in hours** . . . under **Variable 2** (Figure 5.36).

Step 6 Select **Wilcoxon** under **Test Type** and click **Options**. **Two-Related-Samples: Options** dialog box opens (Figure 5.39), select **Descriptive** under **Statistics** and click **Continue**. Click **OK** to run the analysis.

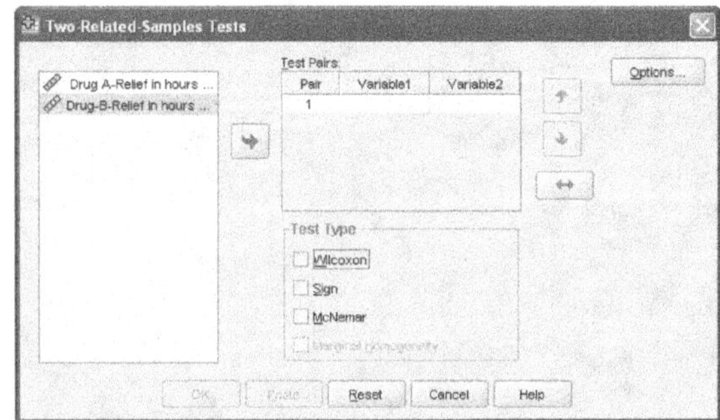

Figure 5.35   Two-Related Samples Tests dialog box

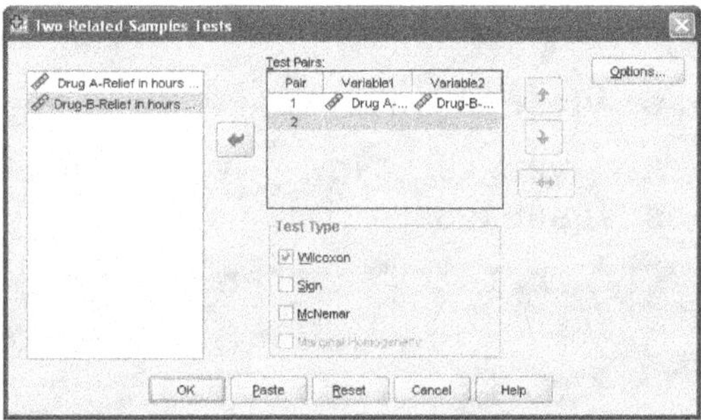

Figure 5.36   Variables transferred and Wilcoxon selected under Test Type in **Two-Related Samples Tests** dialog box

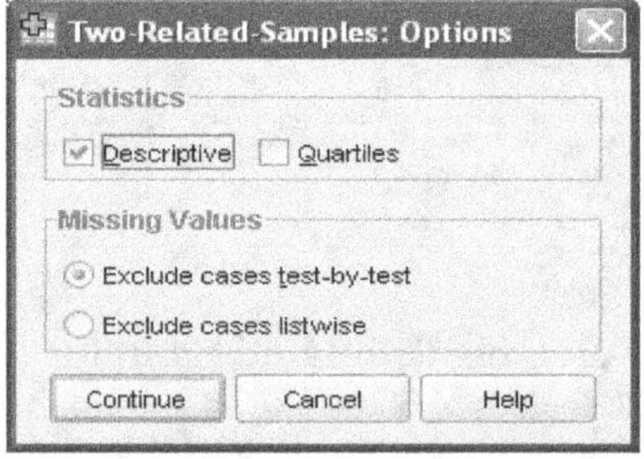

Figure 5.37 Descriptives selected in **Two-Related-Samples: Options**

Output 1

Descriptive Statistics

	N	Mean	Std. Deviation	Minimum	Maximum
Drug A-Relief in hours after taking drug	15	5.720	3.6688	2.0	16.0
Drug-B-Relief in hours after taking drug	15	6.1733	4.28927	1.80	18.70

Output 2

Ranks

		N	Mean Rank	Sum of Ranks
Drug-B-Relief in hours after taking drug - Drug A-Relief in hours after taking drug	Negative Ranks	5[a]	7.00	35.00
	Positive Ranks	10[b]	8.50	85.00
	Ties	0[c]		
	Total	15		

a. Drug-B-Relief in hours after taking drug < Drug A-Relief in hours after taking drug

b. Drug-B-Relief in hours after taking drug > Drug A-Relief in hours after taking drug

c. Drug-B-Relief in hours after taking drug = Drug A-Relief in hours after taking drug

Interpretation

Output 1 gives the average hours of relief after taking the drug A and B with standard deviation.

Output 2 gives mean ranks. The test statistics is given in output 3. Since the Asymp. Sig. (2-tailed) *p*-value is 0.155 which is >0.05, the null hypothesis, Drug A and Drug B provides similar relief can be accepted at 0.05 level of significance. Therefore, there is no evidence that one drug provides longer relief than the other.

Review Exercises

1. Following data show the nitrate content of water (mg/l) from two lakes. Analyze the data and infer whether the two lakes differ significantly in their nitrate content.

Lake 1	0.50	0.65	0.63	0.50	0.54	0.60	0.66	0.68	0.71	0.64
Lake 2	1.62	0.72	1.68	1.58	0.65	0.70	0.72	1.70	0.91	0.99

2. Two athletes were tested according to the time (seconds) to run a particular track and the results are given below. Test whether the two athletes have the same running capacity?

Athletes 1	28	30	32	33	33	29	34	30	32	31
Athletes 2	29	30	32	29	28	28	30	30	31	28

3. Following are the FOOD consumed in gram by two groups of rats. Calculate the mean and standard deviation of two samples given below. Find the significance of difference between two samples and infer the preference of one diet over the other. Draw bar diagram with error bars.

Bengal gram	65	63	67	64	68	70	71	69	75	73
Rice	58	60	61	63	62	67	66	62	68	69

4. The breath of leaves (cm) for two groups of trees is given below. Calculate the mean and standard deviation of two groups and find the significance of difference between two groups. Based on the difference is it possible to infer whether they are from two different species of trees? Draw bar diagram with error bars.

Group I	50	65	63	50	54	60	66	68	71	64
Group II	62	72	68	58	65	70	72	70	71	70

5. The cholesterol levels (mg/100 of serum) in a group of 10 individuals after taking a drug are 231, 245, 208, 258, 245,199, 252, 195,208, and 205. Find whether the drug is effective in reducing the cholesterol level in man. The normal cholesterol level in human is 190mg/100 of serum.

6. An anti-depressive drug was administered to 8 patients and the blood pressure (mm Hg) before and after the administration of the drug is given below. Find the effect of the drug in reducing the blood pressure.

Before drug administration	145	135	135	136	150	131	136	154
After drug administration	123	130	134	127	123	124	119	118

7. A Pharmaceutical company developed a drug, which it claims to increase hemoglobin content in aged people. The hemoglobin content (g/100 ml) of ten subjects is measured before and after the administration of drug. Determine whether the company's claim is valid after observing the following data.

Subject	1	2	3	4	5	6	7	8	9	10
Before	10	9	11	12	8	7	12	18	10	9
After	12	11	13	14	9	10	12	14	11	12

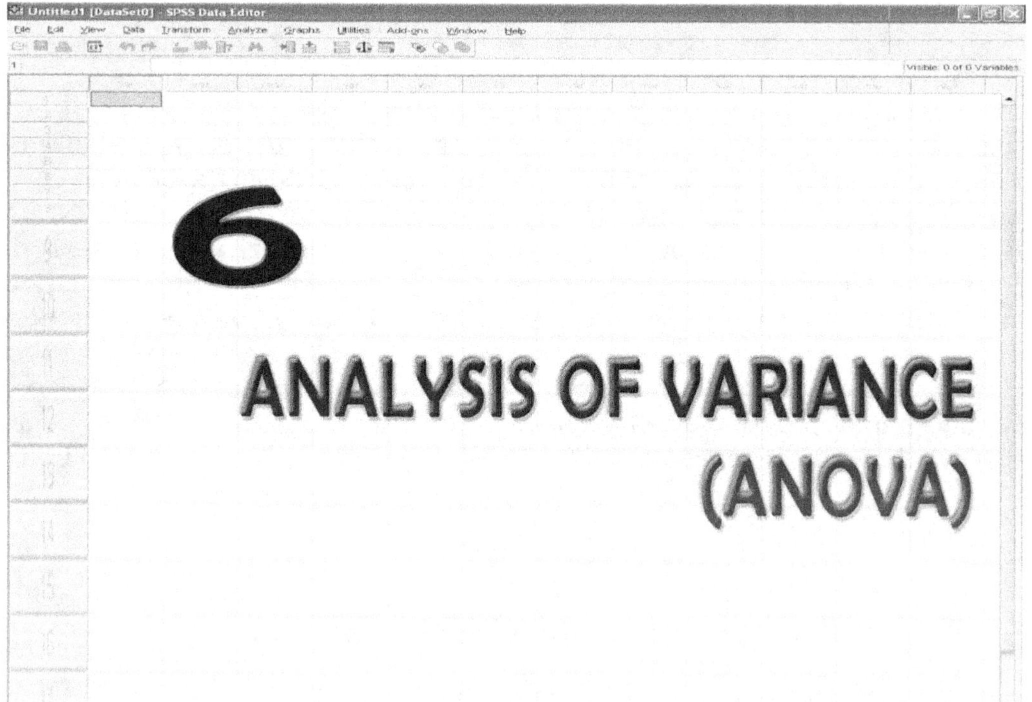

6

ANALYSIS OF VARIANCE (ANOVA)

In Chapter 5, the measurements of variables were obtained for two samples and one sample. t-test or non-parametric equivalents of t-test were used in hypothesis testing and deriving inferences. Often researchers obtain measurement of a variable on three or more samples from three or more populations. If we apply two-sample test and state the null hypothesis as $H_0 : \mu_1 = \mu_2; \mu_1 = \mu_3; \mu_2 = \mu_3$, it not will be appropriate. Employing such a series of two-sample tests for hypothesis testing is invalid for the following reason. When we perform each two-sample test at 5% (confidence) level of significance, there is 95% probability that we shall accept H_0 when the two population means are equal. For a set of three hypothesis proposed above, the probability of accepting all of them is only $0.95^3 = 0.86$. The probability of incorrectly rejecting at least one of the null hypothesis is $1 - 0.86 = 0.14$. The level of significance becomes 0.14 instead of 0.05. For this reason, we do not prefer t-test in hypothesis testing for more than two means; instead we select a procedure that tests the equivalence of mean. The appropriate procedure is single factor analysis of variance, often abbreviated as ANOVA, namely the F-test. Here, the appropriate null hypothesis is $H_0 : \mu_1 = \mu_2 = \mu_3 = \mu_4$. If there is significant difference, there is provision to go for post hoc-multiple comparison tests. Post hoc-multiple comparison tests enable us to find the range in response and test the significance of difference between means in pair as well.

ANALYSIS OF VARIANCE—ONE FACTOR BETWEEN SUBJECTS (ANOVA)

Analysis of Variance, abbreviated as ANOVA, was developed by R.A. Fisher; in fact the F-test was named in his honour. R.A. Fisher emphasized the importance of randomness, that is, identical sample size is not required for single-factor ANOVA, but the sample sizes should be as nearly equal as possible. The single factor ANOVA is said to represent a **completely randomized experimental design**. In ANOVA we assume that $\sigma_1^2 = \sigma_2^2 = \sigma_3^2 = \sigma_4^2$ and we estimate population variance and compartmentalize the variance as **total variance, between variance and within variance**. Thus, ANOVA is based on portioning the variation in the dependent variable. It compares the variance between groups with the variance within groups. If there is more difference between groups than there is within group, then it is the groups that make the difference and the result is statistically significant.

$$F = \frac{MS_{between}}{MS_{within}}$$

$MS_{between}$—mean sum of square between samples,

MS_{within}—mean sum of square within sample.

The larger the value of F-ratio, the larger is the variance between groups.

One-Way ANOVA

If the effect is tested only for one factor (one independent variable) on the variable (dependent) in question, then it is called univariate analysis.

Note Identical sample size is not required for single factor ANOVA, but the sample size could be as nearly equal as possible. There are no firm rules for the number of observations required. This is decided by the researcher in the field.

Basics and meaning One-way ANOVA is performed for only one independent variable and samples belong to different groups of same population. If an investigator wishes to test whether four different feeds result in different body weights in poultry, "feed" is the factor and "body weight" is the variable. The different types of feed are said to be levels of the factor. When the investigator designs his experiment, the experimental animal is assigned at random to receive one of the four feeds with approximately equal number of pigs receiving each feed. The data given below with manual calculation of F-value clearly explains the basics of one way ANOVA.

A	B	C
2	9	10
3	6	6
1	8	9
5	7	7
4	5	8
$K_A = 5$	$K_B = 5$	$K_C = 5$

Null hypothesis   There is no significant difference between different groups.

Grand mean = 6

$N = 15$, $\sum X_A = 15$, $\sum X_B = 35$, $\sum X_C = 40$, $\sum X^2 = 640$, $\sum X = 90$

Mean of A = 3   Mean of B = 7   Mean of C = 8

Step 1 *Compute total sum of squares*   Let us recall that the "sum of squares" refers to the sum of squared deviations of all members of a distribution from the mean of that distribution $SS_{total} = \sum (X - \bar{X})^2$.

$$= (2 - 6)^2 + (3 - 6)^2 + (1 - 6)^2 + \ldots + (8 - 6)^2$$
$$= 100$$

Step 2 *Compute SS between groups*   The term "between groups" is traditionally used. This process involves summing the squared deviations between each group mean and the grand mean making sure that we multiply each squared deviation by the number (K) in each group.

Thus,

$$SS_{between} = K_A (X - \bar{X}_A)^2 + K_B (X - \bar{X}_B)^2 + K_C (X - \bar{X}_C)^2$$

$$= 5(6 - 3)^2 + 5(6 - 7)^2 + 5(6 - 8)^2$$

$$= 45 + 5 + 20 = 70$$

Step 3 *Compute within-group (error) SS*   First sumup the squared deviations between each measurement in a specific group and then sum the within squares of all three groups.

Thus,

A	$(X_A - \bar{X}_A)^2$	B	$(X_B - \bar{X}_B)^2$	C	$(X_C - \bar{X}_C)^2$
2	1	9	4	10	4
3	0	6	1	6	4
1	4	8	1	9	1
5	4	7	0	7	1
4	1	5	4	8	0
Total	**10**		**10**		**10**

$$SS_{within} = 10 + 10 + 10 = 30$$

We have now partitioned the total variability of the data into a "between-group" component and a "within-group," or error component. The next step is to compute the two variances involved and compare them, for which an ANOVA table is formulated.

Step 4 Formulate ANOVA table

ANOVA table

Source	Degrees of freedom	Sum of squares	Mean square
Between	2	70	35.00
Within (error)	12	30	2.50
Total	**14**	**100**	

The degrees of freedom is $N - 1$. Since there is a total of 15 variates, the degrees of freedom for total is $15 - 1 = 14$ for total. The number of between-group degrees of freedom is found by subtracting 1 from the total number of groups; since there are 3 groups, the number of degrees of freedom for between-group is $3 - 1 = 2$. Within group degrees of freedom $= 15 - 3 = 12$. There are three groups, each with 5 variates; therefore $(5–1) + (5–1) + (5–1) = 12$.

Step 5 Find mean sum of square (MS)

$$MS_{between} = 70/2 = 35.00$$
$$MS_{within} = 30/12 = 2.50$$

Step 6 Find the F-ratio

The final step in the analysis of variance involves a comparison of between-group variance with within-group variance in order to determine whether between-group variance is significantly larger. In other words, we want to know if the treatment effects are significant or if differences between groups can be explained simply on the basis of random variation.

$$MS_{between} = 70/2 = 35.00$$
$$MS_{within} = 30/12 = 2.50$$

Interpretation

We read the F-value for 2 and 12 *df* from F-table (we go down the second column to the twelfth row). 2 degrees of freedom are associated with the numerator and 12 degrees of freedom with the denominator. Where the column and row intersect, we locate 3.88 as the critical F-value for the 0.05 level and 6.93 as the critical value for the 0.01 level. Since the calculated F-value is 14.00, which is greater than table F-value at 0.01 level of significance. We reject the null hypothesis. We may therefore, conclude that the treatment effect has produced statistically significant differences among the groups. In a single factor analysis, when there is significant difference in variance between samples the null hypothesis is rejected and a multiple comparison test is carried out to determine between which of sample means the difference occurs. In a single factor analysis, if F-value is insignificant, there is no need to go for post hoc-multiple comparison tests.

Post hoc multiple comparisons

In doing a single-factor analysis of variance, we test the null hypothesis H_0: $\mu_1 = \mu_2 = \mu_3 = \dots \mu_4$ and so on. However, when we reject the null hypothesis, it does not mean that all population means (μ_1, μ_2, μ_3, μ_4, etc.) are different from one another. Further, we do not know how many means are different from one another and where the differences are located among the given number of population means. This problem is tackled by multiple comparison tests. Multiple comparison tests are desired for one-factor analysis (Model I ANOVA and not for Model II ANOVA). In general multiple comparison tests for means have the same underlying assumptions like analysis of variance namely population is/are normally distributed and variance is homogenous. In all multiple comparisons testing, equal sample sizes are desirable, but sometime it is performed with unequal samples also.

There are as many as 18 post hoc–multiple comparison tests. Most of the tests are designed to examine the pair-wise differences. They give additional information on the same variable. Choice of comparison depends on the exact situation one has.

The conclusions on multiple comparison testing depend upon the order in which the pair-wise comparisons are considered. The proper procedure is to first compare the largest mean against the smallest, then the largest against next smaller and so on, until the largest can be compared with the second largest. Then one compares the second largest with smallest, the second largest with the next smallest and so on.

There are a number of multiple comparison tests, yet there is no agreement as to the best procedure to routinely employ. The most widely and commonly used tests are the Tukey test, Newman–Keuls test and Duncan's test, often referred as "Duncan Multiple Range Test".

Sometimes multiple comparison tests will yield ambiguous conclusions in the form of overlapping sets of similarities. In some cases, for example, sample 1 and 2 form a single subset indicating that both the samples have come from population 1 and sample 2, 3 and 4 form a single subset indicating that these three samples have come from population 2. In this case, sample 2 is assigned to population 1 and population 2 which is impossible). Thus we can only state that $\mu_1 \neq \mu_2 \neq \mu_4$ but we cannot conclude how μ_2 is related to μ_1, μ_2, μ_3 and μ_4. In this situation raising the sample size (larger number of data) would give appropriate conclusion.

If the sample size is larger, then results of multiple comparison tests would locate differences among means. One limitation of multiple comparison tests is its inability to determine the position of some means accurately.

Tukey test multiple comparison test   This test is a much-used multiple comparison test. It consists of a null hypothesis $H_0 : \mu_B = \mu_A$ versus alternate hypothesis $H_0 : \mu_B = \mu_A$. For example, if there are 4 groups (1, 2, 3 and 4). Tukey's test compares 1 and 2, 1 and 3, 1 and 4 and then 2 and 1, 2 and 3 and 2 and 4 and so on.

Tukey's test, also known as the Tukey range test, Tukey method, Tukey's honest significance test, Tukey's HSD (Honestly Significant Difference) test, or the Tukey–Kramer method, is a single-step multiple comparison procedure and statistical test generally used in conjunction with an ANOVA to find which means are significantly different from one another. Named after John Tukey, it compares all possible pairs of means and is based on a studentized range distribution (this distribution is similar to t-distribution. The test compares the means of every treatment to the means of every other treatment; that is, it applies simultaneously to the set of all pair-wise comparisons and identifies where the difference between two means is greater.

Duncan multiple range test   Duncan's new multiple range test (MRT) is a multiple comparison procedure developed by David B. Duncan in 1955. Duncan's MRT belongs to the general class of multiple comparison procedures that use the studentized range statistic to compare sets of means. This test is a variant of the Student–Newman–Keuls method that uses increasing alpha levels to calculate the critical values in each step. It is especially protective against false negative (Type II) error at the expense of having a greater risk of making false positive (Type I) errors. It is commonly used in agronomy and other agricultural research. Duncan's test has been criticized as being too liberal by many statisticians including Henry Scheffé and John W. Tukey. Duncan argued that a more liberal procedure was appropriate because in real world practice the global null hypothesis H_0 = "All means are equal" is often false and thus traditional statisticians overprotect a probably false null hypothesis against type I errors. If a researcher wants to find the range in response of different treatment groups to a particular treatment or homogenous response in different treatment groups then Duncan's multiple range test is the most appropriate one.

Example 6.1

The following data on blood sugar level (mg/100 ml) are obtained from a clinical lab. Analyse the variance between groups and find the effectiveness of the herbs on blood sugar level.

Normal	Diabetic	Herb 1	Herb 2
96.00	180.00	180.00	120.00
100.00	225.00	190.00	130.00
111.00	260.00	185.00	130.00
98.00	250.00	190.00	135.00
106.00	265.00	180.00	136.00
105.00	280.00	170.00	140.00

Null hypothesis   The group means are equal to one another.

One-way ANOVA with SPSS

> **Step 1 Open Data Editor**, click **Variable View**, (before beginning to enter the data, assign "factor" and "levels" and the variable to be tested, in this case the four groups are levels of same factor, namely treatment (experiment) and Sugar level is the variable. Name the variable as "Sugarlevel" under **Name**,

select **Numeric** under **Type**, label as "Blood Sugar level in mg/100 ml" (Figure 6.1).

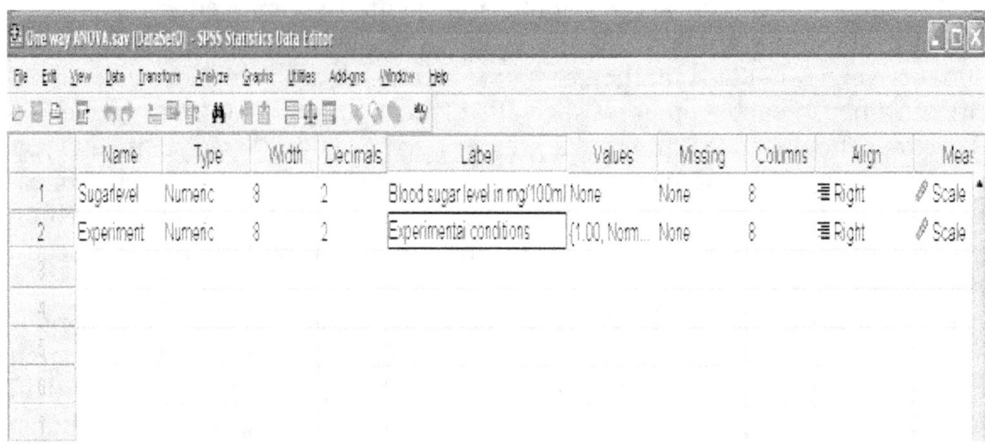

Figure 6.1   Appearance of **Variable View** with the details of 2 variables

Step 2 Go to the second row name the variable as "Experiment" under **Name**, select Numeric under Type, label as "Experimental conditions" under Label. Click Values column and double click on the grey area under Values. A popup window opens as in Figure 6.2, type "1" in the Value box and Normal in Label box and click **Add** to transfer it to the box down. Type "2" in the Value box and "**Diabetic**" in Label box and click **Add** to transfer it to the box down, proceed in a similar way for the rest of the data as "3" for "Herb "1" and "4" for "Herb "2"" by adding each time and click OK.

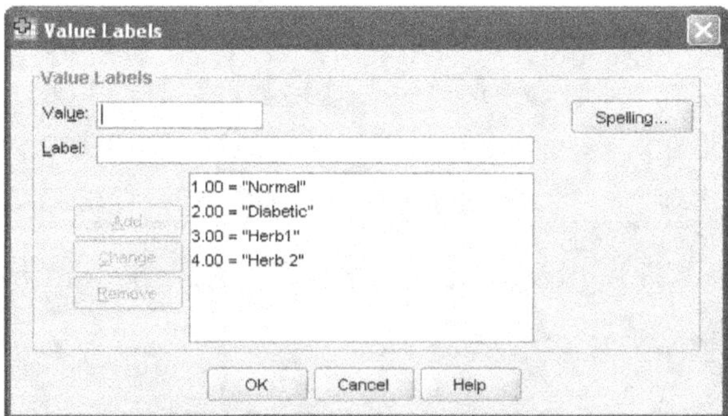

Figure 6.2   **Value Labels** dialog box with coded categorical variable

Step 3 Type data in **Data View** under each head. Choose Analyze from the Pull down menu select **Compare Means** and then click **One-way ANOVA** (Figure 6.3).

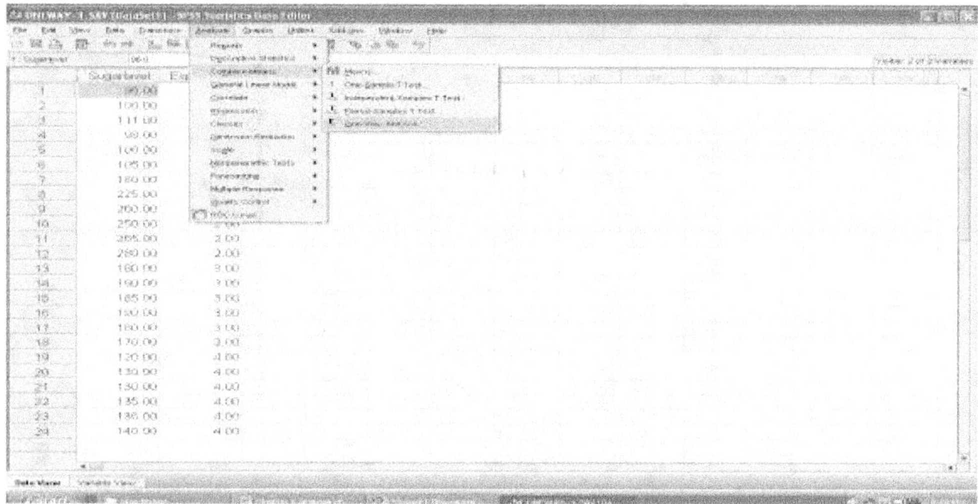

Figure 6.3   Selecting **One-way ANOVA** from main menu

Step 4 One-way ANOVA dialog box opens (Figure 6.4). Transfer (Blood sugar level in mg/100 ml) to **Dependent List** and Experimental conditions to Factor by clicking the arrow.

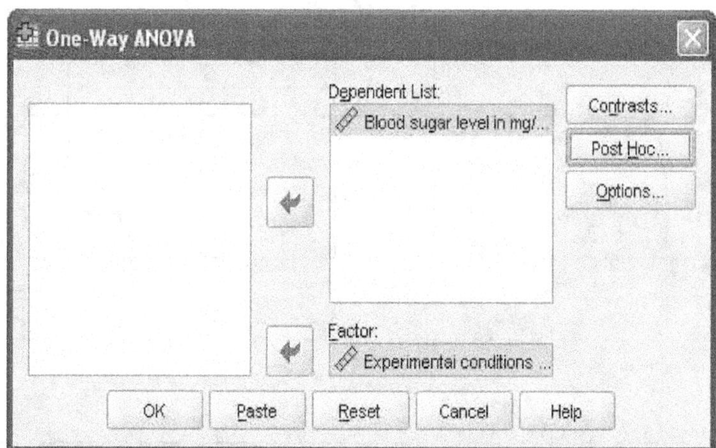

Figure 6.4   **One-way ANOVA** dialog box with variable and **Factor** transferred

Step 5 Click **Options**. A popup window opens with the head as **One-Way ANOVA**: Options (Figure 6.5), select **Descriptive** and click **continue** and click **OK** to run the analysis.

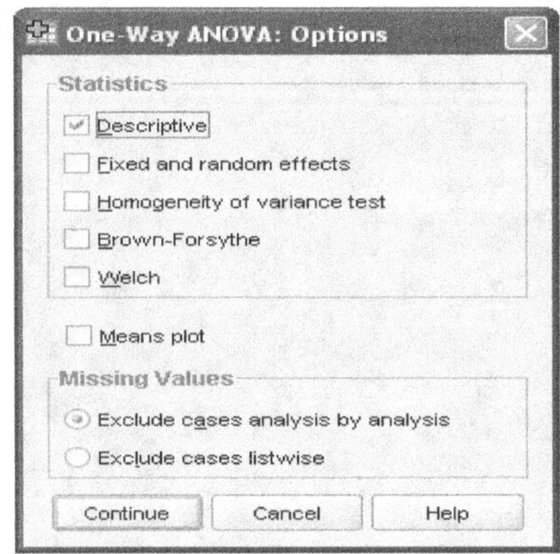

Figure 6.5   One-way ANOVA: Options to select Descriptive

The outputs appear as in Output 1 and Output 2.

Output 1

Descriptives

Blood sugar level in mg/100ml

	N	Mean	Std. Deviation	Std. Error	95% Confidence Interval for Mean		Minimum	Maximum
					Lower Bound	Upper Bound		
Normal	6	102.6667	5.64506	2.30458	96.7425	108.5908	96.00	111.00
Diabetic	6	243.3333	36.00926	14.70072	205.5439	281.1227	180.00	280.00
Herb1	6	182.5000	7.58288	3.09570	174.5423	190.4577	170.00	190.00
Herb 2	6	131.8333	6.94022	2.83333	124.5500	139.1166	120.00	140.00
Total	24	165.0833	57.38422	11.71351	140.8521	189.3146	96.00	280.00

Output 2

ANOVA

Blood sugar level in mg/100ml

	Sum of Squares	df	Mean Square	F	Sig.
Between Groups	68566.833	3	22855.611	63.745	.000
Within Groups	7171.000	20	358.550		
Total	75737.833	23			

Interpretation

The mean, standard deviation and standard errors of four samples are given in Output 1 under the head **Descriptives**. The results of ANOVA are given in Output 2. The significance of variance, i.e., p-value, given under the head Sig. is 0.000. Since, the significance value 0.000 is less than 0.05 ($p < 0.05$), the variance between different experimental conditions is significant. Therefore, we conclude that the four sample means differ from each other significantly.

If we stop the interpretation with this we may not understand whether the difference between sample variance is equal or any two sample variances are equal. In addition, we may not discover the source of significant differences among the group means. Most of the post hoc tests are designed to examine the pair-wise differences. Choice of comparison depends on the exact situation you have. Unplanned multiple comparison among the factor levels can be done by clicking any of the options in post-hoc multiple comparisons, but the researcher should have an idea on his data and knowledge on the post-hoc tests as well, only then he will be able to mine exciting facts about his data. In this case since the sample sizes are equal we can be confident of having similar population variance. Since we need pair-wise comparison and range as well, we go for post-hoc multiple comparison and choose Tukey.

Step 6 Click Post Hoc a popup window opens (Figure 6.6), and select Tukey and click Continue and click OK.

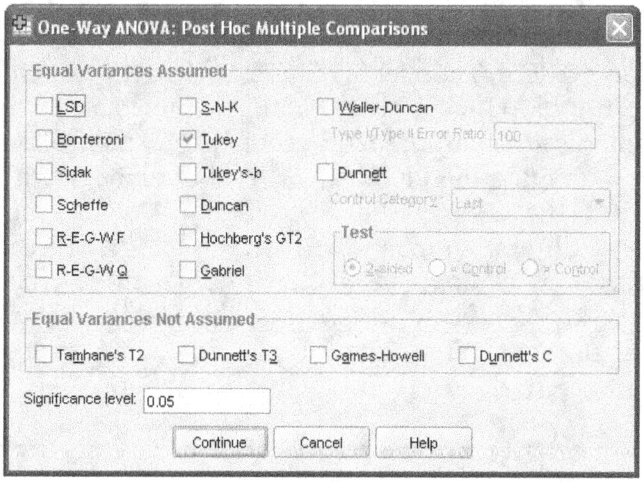

Figure 6.6   Tukey test selected in **One-way ANOVA: Post Hoc Multiple Comparisons** dialog box

Step 7 Now the **One-Way ANOVA: Post-Hoc Multiple comparisons** dialog box opens. Select Tukey and then click Continue. Finally click OK to run the analysis. The output for appears on the screen.

Step 8 Save the outputs (Output 3 and 4) and interpret the results.

Output 3

Multiple Comparisons

Blood sugar level in mg/100ml
Tukey HSD

(I) Experimental conditions	(J) Experimental conditions	Mean Difference (I-J)	Std. Error	Sig.	95% Confidence Interval	
					Lower Bound	Upper Bound
Normal	Diabetic	-140.66667*	10.93237	.000	-171.2657	-110.0677
	Herb1	-79.83333*	10.93237	.000	-110.4323	-49.2343
	Herb 2	-29.16667	10.93237	.065	-59.7657	1.4323
Diabetic	Normal	140.66667*	10.93237	.000	110.0677	171.2657
	Herb1	60.83333*	10.93237	.000	30.2343	91.4323
	Herb 2	111.50000*	10.93237	.000	80.9010	142.0990
Herb1	Normal	79.83333*	10.93237	.000	49.2343	110.4323
	Diabetic	-60.83333*	10.93237	.000	-91.4323	-30.2343
	Herb 2	50.66667*	10.93237	.001	20.0677	81.2657
Herb 2	Normal	29.16667	10.93237	.065	-1.4323	59.7657
	Diabetic	-111.50000*	10.93237	.000	-142.0990	-80.9010
	Herb1	-50.66667*	10.93237	.001	-81.2657	-20.0677

*. The mean difference is significant at the 0.05 level.

Interpretation

In Output 3, in the first row, Normal is compared pair-wise with other three groups. From this we can infer that blood sugar in Normal differ significantly from Diabetic and Herb 1 but Normal do not differ significantly from Herb 2 (p-value = 0.065). The scientific inference is that the patients treated with Herb 2 have the blood sugar level similar to normal person, therefore Herb 2 may be used as antidiabetic agent ($p > 0.05$). The results given in second row compare the blood sugar level of diabetic with other three groups. Since all the values under Sig. column is 0.000, the blood sugar level of diabetic differs significantly the from the other three groups ($p < 0.01$). The third row compares Herb 1 with other three groups pair-wise. Here also there are significant differences. The fourth row infers the same an stated in the previous three rows in pairwise comparison.

Output 4

Homogenous subsets

Blood sugar level in mg/100ml

Tukey HSD[a]

Experimental conditions	N	Subset for alpha = 0.05		
		1	2	3
Normal	6	102.6667		
Herb 2	6	131.8333		
Herb1	6		182.5000	
Diabetic	6			243.3333
Sig.		.065	1.000	1.000

Means for groups in homogeneous subsets are displayed.

a. Uses Harmonic Mean Sample Size = 6.000.

Interpretation

The **Output 4** gives the Homogenous subsets. In this Subset 1 is formed by Normal and Herb 2, Subset 2 is represented by Herb 1 and Subset 3 by diabetic. From this we can conclude that blood sugar level in normal group is towards the lower end of range in blood sugar, which is followed by Herb 1 and the **Diabetic** is towards the higher end. Since, **Normal** and Herb 1 form a single subset, treatment with Herb 2 would bring down the blood sugar level and not Herb 1.

If the researcher is not interested in pair-wise comparison and if he needs to find only a range in response then he can run Duncan's post-hoc test.

Step 9 In **One-Way ANOVA: Post-hoc multiple comparisons**, select **Duncan** and click **Continue** and then click **OK**. The output appears as in Output 5.

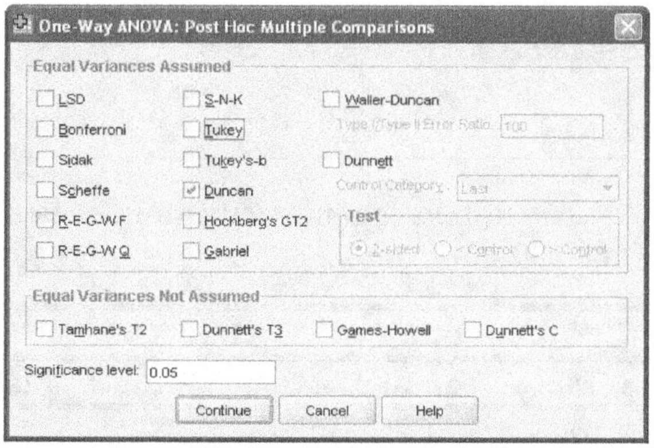

Figure 6.7   **One-way ANOVA: Post Hoc Multiple Comparisons** dialog box with **Duncan** selected

Output 5

Blood sugar level in mg/100ml

Duncan[a]

Experimental conditions	N	Subset for alpha = 0.05			
		1	2	3	4
Normal	6	102.6667			
Herb 2	6		131.8333		
Herb1	6			182.5000	
Diabetic	6				243.3333
Sig.		1.000	1.000	1.000	1.000

Means for groups in homogeneous subsets are displayed.

a. Uses Harmonic Mean Sample Size = 6.000.

Interpretation

Output 5 gives the results of Duncan's multiple comparison test. Here the results get categorized into four subsets indicating that none of the four groups are similar to each other. The blood sugar level of Herb 2 group is closer to normal, whereas the diabetic group is far away from the normal. Therefore, this test is useful in categorizing the different group means from lower to higher value and finding the closeness of the groups.

Two-way ANOVA—Two Treatment Factor Experiment and Analysis

This is a procedure to analyse the difference in mean of three or more groups of means of a dependent variable affected by more than one independent factor. The study design consists of finding the effect of two independent variables on a single dependent variable at the same time, that is, simultaneous effect of both independent variables on the dependent variable. It shows overall effect of two independent variables and also whether there is interaction between them.

Two-way ANOVA with SPSS

Example 6.2

Perform two-way ANOVA to find the interactive influence of herb and sex on blood sugar level (mg/100 ml).

Normal		Diabetic		Herb 1		Herb 2	
Male	**Female**	**Male**	**Female**	**Male**	**Female**	**Male**	**Female**
96	101	180	270	180	192	120	130
100	97	225	250	190	170	130	125
111	110	260	230	185	169	130	126

Normal		Diabetic		Herb 1		Herb 2	
Male	**Female**	**Male**	**Female**	**Male**	**Female**	**Male**	**Female**
98	108	250	220	190	198	135	140
106	102	265	267	180	174	136	138
105	111	280	284	170	180	140	119

Step 1 **Open Data Editor**, click **Variable View** (before starting to enter data, assign factor and levels and the variable to be tested. In this case, the four groups are levels of two factors namely **Experiment** and **Gender. (Blood Sugar** level is the **variable**), in the first column, type as "Experiment", select **Numeric** under **Type**, label as "Experimental conditions" under Label (Figure 6.8). In the Values column type as "Experimental group", and click on the grey area, a popup window opens (the details can be entered as in the previous example), type "1" in the **Value** box and "**Normal**" in the **Label** box and click **Add** to transfer it to the box down. Type "2" in the Value box and "Diabetic" in the **Label** box and click **Add** to transfer it to the box down and proceed in a similar way for the rest of data as "3" for Herb 1 and "4" for Herb 2 by adding each time and click OK.

Step 2 In the second row, type "Gender" under **Name**, select "**Numeric**" under Type, label as "Gender" under **Label** (Figure 6.7). In the **Values** column, type as "Gender", and click on the grey area, in the popup window type "1" in the **Value** box and Male in **Label** box and click Add to transfer it to the box down. Type "2" in the **Value** box as "Female" in **Label** box, click **Add** and click **OK**.

Step 3 In the third row type "Bloodsugar" under **Name**, select **Numeric** under **Type**, label as "Blood sugar level mg 100 ml under **Label**.

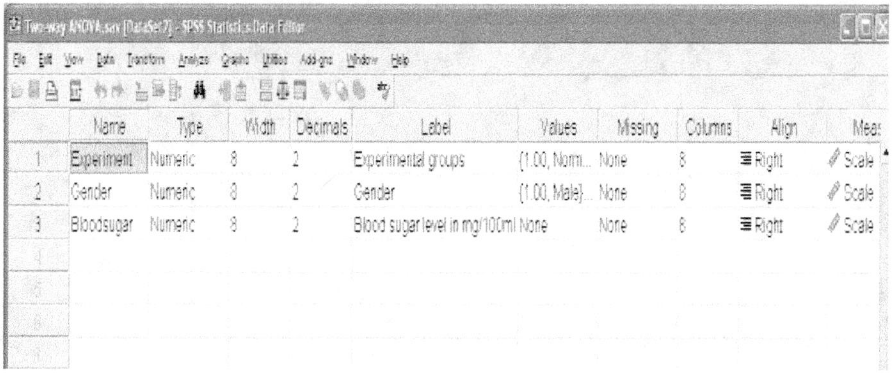

Figure 6.8 **Variable View** with details of three variables

Step 4 Type data in **Data View** under each head (Figure 6.8). Take care to enter data in such a way that four categories in the first column and in the second column 1 (male) and 2 (female) against each experimental group and enter the sugar level in the third column in accordance with experiment and gender.

Step 5 Choose **Analyze** from pull down menu, select **General Linear Model** and then click Univariate.

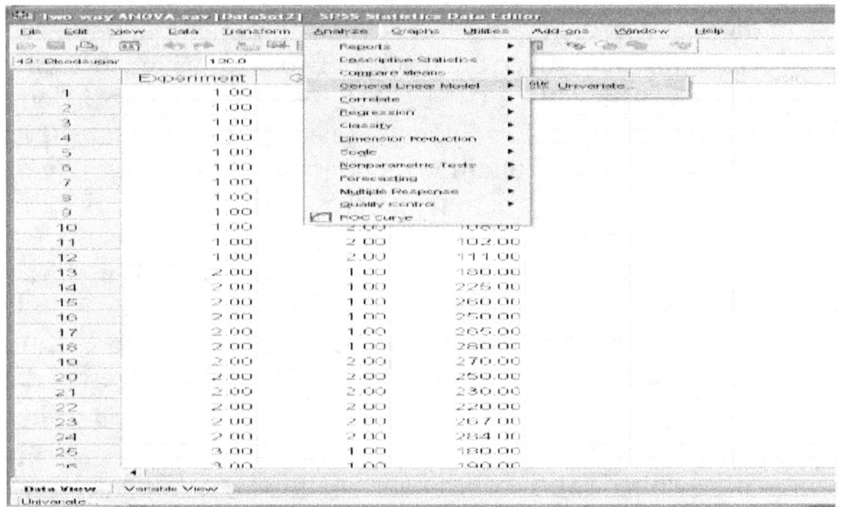

Figure 6.9 Selecting **Univariate** from main menu

Step 6 Univariate popup window opens as in Figure 6.9. Transfer Blood sugar level in mg/100 ml to **Dependent Variable** box, and **Experimental groups** and **Gender** to **Fixed Factor(s)**.

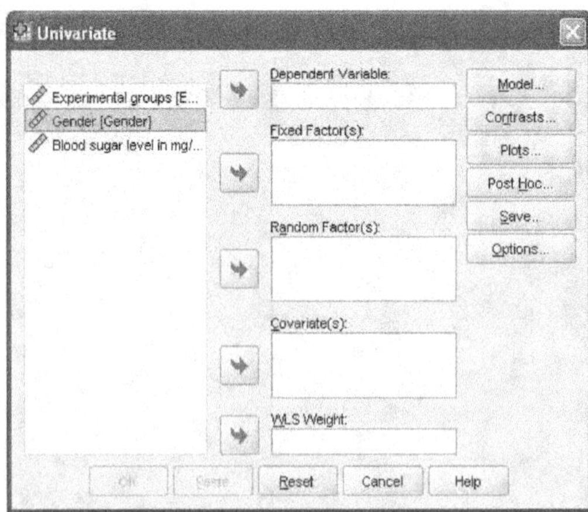

Figure 6.10 **Univariate** dialog box to transfer variables

Step 7 Click **Options** to get **Univariate**: **Options** box and transfer **Experiment**, **Gender** and **Experiment* Gender** to **Display Means for**: box (Figure 6.10). Select **Descriptive statistics** under Display and click Continue.

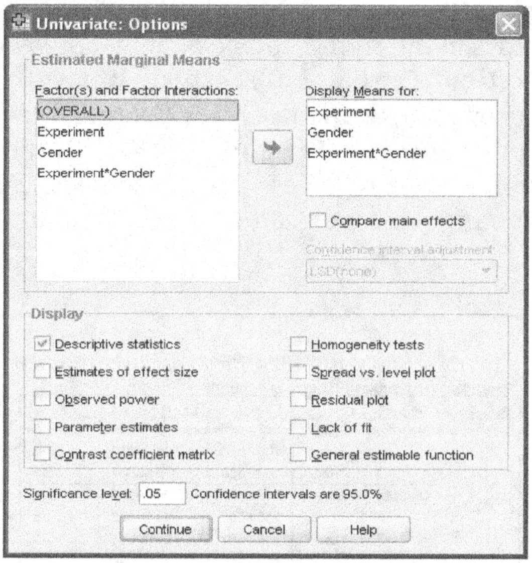

Figure 6.11   **Univariate:Options** dialog box with **Display Means for** and **Descriptive statistics** selected

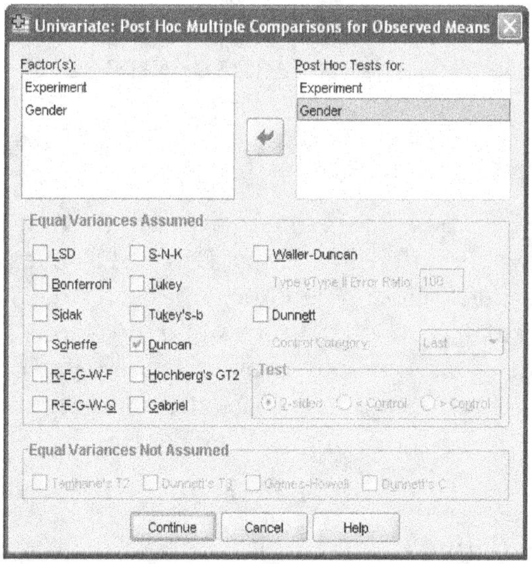

Figure 6.12   **Univariate: Post Hoc Comparisons for Observed Means** dialog box with variables for Post Hoc test for and Duncan selected

Step 8 Click **Post-Hoc**, a popup window (**Univariate: Post-Hoc Multiple Comparison for Observed Means**) opens (Figure 6.12). Transfer **Experiment** and **Gender** to the **Post-Hoc Tests for**: box. Select **Duncan** under **Equal Variances Assumed** and click **Continue** and click **OK** to run the analysis.

The output appears in different heads; you may not need all outputs. Select **Descriptive Statistics** (Output 1), **Tests of between Subject Effects** (Output 2), **Experimental groups*Gender** (Output 3) and Duncan's multiple range test with **Blood sugar level in mg/100 ml** (Output 4). In this example since gender has only two categories, **post-hoc test** cannot be performed (to perform multiple range test we need at least three categories).

Output 1

Descriptive Statistics

Dependent Variable:Blood sugar level in mg/100ml

Experimental groups	Gender	Mean	Std. Deviation	N
Normal	Male	102.6667	5.64506	6
	Femal	104.8333	5.63619	6
	Total	103.7500	5.49587	12
Diabetic	Male	243.3333	36.00926	6
	Femal	253.5000	24.78508	6
	Total	248.4167	29.94680	12
Herb 1	Male	182.5000	7.58288	6
	Femal	180.5000	12.02913	6
	Total	181.5000	9.64365	12
Herb 2	Male	131.8333	6.94022	6
	Femal	129.6667	8.06639	6
	Total	130.7500	7.26292	12
Total	Male	165.0833	57.38422	24
	Femal	167.1250	59.64264	24
	Total	166.1042	57.90757	48

Interpretation

From **Output 1** we can write the mean and standard deviation to describe the blood sugar level in different groups. **Output 2** gives the results of two-way ANOVA univariate analysis (here the variable tested is blood sugar level). To interpret our results, we need to understand the results given in **Output 2**. The column heads gives the source of variance, sum of squares, degrees of freedom, mean sum of squares, F(F-ratio) and significance. From this, we can state the effects of treatment. We take the F-value and Significance given against Experiments, the F-value is 169.784 and significance (*p*-value) is 0.000. Since the *p*-value is less than 0.01, there is significant difference between treatment groups.

Next, we can state whether there is significant difference between male and female for which we take the values given against **Gender**, here, the **F-value** is **0.175** and significance is 0.678. Since the *p*-value is greater than 0.01, the difference in blood sugar level between male and female is considered insignificant.

Then the interactive influence of experimental conditions and gender on blood sugar level is interpreted from the values given against **Experiment *Gender**, where the **F-ratio** is 0.350 and **significance** is **0.790**. Here the *p*-value is greater than 0.01; therefore, the interactive influence of Experiment and Gender is insignificant. Therefore, male and female could be treatedalike to reduce blood sugar level.

Out put 2

Tests of Between-Subjects Effects

Dependent Variable:Blood sugar level in mg/100ml

Source	Type III Sum of Squares	df	Mean Square	F	Sig.
Corrected Model	146154.312^a	7	20879.187	72.939	.000
Intercept	1324348.521	1	1324348.521	4626.478	.000
Experiment	145804.063	3	48601.354	169.784	.000
Gender	50.021	1	50.021	.175	.678
Experiment * Gender	300.229	3	100.076	.350	.790
Error	11450.167	40	286.254		
Total	1481953.000	48			
Corrected Total	157604.479	47			

a. R Squared = .927 (Adjusted R Squared = .915)

Output 3

3. Experimental groups * Gender

Dependent Variable:Blood sugar level in mg/100ml

Experimental groups	Gender	Mean	Std. Error	95% Confidence Interval	
				Lower Bound	Upper Bound
Normal	Male	102.667	6.907	88.707	116.627
	Femal	104.833	6.907	90.873	118.793
Diabetic	Male	243.333	6.907	229.373	257.293
	Femal	253.500	6.907	239.540	267.460
Herb 1	Male	182.500	6.907	168.540	196.460
	Femal	180.500	6.907	166.540	194.460
Herb 2	Male	131.833	6.907	117.873	145.793
	Femal	129.667	6.907	115.707	143.627

Interpretation

Output 3 gives the mean blood sugar levels in different experimental groups with respect to different sex.

Output 4 gives the range in blood sugar level in different experimental groups irrespective of sex.

MULTIPLE ANALYSIS OF VARIANCE (MANOVA)

MANOVA is a technique which determines the effects of independent categorical variables on multiple dependent variables. It is usually used to compare several groups with respect to multiple continuous or categorical variables. The main distinction between MANOVA and ANOVA is that several dependent variables are considered in MANOVA, while ANOVA tests for inter-group differences between the mean values of one dependent variable. MANOVA uses one or more categorical independents as predictors, like ANOVA, but unlike ANOVA, there is more than one dependent variable.

Multiple Analysis of Variance (MANOVA) with SPSS

Multivariate analysis of variance (MANOVA) in SPSS is similar to ANOVA, instead of one metric dependent variable, we have two or more dependent variables. MANOVA in SPSS is concerned with examining the differences between groups and the group differences across multiple dependent variables simultaneously.

Suppose that four groups, each consisting of 100 randomly selected individuals, are exposed to four different commercial advertisements about some detergents. After watching the commercial, adds each individual provide ratings on his preference for the products, for the manufacturing companies and for the commercial advertisements. Since these three variables are correlated, MANOVA in SPSS should be conducted to determine the commercial that received the highest preference across the three preference variables (product, company and commercial advertisement). Let us understand the basics of doing MANOVA in SPSS, before proceeding with the actual process of doing the same.

BASICS OF DOING MANOVA IN SPSS

MANOVA in SPSS is done by selecting **Analyze, General Linear Model** and **Multivariate** from the main menu. As in ANOVA, the first step is to identify the dependent and independent variables. MANOVA in SPSS involves two or more metric dependent variables. Metric variables are those which are measured using an interval or ratio scale. The dependent variable is generally denoted by Y and the independent variable is denoted by X.

Here, the null hypothesis is the means of multiple dependent variables are equal across groups.

As in ANOVA, MANOVA in SPSS also involves the decomposition of the total variation observed in all the dependent variables simultaneously. The total variation in Y is denoted by SS_Y, which can be broken down into two components:

$$SS_Y = SS_{between} + SS_{within}$$

Here the subscripts 'between' and 'within' refer to the categories of X. $SS_{between}$ is the portion of the sum of squares in Y which is related to the independent variables or factors X. Thus, it is generally referred to as the sum of squares of X. SS_{within} is the variation in Y which is related to the variation within each categories of X. It is generally referred to as the sum of squares for errors in MANOVA. Thus in MANOVA, for all the dependent variables, say, Y_1, Y_2 (and so on), the decomposition of the total variation is done simultaneously.

The next task in MANOVA in SPSS is to measure the effects of X on Y_1, Y_2 (and so on). This is generally done by the sum of squares of X. The relative magnitude of the sum of squares of X in MANOVA increases as the difference among the means of Y_1, Y_2 (and so on) in categories of X increases. The relative magnitude of the sum of squares of X in MANOVA decreases as the variation in Y_1, Y_2 (and so on) within the categories of X decreases.

The final step in MANOVA in SPSS is to calculate the mean square which is obtained by dividing the sum of squares by the corresponding degrees of freedom. The null hypothesis of equal of mean is tested by an F statistic, which is the ratio of the mean square related to the independent variable ($MS_{between}$) to the mean square related to error (MS_{within}).

Example 6.3

Perform a multivariate analysis of variance (MANOVA) on the following data for plasma concentration of calcium (in mg/100 ml) and for the rate of evaporative water loss (in mg/min).

No hormone treatment				Hormone treatment			
Female		Male		Female		Male	
Plasma calcium	Water loss	Plasma calcium	Water loss	Plasma calcium	Water loss	Plasma calcium	Water loss
16.5	76	14.5	80	39.1	71	32.0	65
18.4	71	11.0	72	26.2	70	23.8	69
12.7	64	10.8	77	21.3	63	28.8	97
14.0	66	14.3	69	35.8	59	25.0	56
12.8	69	10.0	74	40.2	60	29.3	52

Step 1 **Open Data Editor**, click **Variable View** and follow Steps 1–4 to name the variables (Figure 5.12). In the first column, type as "Treatment", select **Numeric** under Type, label as "Hormone treatment" under **Label**. In the **Values** column click on the grey area, a popup window opens (the details can be entered as in the previous example), type "1" in the Value box and "No hormone treatment" in **Label** box and click **Add** to transfer it to the box down. Type "2" in the **Value** box and "Hormone treatment" in Label box and click **Add** to transfer it to the box down and click **OK**.

Step 2 In the second row, type "Gender" under **Name**, select **Numeric** under **Type**, label as "Gender" under **Label**. In the **Values** column, click on the grey area, in the popup window type 1 in the Value box and "Female" in **Label** box and click **Add** to transfer it to the box down. Type "2" in the **Value** box and "Male" in **Label** box, click **Add** and click OK.

Step 3 In the third row type "Calcium" under **Name**, select **Numeric** under **Type**, label as "Plasma calcium (mg/100 ml)" under **Label**.

Step 4 In the fourth row, type "Water" under **Name**, select **Numeric** under **Type**, label as "Water loss (mg/min) under **Label**.

	Name	Type	Width	Decimals	Label	Values	Missing	Columns	Align	Meas
1	Treatment	Numeric	8	2	Hormone treatment	{1.00, No ho...	None	8	Right	Scale
2	Gender	Numeric	8	2	Gender	{1.00, Fema...	None	8	Right	Scale
3	Calcium	Numeric	8	2	Plasma calcium (mg /100ml)	None	None	8	Right	Scale
4	Water	Numeric	8	2	Water loss (mg/ min.)	None	None	8	Right	Scale
5										

Figure 6.13 **Variable View** with details entered for four variables

Step 5 Click Data View and type data in **Data View** under each head (Figure 6.14). Take care to enter data in such a way that the two categories "1" is entered for **no hormone treatment** and "2" is entered for **hormone treatment** in the first column. In the second column enter "1" for **female** and "2" for **male** against each treatment correctly. In the third column enter calcium level in accordance with hormone treatment and gender. In the fourth column enter water loss in accordance with hormone treatment and gender.

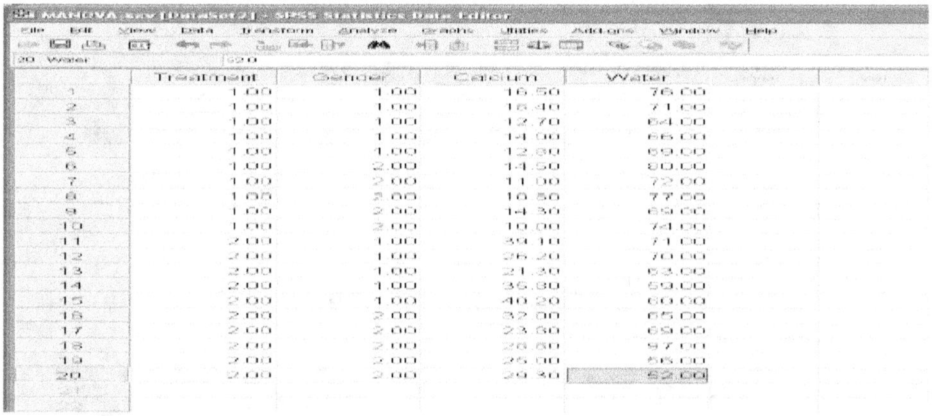

	Treatment	Gender	Calcium	Water
1	1.00	1.00	16.50	76.00
2	1.00	1.00	16.40	71.00
3	1.00	1.00	12.70	64.00
4	1.00	1.00	14.00	66.00
5	1.00	1.00	12.80	69.00
6	1.00	2.00	14.50	80.00
7	1.00	2.00	11.00	72.00
8	1.00	2.00	10.50	77.00
9	1.00	2.00	14.30	69.00
10	1.00	2.00	10.00	74.00
11	2.00	1.00	39.10	71.00
12	2.00	1.00	26.20	70.00
13	2.00	1.00	21.30	63.00
14	2.00	1.00	35.80	59.00
15	2.00	1.00	40.20	60.00
16	2.00	2.00	32.00	65.00
17	2.00	2.00	23.80	69.00
18	2.00	2.00	28.80	57.00
19	2.00	2.00	25.00	55.00
20	2.00	2.00	29.30	62.00

Figure 6.14 Data View with data entered

Step 6 From the main menu select **Analyze**, click **General Linear Model** and then select Multivariate (Figure 6.15).

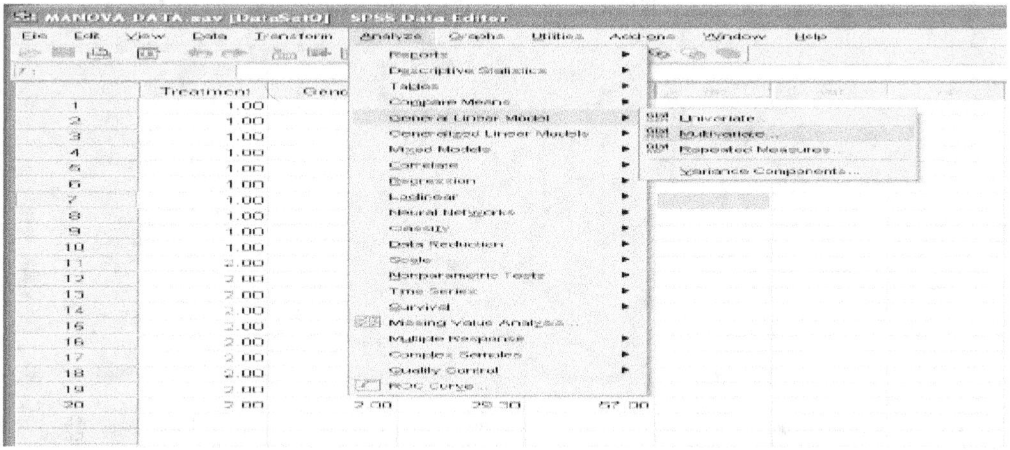

Figure 6.15 Selecting Multivariate from drop down menu

Step 7 A popup window with the head **Multivariate** opens as in Figure 6.16.

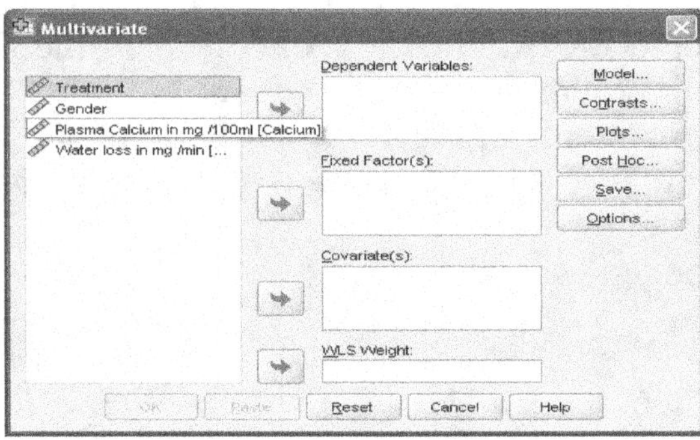

Figure 6.16 Multivariate dialog box to transfer variables

Step 8 Transfer the variables "Plasma Calcium in mg/100 ml" and "Water loss in mg/min" to **Dependent Variables**: box and Treatment and Gender to Fixed Factor(s): box (Figure 5.17). Since, we have only two categories under Treatment and Gender, we cannot perform **post-hoc tests** for this set of data.

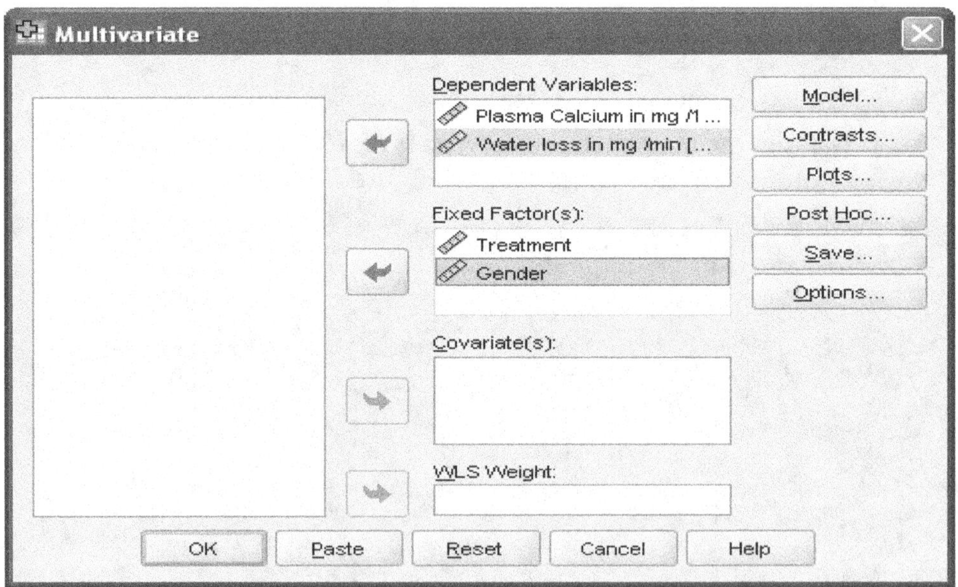

Figure 6.17 **Multivariate:** dialog box with dependent variables and fixed factors transferred

Step 9 Click **Options** to open the **Multivariate: Options** dialog box. Transfer (OVERALL) from **Factor(s)** and

Factor Interactions: to **Display Means for:** box. Select **Descriptive Statistics** checkbox under **Display** (Figure 6.18). Click **Continue** to return to **Multivariate** box.

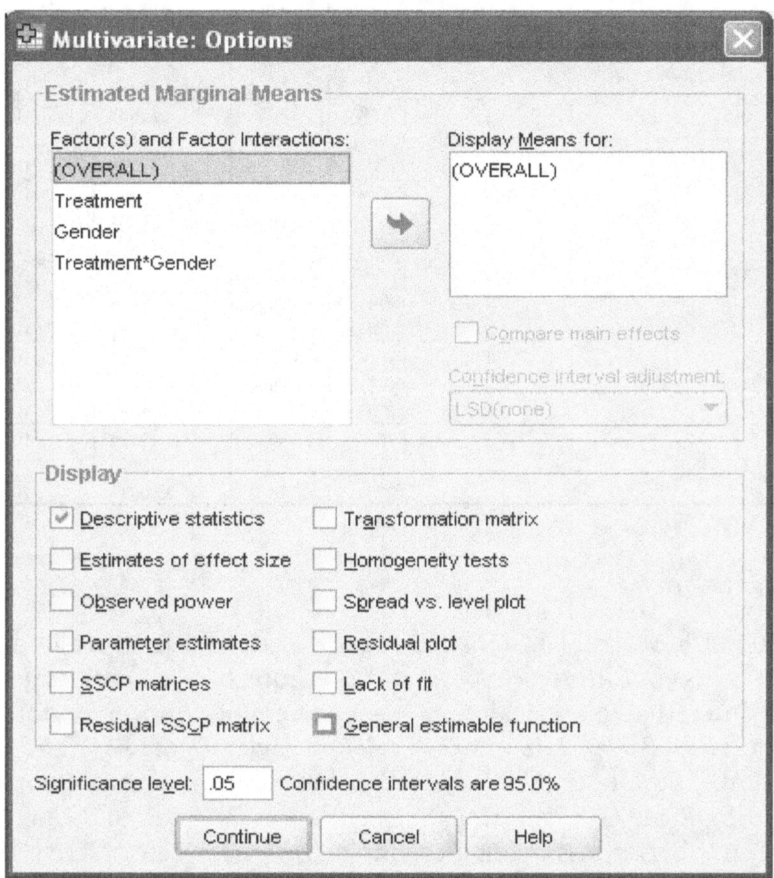

Figure 6.18   Multivariate: Options box to select **Descriptive Statistics**

Step 10   Click **OK** to run the analysis to get the output.

The outputs appears under different heads as **Between Subject Factors, Descriptive Statistics, Multivariate Tests and Tests of Between- Subjects Effects**. However, we use **Descriptive Statistics** (Output 1) and **Tests of Between-Subject Effects** (Output 2) for this example.

Output 1

Descriptive Statistics

	Treatment	Gender	Mean	Std. Deviation	N
Plasma Calcium in mg /100ml	No hormone	Female	14.8800	2.49339	5
		Male	12.1200	2.11589	5
		Total	13.5000	2.62086	10
	Hormone	Female	28.8600	5.52883	5
		Male	28.3800	4.39454	5
		Total	28.6200	4.71518	10
	Total	Female	21.8700	8.40463	10
		Male	20.2500	9.16591	10
		Total	21.0600	8.59923	20
Water loss in mg /min	No hormone	Female	69.2000	4.65833	5
		Male	74.4000	4.27785	5
		Total	71.8000	5.02881	10
	Hormone	Female	64.6000	5.59464	5
		Male	62.8000	5.93296	5
		Total	63.7000	5.51866	10
	Total	Female	66.9000	5.42525	10
		Male	68.6000	7.82020	10
		Total	67.7500	6.60841	20

Interpretation

From Output 1, Descriptive Statistics we can describe the level of blood calcium and water loss in different experimental groups of both male and female. We can infer that blood calcium level in female who does not receive hormone is 14.88 ± 2.49 mg/100ml and that of male is 12.12 ± 2.11 mg/100ml. The blood calcium level in female who receives hormone is 28.86 ± 5.52 mg/100 ml and that of male is 28.38 ± 4.39 mg/100ml. Similarly, the water loss in females who do not receive hormone is 69.20 ± 4.65 mg/min and in male is 74.40 ± 4.28 mg/min. Water loss in females who receive hormone is 64.6 ± 5.59 mg/min and in female is 62.8 ± 5.93 mg/min.

Output 2

From output 2, Tests of Between-Subjects Effects, we can infer the influence of hormone treatment, gender and the interactive influence of both (hormone and gender) on blood calcium and water loss. There are 7 columns and 8 rows in the output. The first column gives the source of variance. From that column we can formulate ANOVA table by taking the values against Treatment, Gender and Treatment * Gender, Error and Total. We can take the results given against Treatment, Gender and Treatment * Gender to answer our problem.

The F-value for treatment for plasma calcium is 75.48 and the significance is 0.000 ($p < 0.01$). The F-value for and for water loss is 12.32 and the significance is 0.003 ($p < 0.05$). Therefore, hormone treatment has a significant effect on both plasma calcium level and water loss.

Tests of Between-Subjects Effects

Source	Dependent Variable	Type III Sum of Squares	df	Mean Square	F	Sig.
Corrected Model	Plasma Calcium in mg /100ml	1162.692*	3	387.564	25.593	.000
	Water loss in mg /min	403.750b	3	134.583	5.055	.012
Intercept	Plasma Calcium in mg /100ml	8870.472	1	8870.472	585.761	.000
	Water loss in mg /min	91801.250	1	91801.250	3.448E3	.000
Treatment	Plasma Calcium in mg /100ml	1143.072	1	1143.072	75.483	.000
	Water loss in mg /min	328.050	1	328.050	12.321	.003
Gender	Plasma Calcium in mg /100ml	13.122	1	13.122	.867	.366
	Water loss in mg /min	14.450	1	14.450	.543	.472
Treatment * Gender	Plasma Calcium in mg /100ml	8.498	1	8.498	.429	.522
	Water loss in mg /min	61.250	1	61.250	2.300	.149
Error	Plasma Calcium in mg /100ml	242.296	16	15.143		
	Water loss in mg /min	426.000	16	26.625		
Total	Plasma Calcium in mg /100ml	10275.460	20			
	Water loss in mg /min	92631.000	20			
Corrected Total	Plasma Calcium in mg /100ml	1404.988	19			
	Water loss in mg /min	829.750	19			

a. R Squared = .828 (Adjusted R Squared = .795)

b. R Squared = .487 (Adjusted R Squared = .390)

The F-value for gender for plasma calcium is 0.867 and the significance is 0.336 ($p > 0.05$). The F-value for water loss is 0.543 and the significance is 0.472 ($p > 0.05$). Therefore, plasma calcium level and water loss do not differ significantly in male and female or gender does not have any influence on calcium level and water loss.

The F-value for interactive influence of treatment and gender on plasma calcium is 0.429 and the significance is 0.522 ($p > 0.05$). The F-value for water loss is 2.3 and the significance is 0.149 ($p > 0.05$). Hence, the interactive influence of both hormone and gender is insignificant. The results can be concluded by saying that male and female do not differ significantly in their plasma calcium level and water loss and hormone treatment only has significant influence on both. Therefore, male and females can be treated alike with hormones to control plasma calcium and water loss.

Review Exercises

1. Two samples are drawn from two normal populations and the following data are obtained. Test whether the two samples have the same variance at 5% level of significance.

Sample 1	60	65	71	74	76	82	85	87
Sample 2	61	66	67	85	78	63	86	85

2. The Chloride content (mg/lit) of a river at a particular site collected from four different seasons are given below. Find the mean and standard deviation. Analyze the significance of variance. Infer the variance in oxygen content for four different seasons. Find the range in chloride content for different seasons.

Winter	Summer	Monsoon	Post monsoon
68	102	99	88
69	103	98	90
70	110	100	83
71	106	86	91
72	105	88	80
75	108	89	82

3. In a river where the sewages are allowed to mix, the BOD (oxygen in mg/L) values are calculated at different sites and given below. Calculate the mean and standard deviation. Analyze the significance of variance between different sites.

Site A	Site B	Site C	Site D
1.2	2.2.	3.2.	4.3
1.0	2.3	2.9	3.9
1.3	2.2	2.1	3.6
1.0	2.3	3.0	3.4
1.0	2.0.	2.9	3.5
1.1	1.9	2.8	3.9
1.2	1.8	3.3	3.8

4. The haemoglobin levels of four groups of children fed on four different diets are given below. Calculate the mean and standard deviation. Analyze the significance of varince and range in response of diet on haemoglobin.

Diet A	Diet B	Diet C	Diet D
11.6	13.2	10.1	12.2
10.6	13.1	10.1	13.1

Diet A	Diet B	Diet C	Diet D
11.1	13.	9.9	13.
11.2	14.2	9.8	12.2
10.3	13.5	10.1	12.5
11.5	12.8	10.1	11.8
12.1	13.0	11.1	13.0
12.6	12.5	10.5	12.5

5. In an experiment conducted on fortification of mulberry leaves with different nutrient supplementation, the following data are obtained on the cocoon weight (gm) of mulberry silkworm Bombyx mori. Calculate the mean and standard deviation. Analyze the significance of variance between different groups. Infer the range in response.

Control	Vitamin	Spirulina	Soya
1.5	1.6	1.9	1.9
1.6	2.0	2.1	2.0
1.7	2.1	2.2	1.95
1.6	1.9	2.3	2.0
1.8	2.1	2.1	2.4
1.6	2.0	1.9	2.3
1.6	1.9	2.3	2.2

6. The following data gives the production of wheat in tons/hectare of three different varieties A, B and C. Is there a significant variance in the production of three varieties?

Variety A	Variety B	Variety C
68	102	99
69	103	98
70	110	86
71	106	86
72	105	88
75	108	89

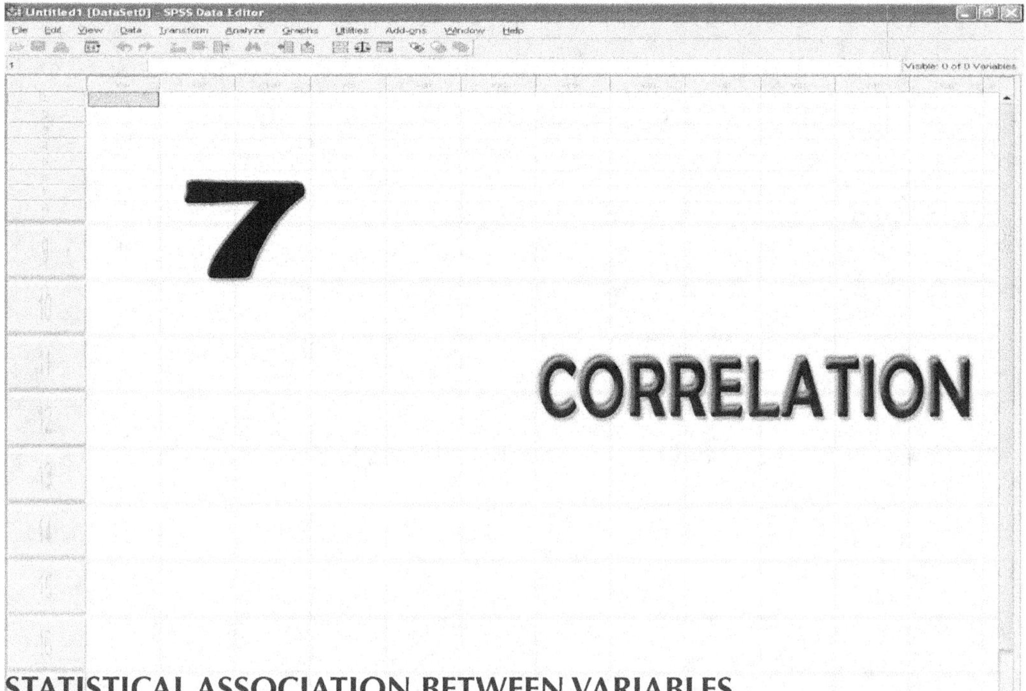

STATISTICAL ASSOCIATION BETWEEN VARIABLES

In real life situations, a kind of relationship or association exits between characters or variables. For example, if we measure the heights and weights of a group of individuals we obtain a series in which each individual of the series has 2 values, one relating to height and the other relating to weight. Such a **distribution** in which each individual (unit) has two values is called **bivariate distribution.** If we measure more than two variables on each unit of a distribution it is called **multivariate distribution**. In both of these, change in one variable is found or apparently found to be associated with the change in the other variable. This relationship may be casual or causal. The statistical tools used in such relationships are correlation and regression respectively. There are many kinds of data in life sciences and social sciences where the relationship between two variables is not one of dependence. In such cases, the magnitude of one of the variables changes as the magnitude of the second variable changes, but it is not reasonable to consider them as independent or dependent variable. In such situations, correlation analyses are called for.

An example of data suitable for correlation analysis would be measurements of human arm and leg lengths. It might be found that an individual with long arms will in general possess long legs, so a relationship may be desirable; but there is no justification in stating that the length of one limb is dependent upon the length of the other. But for variables like age and blood pressure of persons, age influences blood pressure. Regression analysis is the most suitable one for these kinds of variables, though we can apply correlation analysis to find the degree of association. The degree to which the two or more variables co-vary in some linear fashion is given by correlation analysis.

"When the relationship is of a quantitative nature, the appropriate statistical tool for discovering and measuring the relationship and expressing it in a brief formula is known as correlation."

Croxton and Cowden

"Correlation is an analysis of covariation between two or more variables".

A.M. Tuffle

Thus two variables are said to correlate if the change in one variable results in a corresponding change in the other variable. Therefore, correlation is a statistical tool which studies the relationship between 2 variables.

CORRELATION—SIMPLE AND MULTIPLE CORRELATION

Two variables, for example, age and blood pressure are found to vary in some linear fashion. The apt way to express the degree of linear relationship between these two variables is by the calculation of correlation coefficient. Hence, when one studies the relationship between two variables it is called simple correlation analysis and if more than two variables are involved it is multivariate analysis.

Types of Correlation

Positive and negative correlation   If the value of the two variables move in the same direction, i.e., if the increase in the values of one variable results in a corresponding increase in the values of the other variable or if the decrease in the values of one variable result in a corresponding decrease in the values of the other variable, there exists a positive correlation.

On the other hand, if the variables deviate in the opposite direction, i.e., if the increase in the values of one variable results in a corresponding decrease in the values of other variable there exists a negative correlation.

Linear and non-linear correlation If a unit change in one variable corresponds to a constant change in the other variable over the entire range of data, then the correlation between the two variables is said to be linear. For example, the following data shows a linear correlation between two variable X and Y.

X	1	2	3	4	5
Y	5	7	9	11	13

Thus for a unit change in the value of X, there is a constant change i.e., 2 in the corresponding values of Y. When these data are plotted on graph sheet, these give a straight line. But such an ideal condition never exists in nature. In most situations in social and biological sciences the relationship between 2 variables is not linear one and may fluctuate.

The relationship between two variable is said to be non-linear or curvilinear, if a unit change in one variable does not correspond to the change in the other variable at a constant rate but at a fluctuating rate. Such kinds of data, when plotted on a graph sheet we do not get a straight line. Mathematically, the correlation is said to be non-linear if the slope of the plotted curve is not constant.

The technique for its analysis and measurement of non-linear relationship are quite tedious and complicated when compared to methods of studying and measuring linear relationship.

Methods of Studying Correlation

There are different methods of studying the degree of correlation depending on the type of variable and the number of variables involved. If only two variables are studied in any investigation, it is bivariate analysis. The degree of relationship between two measurement variables can be done both graphically and mathematically.

Graphical Method: Scatter Diagram

The simplest way to ascertain the correlation between two variables is by scatter diagram. In this method, if n pairs of value $(X_1Y_1, X_2Y_2, \ldots X_nY_n)$ of two variables X and Y are given, then one is represented along the abscissa (X-axis) and the other along the ordinate (Y-axis) on a graph sheet. In the example of the two variables (*Refer* Chapter 4) namely age of the person and blood pressure, for each case or each person a single point is plotted for his age and blood pressure (Age is taken in X-axis and blood pressure in Y-axis). When all "n" pairs are plotted for the entire set of data, the diagram of dots obtained is called Scatter diagram. The scatter diagram for the same data is given below. From the scatter diagram we can form a fairly good but rough idea on the relationship between the two variables.

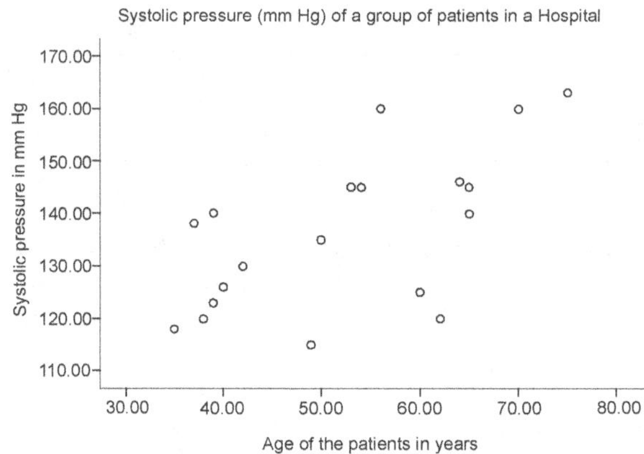

Figure 7.1   **Scatter diagram of systolic pressure (mm Hg) and age (years)**

In a scatter diagram if the points start from the lower left hand corner and extend to the upper right hand corner as shown in Figure 7.2, there is positive correlation between these two variables. On the other hand, when the points move from the lower right hand corner to the upper left hand corner as shown in Figure 7.3, there is negative correlation between these two variables. If the points are scattered throughout as in Figure 7.4, then there is no correlation.

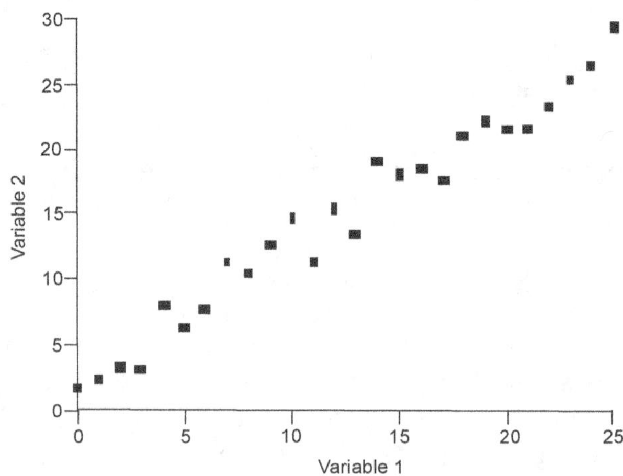

Figure 7.2   **Scatter diagram showing positive correlation between variables**

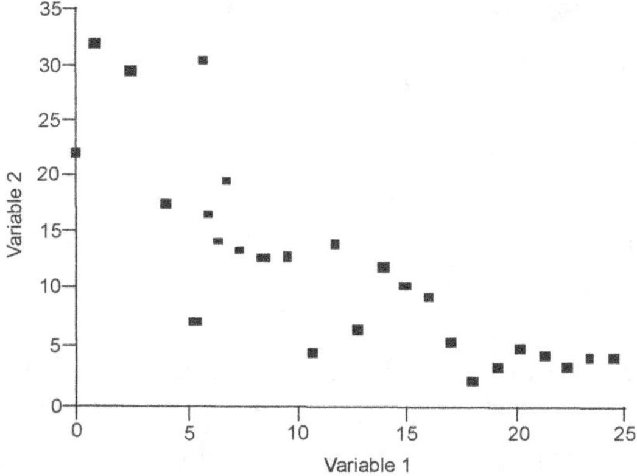

Figure 7.3   Scatter diagram showing negative correlation between two variables

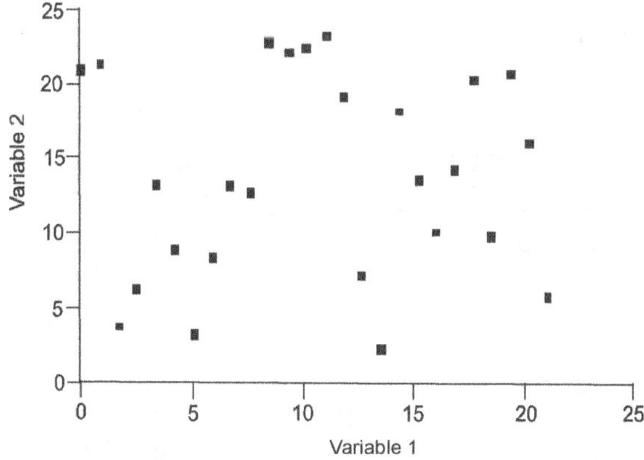

Figure 7.4   Scatter diagram—no correlation between two variables

Mathematical Method: Pearson's Correlation Coefficient

The relationship between two measurement variables is studied by a method introduced by Karl Pearson and is called Pearson's correlation coefficient. The following formula is used to find the relationship between two variables.

$$r = \frac{\sum \left(x_i - \bar{x} \right)\left(y_i - \bar{y} \right)}{\sqrt{\sum \left(x_i - \bar{x} \right)^2 \left(y_i - \bar{y} \right)^2}}$$

where,

r—correlation coefficient

x_i—value of ith item of variable x

$\bar{x}$—mean of variable x

y_i—value of ith item of variable y

$\bar{y}$—mean of variable y and

$\sum$—sum

The value of Pearson's correlation coefficient falls between $+1$ and -1. If the variables are negatively correlated the value of r lies between 0 and -1, if they are positively correlated the value is between 0 and $+1$. If there is no correlation the value is 0. But the values from 0 to 1 is interpreted based on the test of significance.

BIVARIATE ANALYSIS WITH SPSS

Calculation of correlation coefficient with mathematical formula becomes tedious when one likes to calculate greater number of variables from a very large sample. SPSS allows us to do the analysis for a large number of variables at a time. Let us work out correlation coefficient for a pair of variables first with the familiar example.

Example 7.1

Find out correlation coefficient for the variables, age (years) and systolic blood pressure (mmHg) in man.

Age	Group	Age	Group
56	160	40	126
42	130	53	145
60	125	35	118
50	135	38	120
54	145	39	123
49	115	37	138
39	140	70	160
62	120	75	163
65	140	65	145
70	160	64	146

Before going into SPSS, it is important to propose a null hypothesis and alternate hypothesis.

***Null hypothesis* (H$_0$)**   There is no correlation between age and systolic blood pressure.

***Alternate hypothesis* (H$_A$)**   There is correlation between age and systolic blood pressure.

> **Step 1** Open the **Data Editor** and click **Variable View** and then enter the name of variables and details of the variables (Figure 7.5).

	Name	Type	Width	Decimals	Label	Values	Missing	Columns	Align
1	Age	Numeric	8	2	Age of the patients in years	None	None	8	Right
2	Bloodpress	Numeric	8	2	Blood pressure (mm Hg)	None	None	8	Right
3									
4									
5									
6									
7									
8									
9									
10									

Figure 7.5   **Variable View** with two variables entered

> **Step 2** Click **Data View** and enter data under appropriate variable (Figure 7.6).

> **Step 3** Select Analyse from the main menu and select **Correlate** from the drop down menu and then select **Bivariate** is shown in Figure 7.7.

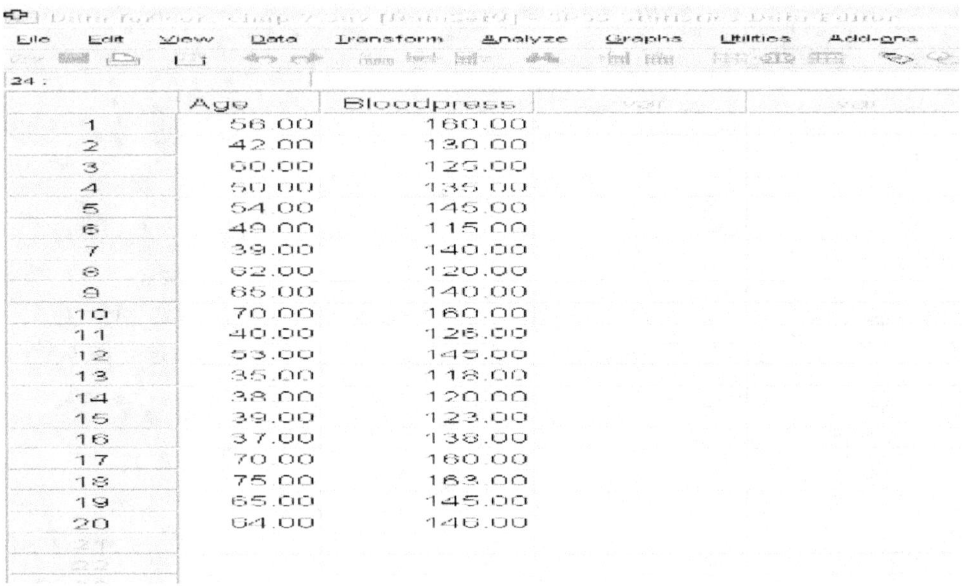

Figure 7.6   Data View with data for two variables

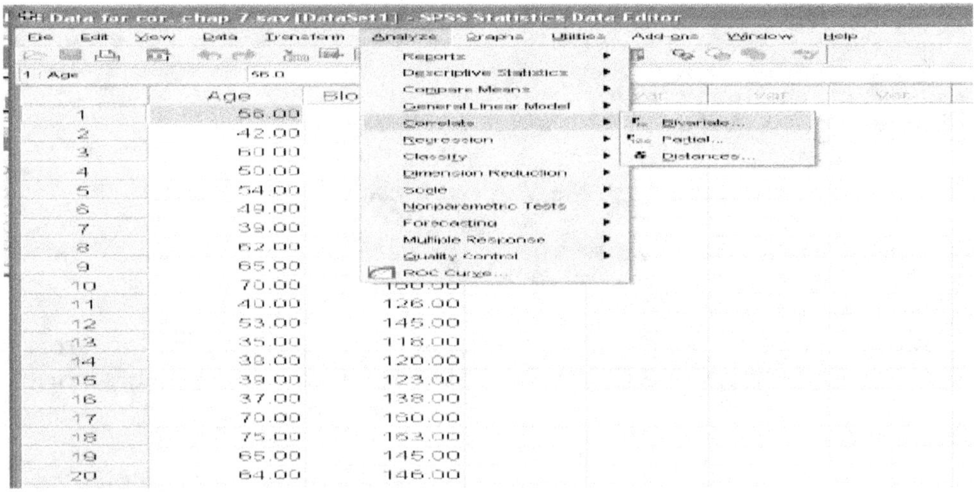

Figure 7.7   Selecting **Bivariate option from main menu

Step 4 Bivariate Correlations dialog box opens as in Figure 7.8.

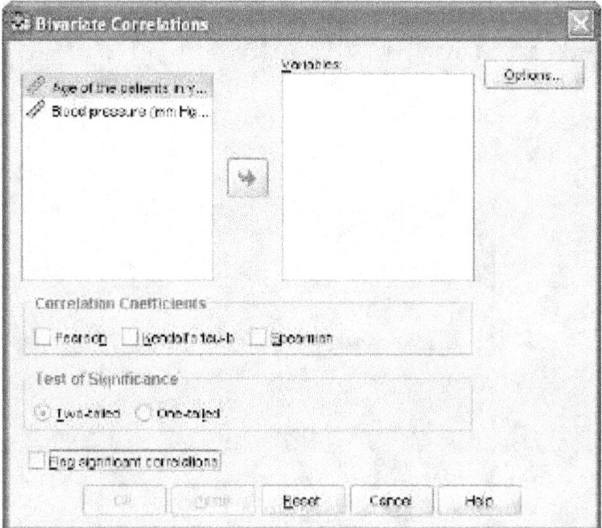

Figure 7.8   Bivariate Correlations dialog box to select

Step 5 Transfer variables into **Variables** box , select **Pearson** under
Correlation Coefficients and select **Two-tailed** under Test of
Significance and Flag Significant Correlations (Figure 7.9).

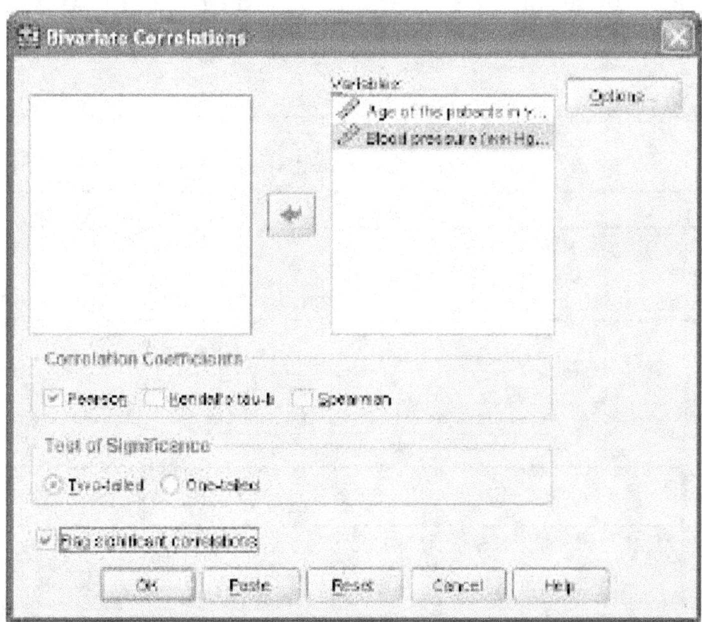

Figure 7.9   Bivariate Correlations dialog box with options selected for **Pearson correlation
coefficient**

Step 6 Click **Options** to open **Bivariate Correlations**: **Options**, select **Mean** and **Standard Deviation** under **Statistics**, so that you can get some descriptive statistics in the output, although these options are not needed to run the actual Pearson's correlation coefficient (Figure 7.10).

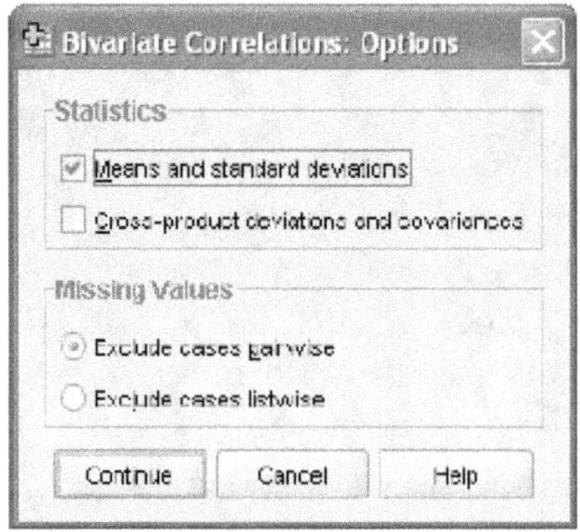

Figure 7.10   Bivariate Correlations: Options dialog box with to select mean and standard deviation

Step 7 Click Continue and click OK to run the analysis. Two outputs, one for descriptive statistics (Output 1) and the other for Correlations (Output 2) appear is shown below.

Output 1

Descriptive Statistics

	Mean	Std. Deviation	N
Age of the patients in years	53.1500	12.81970	20
Blood pressure (mm Hg)	137.7000	15.35921	20

Output 2

Correlations

		Age of the patients in years	Blood pressure (mm Hg)
Age of the patients in years	Pearson Correlation	1	.661**
	Sig. (2-tailed)		.002
	N	20	20
Blood pressure (mm Hg)	Pearson Correlation	.661**	1
	Sig. (2-tailed)	.002	
	N	20	20

**. Correlation is significant at the 0.01 level (2-tailed).

Interpretation

Output 1 gives the mean age and blood pressure with standard deviation.

Output 2 gives the main matrix of the Pearson's correlation coefficient. Variables have been arranged in a matrix such that their columns/rows intersect. In the cells there are numbers that tell about the statistical interaction between the variables. Three types of information are provided in each cell, i.e., Pearson correlation, significance and number of cases. The values on either side of the diagonal are mirror images of each other, i.e., the values are the same. Hence, one can ignore the information above the diagonal or below the diagonal as one wishes.

The value against Pearson correlation, i.e., 0.661 is the *r*-value. Since, the *r*-value is positive and significance (2-tailed) value of 0.002 (the *p*-value) is below 0.01, we reject the H_0 and accept alternate hypothesis and infer that an increase in age really increases the systolic blood pressure or patients age and blood pressure are positively related.

Example 7.2

The following are the data related to test scores obtained by the students with their studying time and their absence in the class. Perform bivariate analysis for the following data.

Case no.	Test score	Study time in hours/ week	Absence in hours/ week
1	47	8	4
2	51	12	3
3	70	12.5	2
4	70	19.5	3
5	75	13.5	2
6	75	16	2
7	80	14.5	3
8	84	18.5	1
9	80	15	0
10	85	14.5	1
11	90	22.5	3
12	90	18.5	2
13	92	19	1

In this exercise there are three variables, we can find the correlation between test scores and study time and test scores and absence in the class as well. SPSS allows us to carry out bivariate analysis as many variables as we would like to find the relation. In such situations we can propose null hypothesis for any two variables separately. Here, we propose the hypothesis only for two variables at a time, like test scores and study time. Similarly we can propose for test scores and absence in the class and study time and absence in the class. Null and alternate hypothesis is proposed individually for each pair.

Step 1 **Open Data Editor**, and **Click Variable View**. Enter the name of three variables and details for each of the variables.

Step 2 Click **Data View** and enter data under appropriate variables (Figure 7.11).

	Score	Studytime	Absence
1	47.00	8.00	1.00
2	51.00	12.00	3.00
3	70.00	12.50	2.00
4	70.00	19.50	3.00
5	75.00	13.50	2.00
6	75.00	16.00	2.00
7	80.00	14.50	3.00
8	84.00	18.50	1.00
9	80.00	15.00	0.00
10	85.00	14.50	1.00
11	90.00	22.50	3.00
12	90.00	18.50	2.00
13	92.00	19.00	1.00

Figure 7.11   Data View with data for three variables

Step 3 Select Analyze from the main menu and select **Correlate** from drop down menu and **Bivariate**. **Bivariate Correlations** dialog box appears.

Step 4 Now move the variables from the left pan to the **Variables** box on the right by clicking on the arrow.

Step 5 Select **Pearson** under **Correlation Coefficients** and select Two-tailed under test of significance.

Step 6 Click Options and select **Means** and **Standard Deviations** box under **Statistics**.

Step 7 Click **Continue** and click **OK** to run the analysis.

Step 8 Output 1 and 2 appears as given below.

Output 1

Descriptive Statistics

	Mean	Std. Deviation	N
Test score obtained by students	76.0769	14.03841	13
Study time in hours / week	15.6923	3.85972	13
Absence in the class in hours / week	2.0769	1.11516	13

Output 2

Correlations

		Test score obtained by students	Study time in hours / week	Absence in the class in hours / ...
Test score obtained by students	Pearson Correlation	1	.777**	-.597*
	Sig. (2-tailed)		.002	.031
	N	13	13	13
Study time in hours / week	Pearson Correlation	.777**	1	-.255
	Sig. (2-tailed)	.002		.400
	N	13	13	13
Absence in the class in hours / week	Pearson Correlation	-.597*	-.255	1
	Sig. (2-tailed)	.031	.400	
	N	13	13	13

**. Correlation is significant at the 0.01 level (2-tailed).

*. Correlation is significant at the 0.05 level (2-tailed).

Interpretation

1. The **output 1** gives mean, standard deviation and number of cases. With this we can describe the data.

2. The **output 2** is in the form of a matrix. The values on either side of the diagonal are the mirror images of each other, i.e., the values are the same. We can refer and interpret the values on one side of the diagonal. The r-value is positive for the "variables test scores" and "studying time", the p-value 0.003 is below 0.01, so we reject the H_0, accept H_A. Hence, there is significant positive correlation between these two. Therefore, increase in study time really increases the test scores.

3. The *r*-value is –0.637 for the variables test score and absence in the class and the *p*-value (0.026) is below 0.01, so we reject the H_0, therefore significant correlation exists between the two, i.e., the absence in the class really correlate negatively with test scores.

4. The *r*-value 0.360 is negative, for the variables study time and absence in the class and the *p*-value is 0.25, which is above 0.01 so we accept the H_0, i.e., there is no correlation between study time and absence in the class and therefore, study time really do not correlate with absence in the class or *vice versa*.

RANK CORRELATION

Occasionally, we come across statistical data in which the variables under study are **not capable** of accurate quantitative measurements and may not fall in an interval scale also, but can be arranged in **serial order**. Such variables are qualitative characteristics or attributes like intelligence, beauty, morality, teaching method, honesty, etc., which cannot be directly measured quantitatively but can be arranged serially. For such data Karl **Pearson's correlation coefficient** cannot be used as such. One method of analyzing such a data is by ranking the variates and calculating a coefficient of rank correlation. Thus rank correlation is the study of relationship between different rankings on the same set of items. It deals with correspondence between two rankings and assign the significance of this relationship. Data suited to ranking methods are those which can not be measured on absolute scale, but only on an ordinal scale. There are different methods of ranking data and calculating correlation co-efficient. We shall discuss on **Spearman's rank correlation coefficient** and **Kendall's correlation coefficient**.

Spearman's Rank Correlation Coefficient

Charles Edward Spearman, a British Psychologist developed formula to obtain correlation coefficient between ranks of a group of individuals for a given pair of attributes. To calculate Spearman correlation coefficient, ranks are assigned to a **set of variables X** and **Y** individually. In ranking, first the variable X is ranked from low to high (it can be from high to low also); then the variable Y is ranked in the same way. The deviation between the ranks of pairs of variable is, squared and summed up. The values are substituted in the following formula to get **Pearson's correlation coefficient**. As the deviation between ranks form the basis for calculation of **Pearson's correlation coefficient**, it is commonly called as **Rank correlation**.

$$R = 1 - \frac{6\left(\Sigma\, d^2\right)}{n\left(n^2 - 1\right)}$$

where,

R—Rank correlation coefficient

d^2—squared deviations

Σ—sum

n—pair of items

Interpretation

R value lies between −1 and +1 and interpreted as in the case of Pearson's correlation coefficient.

Spearman's Rank Correlation with SPSS

Example 7.3

Compute Spearman's rank correlation coefficient for the data given below on academic achievements and family income.

Grade points	Family income (Rs)
75	8500
73	7000
96	6000
61	12000
71	12000
56	5000
50	18000
85	9000
90	7000
54	8200

Step 1 Name the variables in **Variable View** and data in Data editor

Step 2 Click **Analyse** then select **Correlate** and click **Bivariate**. **Bivariate Correlations** dialog box opens (Figure 7.12).

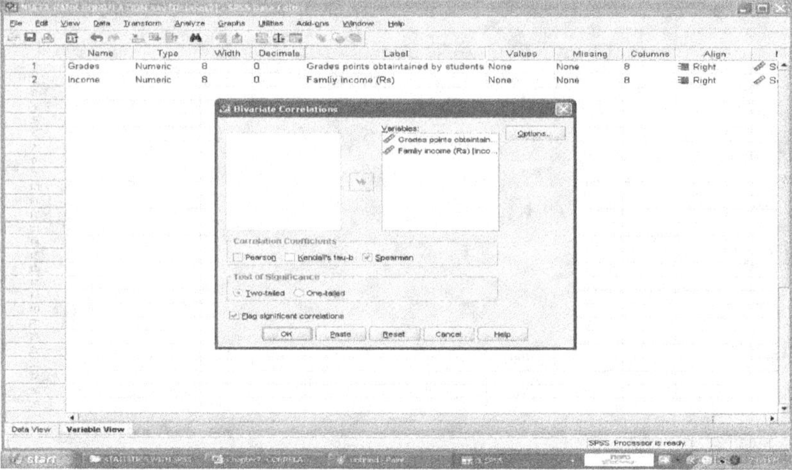

Figure 7.12   Bivariate Correlations dialog box with Spearman correlation coefficient selected

Step 3 Transfer both the variables to **Variables** box and select **Spearman** under **Correlation Coefficients** and **Two-tailed** under **Test of Significance**.

Step 4 Click **OK** to run the analysis.

Step 5 Output appears as shown below.

Output

Correlations

			Grades obtaintained by students	Famliy income (Rs)
Spearman's rho	Grades obtaintained by students	Correlation Coefficient	1.000	-.396
		Sig. (2-tailed)	.	.257
		N	10	10
	Famliy income (Rs)	Correlation Coefficient	-.396	1.000
		Sig. (2-tailed)	.257	.
		N	10	10

Interpretation

In this output Spearman's correlation coefficient is given at the point of intersection between "grade points obtained" and "family income" which is –0.396, and the significance value for two-tailed is 0.257. Since the significance value is greater than 0.05 ($p > 0.05$), the correlation coefficient is insignificant and it is inferred that the academic achievement is not related to family income in this data set.

Kendall's Rank Correlation Coefficient

It is symbolised by τ (tau) and therefore commonly referred to as Kendall's tau (τ) coefficient. A tau test is a non-parametric hypothesis test which uses the coefficient to test for statistical dependence. It is named after Maurice Kendall, who proposed and developed it. The Kendall rank correlation coefficient evaluates the degree of similarity between two sets of ranks given to a same set of objects. This coefficient depends upon the number of inversions of pairs of objects which are needed to transform one rank order into the other.

Kendall's coefficient is different from Spearman's rank correlation coefficient. Specifically, it is a measure of rank correlation, that is, the values are ranked by each of the quantities, but concordance and discordance are considered instead of deviation of rankings . If two random variables X and Y have a set of observations (x_1, y_1), (x_2, y_2), ..., (x_n, y_n), any pair of observations (x_i, y_i) and (x_j, y_j) are said to be concordant if the ranks for both values agree: that is, if both $x_i > x_j$ and $y_i > y_j$ or if both $x_i < x_j$ and $y_i < y_j$; otherwise they are said to be discordant.

The following formula is used to calculate the value of Kendall rank correlation:

$$\tau = \frac{n_c - n_d}{\frac{1}{2}n(n-1)}$$

where,

n_c—number of concordant

n_d—number of discordant

n—total number of possible pairing of observations

Kendall Rank Correlation with SPSS

Example 7.4

Compute Kendall rank correlation coefficient for the data on the IQ of 10 persons and the number of hours of TV watching

IQ	106	86	100	101	199	103	97	113	112	110
No. of hours of TV watching	7	0	27	50	28	29	20	12	6	17

The procedures for Kendall rank correlation will be the same as the Pearson correlation in SPSS.

Step 1 Name the variables in **Variable View** and data in **Data Editor**.

Step 2 Click **Analysis**, then select **Correlate** and then select **Bivariate**, **Bivariate Correlations** dialog box open (Figure 7.13).

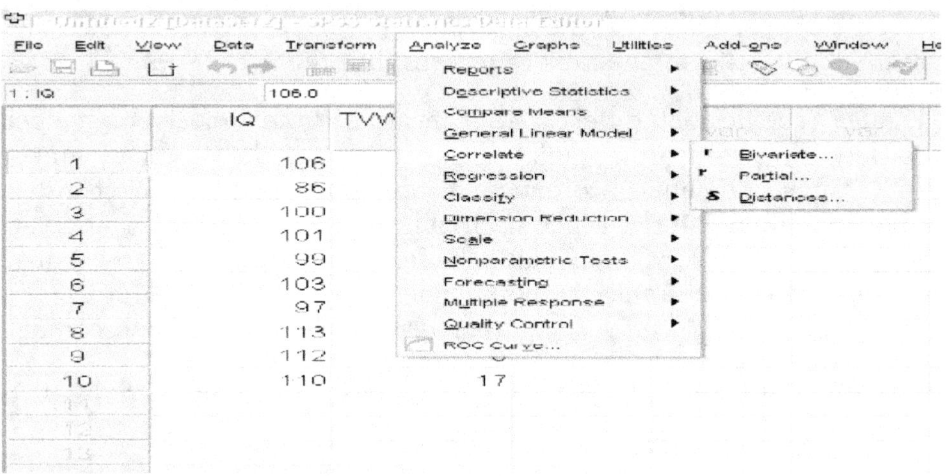

Figure 7.13 Selecting **Bivariate** from main menu

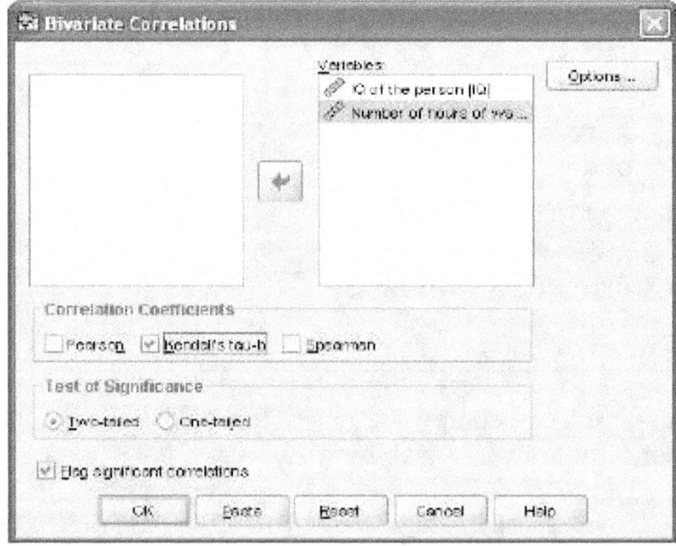

Figure 7.14 **Bivariate Correlatons** dialog box with test variables transferred and **Kendall's tau-b** selected

Step 3 Transfer both the variables to **Variables** box and select **Kendall's tau-b** under **correlation coefficient** and **Two-tailed** under **Test of Significance**.

Step 4 Click **OK** to run the analysis, the output appears as given below

Output

Correlations

			IQ of the person	Number of hours of watching TV
Kendall's tau_b	IQ of the person	Correlation Coefficient	1	-0.11
		Sig. (2-tailed)		0.65
		N	10	10
	Number of hours of watching TV	Correlation Coefficient	-0.11	1
		Sig. (2-tailed)	0.65	
		N	10	10

Interpretation

In this output Kendall's correlation co-efficient b is given at the point of intersect between IQ of the person and the number of hours of watching TV, which is = –0.11, and the significance for two tailed is 0.65. Since, the significance value is greater than 0.05 ($p > 0.05$), the correlation coefficient is insignificant and is inferred that the IQ of the person is not related to number of hours of watching TV in this data set.

MULTIPLE CORRELATION

In the preceding examples we have discussed the relationships between two variables. We shall now expand these considerations to relationship among three or more variables using the procedures of multiple correlation. Multiple correlation (sometimes called multiple regression correlation or multiple linear correlation) is an extension of linear correlation. If none of the variables is assumed to be functionally dependent on one another, then we can apply multiple correlation. In all these cases, the assumption is that the variables are normally distributed. In simple correlation, the sample is from a bivariate normal population; whereas in multiple correlation, the sample (on which the observations or measurements are collected for more than two variables) is from a multivariate normal distribution. In multiple correlation, all variables y, x_1, x_2, x_3,... etc. must be treated as y.

Advantages of multiple correlation over simple bivariate correlation

1. Curvilinear effects can be tested

2. Interaction effects can be tested.

3. Researcher may learn how much variation in the dependent variable is explained by one set of variables as opposed to another.

4. The relative importance of each variable can be identified.

The following formula is used to calculate multiple correlation involving three variables.

$$R = \frac{\sqrt{r^2_{yx_1} + r^2_{yx_2} - 2r_{yx_1}\left(r_{yx_2}\right)\left(r_{x_1x_2}\right)}}{\sqrt{1 - r^2_{x_1x_2}}}$$

where, R = multiple correlation coefficient, r = simple correlation coefficient of two given variables, i.e., between y and x_1, y and x_2, and x_1 and x_2 and so on.

Interpretation

In contrast to simple correlation coefficient r, which tells about the strength and direction of association between variables, multiple correlation coefficient R, tells only the strength of the association. Since it is a measure of the strength of the linear relationship between the variable y and a set of variables x_1, x_2, ...x_p..., the R value is never negative. R can take any value from 0 and $+1$. If the value of R is 1, there is perfect linear association. If R equals zero, then there is no linear association between the variables. For the values ranging from 0 to 1, the significance of R is predicted with test of significance. SPSS enables the researcher to do both simultaneously.

Multiple Correlation with SPSS

Since the working part of multiple correlation and multiple regression deals with the same procedure, the example for multiple correlation is worked out under multiple regression (*Refer* Chapter 8).

DOES CORRELATION COEFFICIENT REVEALS THE RELATIONSHIP BETWEEN THE VARIABLE FULLY?

No discussion of correlation would be complete without a discussion of causation. In correlation analysis, it is possible to say the relationship between two variables, but not to say one variable as cause and another as effect. For example, suppose there is a high correlation between the number of Pepsi bottles sold and the number of drowning deaths in summer. Does that mean that one should not drink Pepsi before one swims? Not necessarily. This is an example of correlation without causation.

On the other hand there is high degree of positive correlation between cigarette smoking and incidences of cancer. The cigarette companies say that people who smoke are more nervous and nervous people are more susceptible to cancer. While doctors say that smoking indeed causes cancer. But the fact is those who smoke more cigarette get cancer or cigarette smoking causes cancer. Here cigarette smoking is the cause and cancer is effect and therefore do not smoke. This is an example of correlation with causation. In the example if we do only correlation, we can only find the strength of association between the variable and can not proceed further to prediction. We can go for prediction with regression analysis. Chapter 8 deals with regression analysis.

Review Exercises

1. Calculate Karl Pearson's correlation between the age of husband and wives and draw a scatter plot.

Age of husband	25	29	30	27	28	40	54	47	35	60
Age of wife	23	27	30	26	26	38	50	44	33	56

2. Draw a scatter diagram for the following data on the length and breadth of 10 fishes, calculate correlation coefficient and interpret your results.

Length of fishes (cm)	13	15	15	16	17	19	21	23	16	20
Breadth of fishes (cm)	4	4	4	4	4	6	6	8	4	5

3. Find out Karl Pearson's correlation coefficient for the following data on the arm width and weight in starfish.

Arm width (in mm)	12	9	8	10	11	13	7
Weight (in g)	14	8	6	9	11	12	3

4. Two judges in a painting competition rank twelve students as follows. Find Rank correlation coefficient and state the degree of agreement between the two judges.

Judge 1	5	11	2	3	4	1	6	8	7	10	9	12
Judge 2	4	8	5	2	1	6	7	10	9	11	12	3

5. Calculate Kendall's coefficient of correlation for the following data on demand and supply.

Year	2000	2001	2002	2003	2004	2005	2006	2007	2009	2009
Supply	125	160	164	174	155	170	165	162	172	175
Demand	112	125	192	190	165	174	124	127	152	169

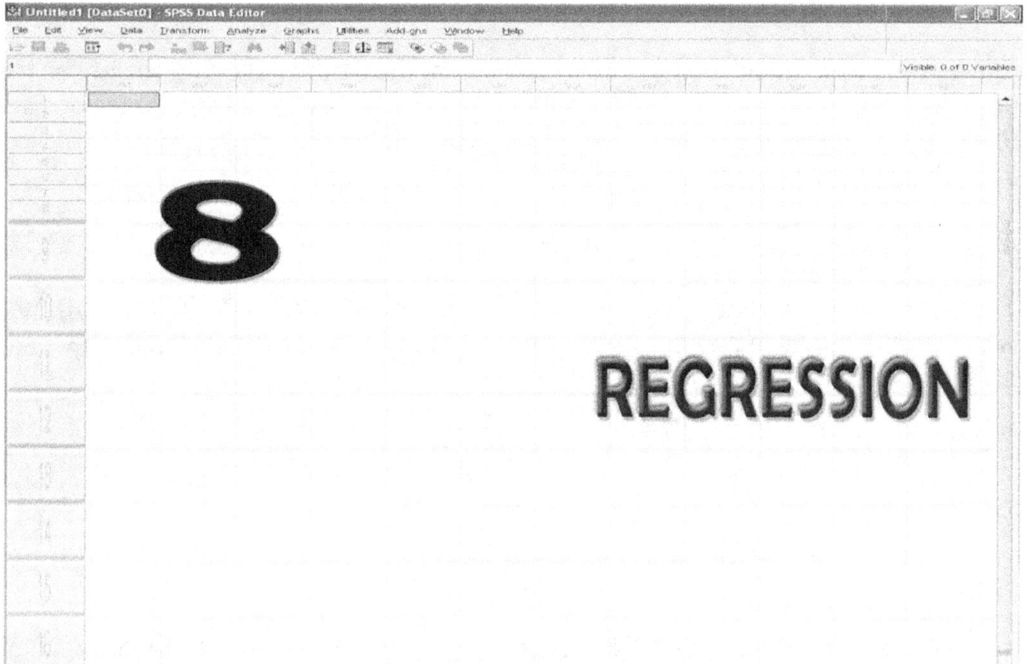

8

REGRESSION

In the previous chapter, we discussed about simple linear correlation and multiple correlation. Both these procedures enable the investigator to find the degree and direction or only degree of relationship between two variables. But these procedures failed to find the functional relationship (i.e., cause and effect relationship) between variables under study. The cause and effect relationship between variables is studied with regression analysis. The term "Regression" was first used by Sir Francis Galton, a British biometrician. The term regression is defined as a mathematical measure of average relationship between two or more variables in a data set.

In most of the cases, the relationship between two variables may be a functional dependence of one on the other. The magnitude of one of the variables (dependent variable) is assumed to be determined by the function of the magnitude of the second variable (independent variable) whereas the reverse is not possible. For example, in the relationship between blood pressure and age in human, blood pressure may be considered as the dependent variable and age as the independent variable. It is reasonably assumed that the magnitude of a person's blood pressure might be a function of age. In this example, age is not the only biological determinant of blood pressure, but it is considered as one of the determining factors. For this reason, the independent variable is called the predictor, or regressor variable and the dependent variable is called as the response, or criterion variable.

SIMPLE LINEAR REGRESSION

The term simple linear regression refers to the fact that only two variables are being considered. Data to which simple regression analysis is applicable consists of a dependent variable and an independent variable. This relationship is studied both mathematically and graphically.

Simple Linear Regression Equation

The simplest functional relationship of one variable to another in a population is the simple linear regression. This kind of relationship is expressed in the form of an equation

$$Y_i = a + bX_i$$

where,

Y_i —ith item of variable Y (dependent)

X_i—ith item of variable X (independent),

a—constant and is called Y intercept, i.e., value of Y on regression line when $X = 0$

b—parameter termed as regression coefficient or the slope (the change in y with a change of one unit in X).

The value of b theoretically can range from $-\infty$ to $+\infty$ including zero.

From the functional relationship of the equation $Y_i = a + bX_i$, we can predict the most probable value of Y for the given value of X. To do this we need to find the constant a and the parameter b in the equation. The constants a and b are calculated from the following formula

$$a = \bar{X} - b\bar{Y}$$

$$b = \frac{\sum XY - \dfrac{\sum X \sum Y}{n}}{\sum X^2 - \dfrac{\sum (X)^2}{n}}$$

where,

$\bar{X}$—mean of variable X,

$\bar{Y}$—mean of variable Y and

$\sum$—summation

When we formulate the regression equation we can predict the most probable value of Y for the given value of X.

Scatter Plot and the Line of Best Fit

As in the previous chapter, we can plot the variables Y and X on a graph sheet using the ordinate (Y-axis) for the dependent variable (Y) and the abscissa (X-axis) for the independent variable (X). One pair of X and Y data may be denoted as (X_1, Y_1), another as (X_2, Y_2), another as (X_3, Y_3), etc. Thus the data appear as scatter points, each point representing a pair of X and Y values. The resulting graphic representation is called scatter plot. This gives the spread of the variables showing the nature of relationship. A line drawn through these points in such a way that the deviations of scatter points from the line are the least. Such a line is called the line of best fit.

Consider the data in Example 1 in Chapter 7 where there are two variables namely age, the independent variable and blood pressure, the dependent variable. From the scatter plot of these data, it appears that blood pressure measurements are linearly related to age. When we draw an "eye fit" curve there is going to be a considerable variability of data around any straight line we might draw through them. Therefore, we seek to draw what is commonly termed the "best fit" line through the data. The line of best fit is called "regression line". The criterion for "best fit" that is generally employed utilises the concept of least squares. Each value of X will have a corresponding value of Y lying on the line that we might draw through the scatter of data points. This value of Y is represented as $\hat{Y}$ to distinguish it from the Y value actually observed in the sample.

The criterion of least squares considers the vertical deviation of each point from the line (i.e., the deviation described as $(Y_i - \hat{Y}_i)$, and defines the best fit line that results in the smallest value for the sum of squares of these deviations for all values of Y_i and $\hat{Y}_i$. That is, $\sum_{i=1}^{n}(Y_i - \hat{Y})^2$ is to be minimum, where n is the number of data points comprising the sample. The sum of squares of these deviations is called the residual sum of squares (or, sometimes, the error sum of squares). Thus there is a functional relationship between regression line and regression equation. The latter is the mathematical expression of the former.

Regression and One-way ANOVA

Simple linear regression equation is based on a and b whose calculations involve the concept of least squares. For this reason one way analysis of variance is carried out along with regression analysis. This procedure enables the investigator to find out how far the variance in independent variable contributes to the change in the dependent variable.

Simple Regression with SPSS

As with correlation analysis, SPSS allows us to do the analysis quickly. Let us calculate the constant a and parameter b for the pair of variables, age (independent variable) and systolic pressure (dependent variable)

Example 8.1

Formulate regression equation of Y (systolic pressure mm Hg) on X (age) in man. Predict the most probable value of systolic pressure for ages 51 and 68.

Age	Group	Age	Group
56	160	40	126
42	130	53	145
60	125	35	118
50	135	38	120
54	145	39	123
49	115	37	138
39	140	70	160
62	120	75	163
65	140	65	145
70	160	64	146

Step 1 **Open Data Editor** and click **Variable View**. Enter the name of variables and details of the variables.

Step 2 Click **Data View** and enter data under appropriate variable.

Step 3 Select **Analyse** from the main menu and select **Regression** and **Linear** from the drop down menu as in Figure 8.1.

Step 4 **Linear Regression** dialog box opens. Transfer **Systolic pressure** to **Dependent** box and **Age** to **Independent** box (Figure 8.2).

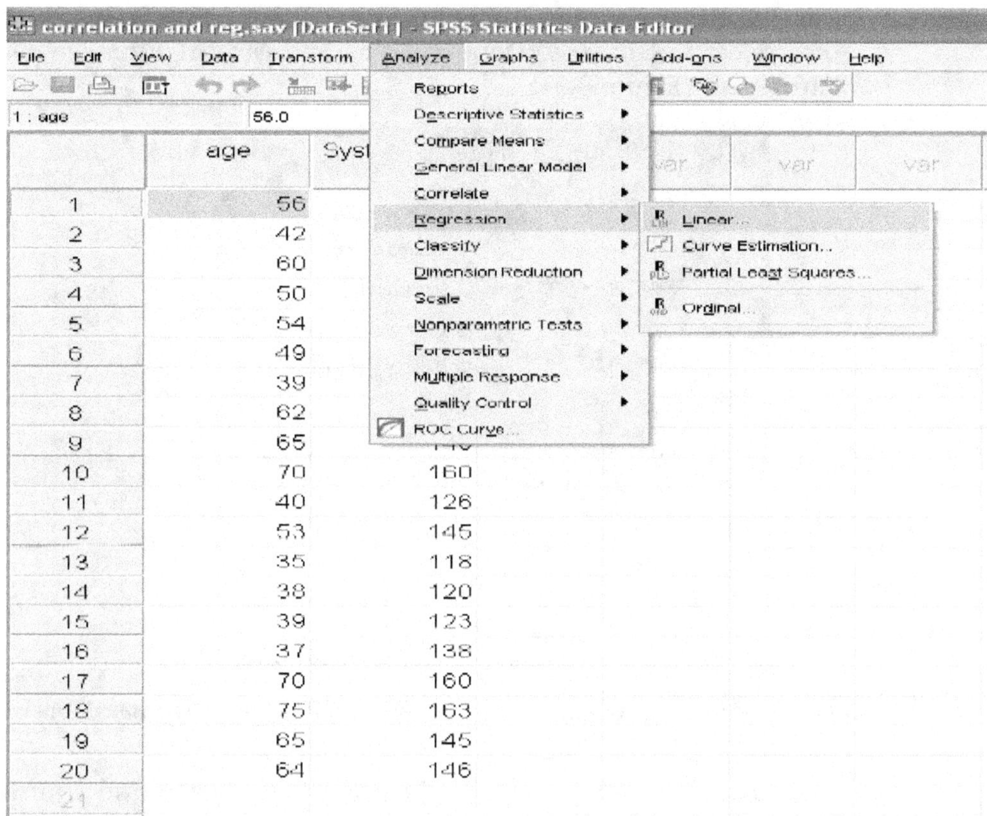

Figure 8.1   Selecting **Linear Regression** from main menu

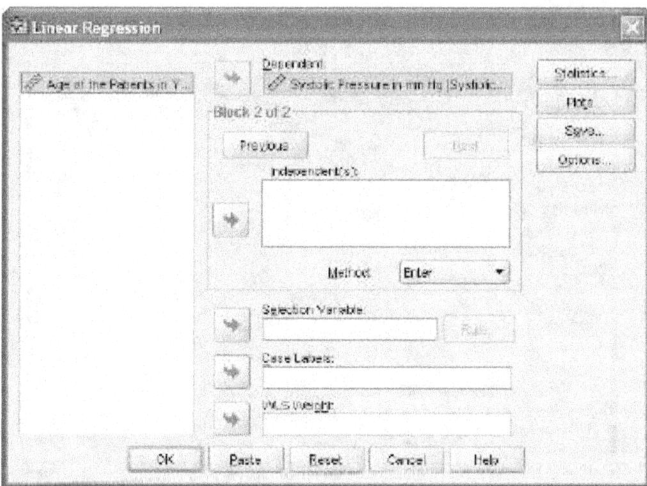

Figure 8.2   **Linear Regression** dialog box to transfer variables

Step 5 Click **Statisics** to open **Linear Regression**: **Statistics** dialog box, select **Estimates**, **Descriptives** and **Model Fit,** then click **Continue** (Figure 8.3).

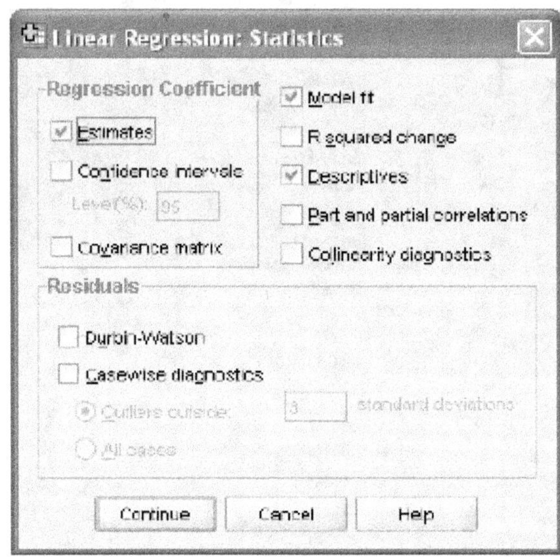

Figure 8.3 **Linear Regression: Statistics** dialog box with options for **Estimates**, **Model Fit** and **Descriptives**

Step 6 Click **Plots** to open **Linear Regression**: **Plots** and transfer *ZRESID (dependent or criterion) to Y: box and * ZPRED (independent or predictor) to X: box (Figure 8.4) and then click **Continue**.

Step 7 Click **OK** to run the analysis.

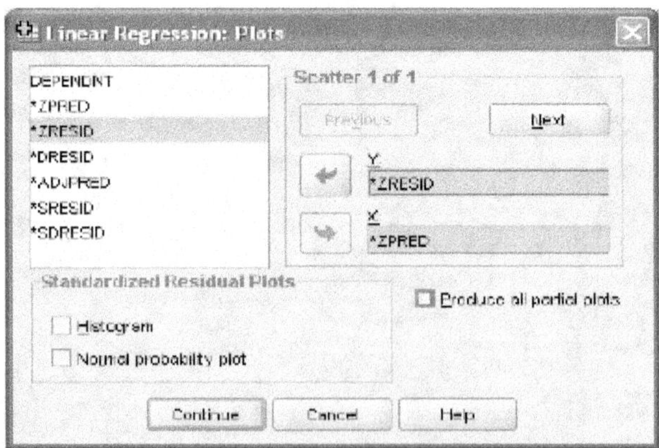

Figure 8.4 **Linear Regression: Plots** to transfer dependent and Independent variables

Step 8   The outputs appear under different headings as given in Outputs 1, 2, 3, and 4

Output 1

Descriptive Statistics

	Mean	Std. Deviation	N
Systolic Pressure in mm Hg	137.70	15.359	20
Age of the Patients in Years	53.15	12.820	20

Output 2

Coefficients[a]

Model		Unstandardized Coefficients		Standardized Coefficients	t	Sig.
		B	Std. Error	Beta		
1	(Constant)	95.625	11.57		8.26	.000
	Age of the Patients in Years	.792	0.21	0.66	3.73	.002

a. Dependent Variable: Systolic Pressure in mm Hg

Output 3

ANOVA[b]

Model		Sum of Squares	df	Mean Square	F	Sig.
1	Regression	1956.827	1	1956.827	13.948	.002[a]
	Residual	2525.373	18	140.299		
	Total	4482.200	19			

a. Predictors: (Constant), Age of the Patients in Years

b. Dependent Variable: Systolic Pressure in mm Hg

Output 4

Residuals Statistics[a]

	Minimum	Maximum	Mean	Std. Deviation	N
Predicted Value	123.33	155.00	137.70	10.15	20
Residual	-24.71	20.04	1.48E-14	11.53	20
Std. Predicted Value	-1.42	1.7	-3.83E-16	1	20
Std. Residual	-2.09	1.69	1.26E-15	0.97	20

a. Dependent Variable: Systolic Pressure in mm Hg

Interpretation

Depending upon the need of the investigator, the values in the output can be taken for interpretation.

1. The mean and standard deviation of the variables is given under **Descriptive Statistics** (Output 1). The mean age of the persons in the sample is 53.15 with a standard deviation of 12. 820 (in research paper it is written as 53.15 ± 12.820 years) and the average systolic pressure is 137.70 with a standard deviation of 15.359 (137.70 ± 15.359 mm Hg).

2. The constant and parameter needed for the formulation of regression equation $Y_i = a + bX_i$ are given in **output 2** under the heading coefficients. The value given under the column B against **Constant** is the a-value (95.625) and against **Age of the patients in Years** is the b-value (0.792).

   Therefore, regression equation $Y_i = a + bX_i$ is formulated as

   $$Y_i = 95.625 + 0.792X_i$$

   To predict the most probable systolic pressure for the ages 51 and 68 years:

   i.   Systolic pressure for a person of age 51 years

   Here the equation is formulated as

   $$Y_i = 95.625 + 0.792 \times 51$$
   $$Y_i = 95.625 + 40.392$$
   $$Y_i = 136.017 \text{ mm Hg.}$$

   ii. Systolic pressure for a person of age 68 years

   Here the equation is formulated as

   $$Y_i = 95.625 + 0.792 \times 68$$
   $$Y_i = 95.625 + 53.856$$
   $$Y_i = 149.481 \text{ mm Hg.}$$

3. Output 3 gives the results on analysis of variance. The F-ratio given under column F is 13.948, and p-value, 0.002 is given under Sig. column. Since p-value is less than 0.01, it implies that the calculated regression coefficient is significant and the variance in independent variable contributes to the change in dependent variable. Therefore, it is inferred that the variance in age really contribute to change in systolic pressure.

Drawing regression line with SPSS

Example 8.2

Draw a regression line for the data given in Example 8.1.

> **Step 1** Choose **Graph** from main menu, click **Legacy Dialog**, then click **Interactive** and then **Scatter plot** (Figure 8.5) to open **Create Scatterplot**.

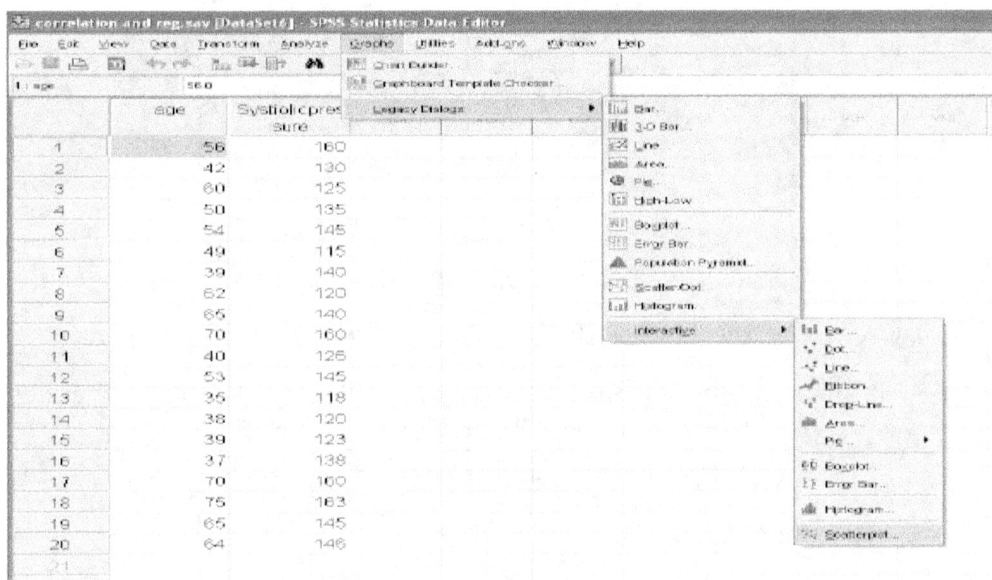

Figure 8.5   Selecting Scatter Plot from main menu

> **Step 2** Click **Assign Variable** and drag the variable "Age of the Person" to *X*-axis and "Systolic Pressure" to *Y*-axis (Figure 8.6) and click **Fit**.

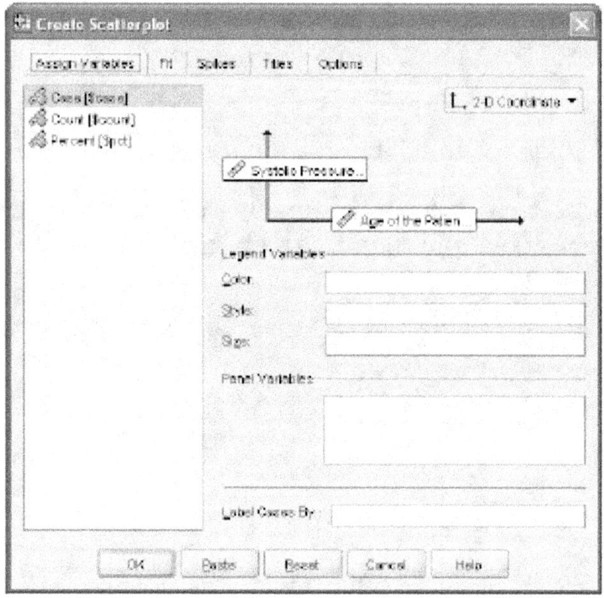

Figure 8.6   Assigning variables to X and Y-axis in **Create Scatter Plot** dialog box

Step 3   It opens another **Create Scatterplot**, click the down arrow under **Methods** and select **Regression** (Figure 8.7).

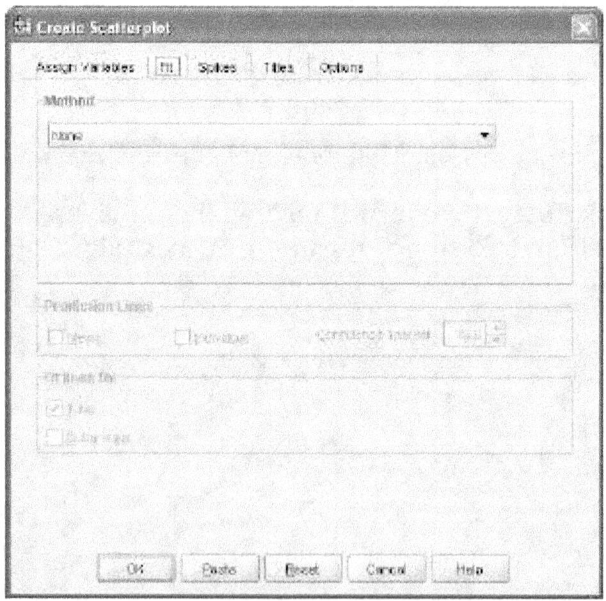

Figure 8.7   Create Scatterplot dialog box with option **Fit** selected

Step 4 When you select **Regression**, all squares in that dialog box gets highlighted, now select **Constant in Equation** and **Mean** under **Prediction lines** and click **OK** (Figure 8.8).

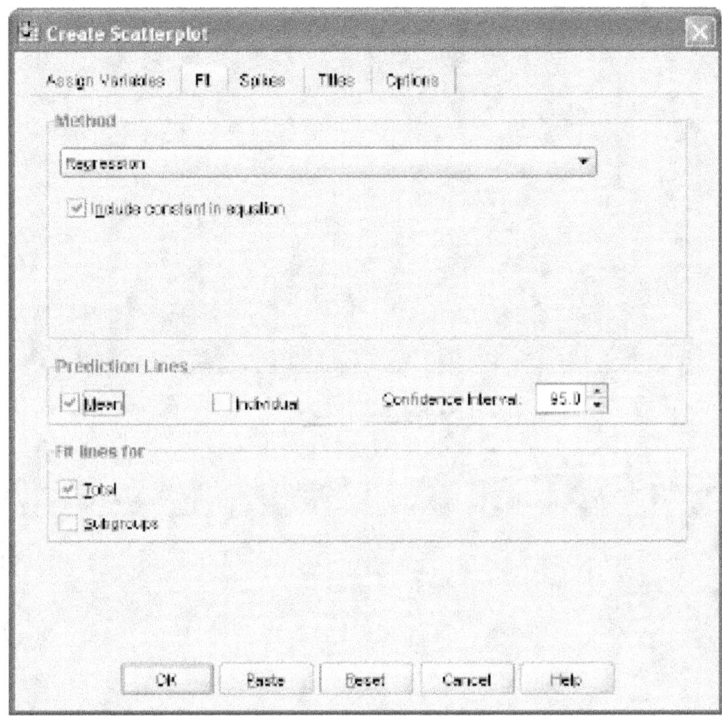

Figure 8.8   Create Scatterplot dialog box with options selected under **Method**, **Prediction line** and **Fit lines for**

Step 5 The result appears in output as in Output 1. The central line is the regression line, i.e., the line of "**best fit**" and the other two lines, one below and the other above the regression line gives the confidence limit (95%). The scatter points are the plot for each pair of variable for a single individual.

Output 1

Step 6 To denote the deviation of various points from the regression line or line of best fit click **Spike** under **Create Scatterplot** and select **Fit Line** under **Spike** (Figure 8.9).

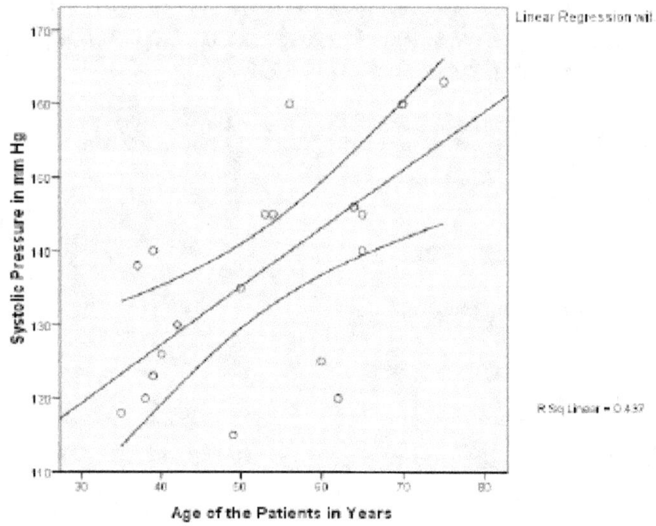

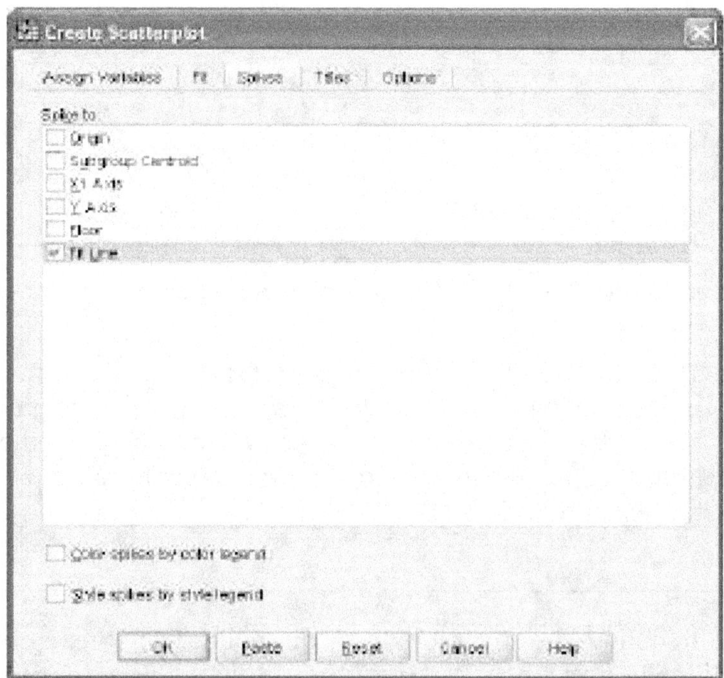

Figure 8.9   Create Scatterplot dialog box with "**Fit Line**" selected under **Spikes**

Step 7 Click **OK** to get the output as shown in Output 2.

Output 2

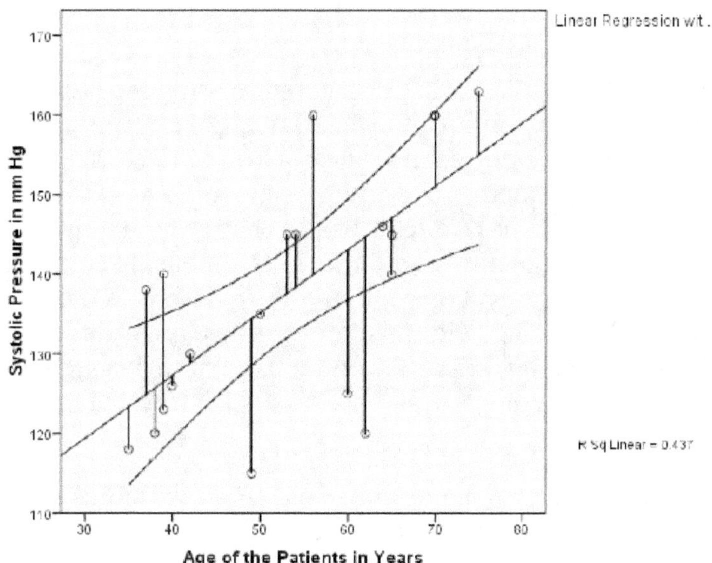

In Output 2 the vertical line from the line of best fit to the scatter points show the deviation.

MULTIPLE REGRESSION ANALYSIS

The general purpose of multiple regression is to learn more about the relationship between several independent or predictor variables and a dependent or criterion variable. In the social and natural sciences research multiple regression procedures are very widely used. For example, educational researchers might want to learn the best predictors of success in college. Biologists may want to determine the best predictor for the survival of the fish in polluted water. Psychologists may want to determine which personality variable best predicts social adjustment. Sociologists may want to find out which of the multiple social indicators best predict whether or not a new immigrant group will adapt to the new situation.

Simple linear regression for paired variables in a population is

$$Yi = a + bX_i$$

In this relationship, Y and X represent the dependent and independent variables respectively, b is the regression cocfficient in the population, a (Y intercept) is the value of Y when X is zero.

In many situations, however, Y may be considered dependent upon more than one variable. Then,

$$Y_j = a + b_i X_{ij} + b_2 X_{2j}$$

Here, one variable (Y) is linearly dependent upon a second variable (X_1) and Y is also linearly dependent upon a third variable (X_2). In this particular multiple regression model we have one dependent variable and two independent variables. The two population parameters b_1 and b_2, are termed as **partial regression coefficients**; b_1 expresses how much Y would change for a unit change in X_1, if X_2 was held constant. It is sometimes said that b_1 is a measure of the relationship of Y to X_1 after removing the effect of X_2. Similarly, b_2 describes the rate of change of Y as X_2 changes, with X_1 being held constant. b_1 and b_2 are called partial regression coefficients, because each one expresses only a part of the dependence relationship. The Y intercept, a (sometimes designated as b_0) is the value of Y when both X_1 and X_2 are zero.

If we sample a population containing the three variables (Y, X_1 and X_2) the multiple regression equation may be expressed as

$$Y_j = a + b_1 X_{1j} + b_2 X_{2j}$$

where Y_j = dependent variable, a is a constant called Y intercept where the value of independent variable X_1 and X_2 is 0, b_1 slope of X_1 with X_2 being held constant, b_2 = slope of X_2 with X_1 being held constant.

Note   The above descriptions and formulae are explained to make the reader to have a better understanding on the principles of carrying out multiple regression and enable them to interpret the results.

Multiple Regression with SPSS

Example 8.3

A hospital record gives the data on forced expiratory air volume (litres), vital capacity (litres) and total lung capacity (litres). The forced expiratory air volume of the lung depends on vital capacity and total lung capacity. Calculate multiple regression coefficient and formulate multiple regression equation.

In this example only three variables are given. Out of these three, forced expiratory air volume is the dependent variable and vital capacity and total lung capacity are independent variables.

Vital capacity (litre)	2.2	1.5	1.6	3.4	2.0	1.9	2.2	3.3	2.4	0.9	1.0	2.1	2.8	1.5	1.6
Total lung capacity (litre)	2.5	3.2	4.0	4.4	4.4	3.3	3.2	3.3	3.7	2.8	3.6	3.6	4.3	3.2	5.0
Expiratory air volume (litre)	1.0	1.0	1.4	2.6	1.2	1.5	1.6	1.6	2.1	0.7	0.7	1.1	2.5	1.0	1.4

Step 1 Enter the variable names in **Variable view** and data in **Data editor.**

Step 2 Select **Analyze** from main menu, then **Regression** and then select **Linear** to open **Linear Regression** dialog box.

Step 3 Transfer **forced expiratory air volume** to **Dependent box** (Figure 8.10) and **Vital capacity** and **Total lung capacity** to **Independent** box.

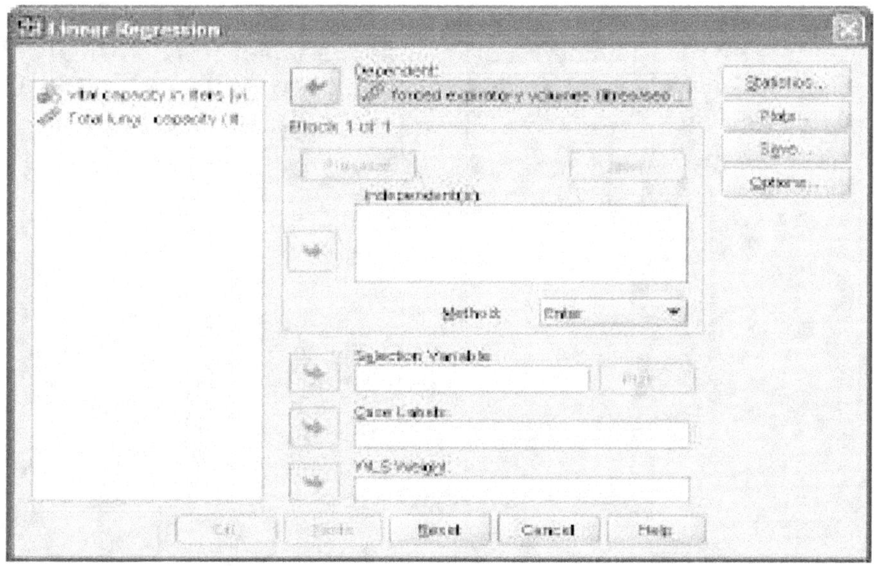

Figure 8.10   **Linear Regression** dialog box to trnasfer Dependent and Independent variables

Step 4 Click **Statistics** to open **Linear Regression**: **Statistics** dialog box. In this select **Estimates** and **Model Fit**, **Descriptive** then click **Continue** (Figure 8.11).

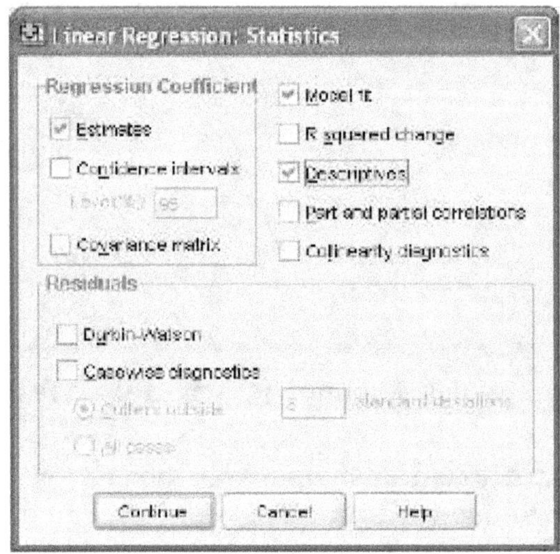

Figure 8.11   **Linear Regression: Statistics** dialog box to select **Estimates, Model Fit** and **Descriptives**

Step 5 Click Plots to open **Linear Regression**: **Plots** and transfer *ZRESID (dependent or criterion variable) to *Y*: box and * ZPRED (independent or predictor variable) to *X*: box (Figure 8.12) and then click **Continue**.

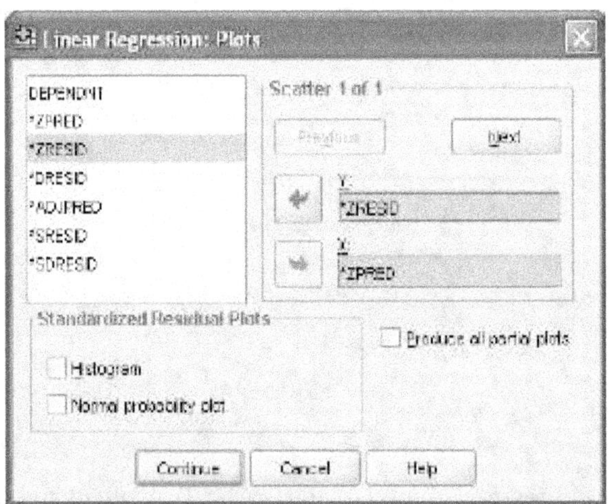

Figure 8.12   **Linear Regression: Plots** dialog box to set transfer Y and X variables

Step 6 Click **OK** to run the analysis, the outputs (1, 2, 3, 4 and 5) appear.

Output 1

Descriptive Statistics

	Mean	Std. Deviation	N
forced expiratory volumes (litres/second)	1.428	.5844	15
vital capacity in liters	2.027	.7353	15
Total lung capacity (liters)	3.633	.6758	15

Output 2

Model Summary[b]

Model	R	R Square	Adjusted R Square	Std. Error of the Estimate
1	.870[a]	.758	.717	.3108

a. Predictors: (Constant), Total lung   capacity (liters), vital capacity in liters

b. Dependent Variable: forced expiratory volumes (litres/second)

Output 3

ANOVA[b]

Model		Sum of Squares	df	Mean Square	F	Sig.
1	Regression	3.622	2	1.811	18.753	.000[a]
	Residual	1.159	12	.097		
	Total	4.781	14			

a. Predictors: (Constant), Total lung   capacity (liters), vital capacity in liters

b. Dependent Variable: forced expiratory volumes (litres/second)

Output 4

Coefficients[a]

Model		Unstandardized Coefficients		Standardized Coefficients	t	Sig.
		B	Std. Error	Beta		
1	(Constant)	-.796	0.47		-1.69	0.12
	vital capacity in liters	.581	0.12	0.73	5	3.08E-4
	Total lung capacity (liters)	.288	0.13	0.33	2.28	0.04

a. Dependent Variable: forced expiratory volumes (litres/second)

Output 5

Residuals Statistics[a]

	Minimum	Maximum	Mean	Std. Deviation	N
Predicted Value	0.53	2.45	1.43	.5086	15
Residual	-.4714	.4360	.0000	.2877	15
Std. Predicted Value	-1.76	2	1.85E-16	1	15
Std. Residual	-1.52	1.4	-7.4E-17	0.93	15

a. Dependent Variable: forced expiratory volumes (litres/second)

Interpretation

1. The output 1 gives the descriptive statistics namely mean and standard deviation for the three variables and number of variates. Mean expiratory volumes is 1.428 ± 0.584 (litres/second), the vital capacity is 2.027 ± 0.735 (litres) and the lung capacity is 3.633 ± 0.676 (litres).

2. In Output 2, Model Summary[b], the value 0.870 given under the column R is multiple correlation coefficient. These three variables are correlated significantly.

3. Output 3 gives the results on ANOVA, since the p-value given under significance column is < 0.01. This tells that the variance in vital capacity and total lung capacity (two independent variables or predictor variables) contribute significantly to the change in forced expiratory air volume (dependent variable).

4. Output 4 gives the coefficients; these values are needed to formulate regression equation. The value under column B against constant is the "a" value (Y-intercept) in the regression equation and the values against total lung capacity (0.288) and vital capacity (0.581) define the slope of the regression lines and are the values of b_1 and b_2 in the multiple regression equation

$$Y_j = a + b_1 X_{1j} + b_2 X_{2j}$$

Hence, the multiple regression equation is formulated as

$$Y_j = -0.796 + 0.288 X_{1j} + 0.581 X_{2j}$$

5. Output 5 gives the residual statistics in which the number of cases, mean and standard deviation for the predicted values of the dependent variable are given.

CORRELATION ANALYSIS VS REGRESSION ANALYSIS

1. In correlation analysis, we identify the **strength** and **direction** of a **linear relation** between two random variables. It simply tells how much one variable tends to change when the other one changes. Regression analysis aims at establishing the functional relationship between the two variables under study and by using this relationship the value of one variable is predicted or estimated for any given value of the other variable.

2. In correlation, it does not matter which of the two variables is called "X" or "Y". We will get the same correlation coefficient even if we interchange the two variables i.e., considering X as Y.

3. In regression the two variables 'X' and 'Y' are considered as 'independent or predictor" and 'dependent or criterion" variables respectively. We can not interchange the variables, if we interchange the two variables, we will get different results.

4. Correlation coefficient r is a relative measure of the linear relationship between the variables under study and is a pure number lying between ± 1. On the other hand, the regression coefficient b_{yx} is an absolute measure representing the change in the value of the variable Y for a unit change in the value of the variable X.

5. Correlation does not study 'cause' and 'effect' relationship. It simply quantifies how well two variables relate to each other. In regression we study cause and effect relationship and we can predict the most probable value of a dependent variable for a given independent variable.

6. In correlation we can not experimentally manipulate the variables. With linear regression, the X variable is often something we experimentally manipulate (time, concentration...) and the effect on Y variable is measured.

Review Exercises

1. Formulate regression equation for the height of son and father for the following data. Find the most probable height of the son when the father's height is 166 and 172. Draw a scatter diagram and the line of best fit.

Height of father (cm)	165	160	157	158	168	170	171	169	165	163
Height of son (cm)	160	162	155	156	165	168	170	159	161	164

2. Draw a scatter plot. Formulate regression equation of weight on height for the following data on the partial pressure of oxygen (mm Hg) in water and the oxygen consumed (mg/hr) by the fish.

Partial pressure of oxygen (mmHg)	117	115	109	105	100	95	93	89	85	75
Oxygen consumed (mg)	6.9	6.9	6.7	6.5	6.4	5.0	5.5	3.3	2.3	1.9

3. Following data show concentration of the pesticide aldrin (mg/l) and the mortality of fish in %. Draw a scatter plot and the line of best fir with spikes. Formulate regression equation of mortalility on pesticide concentration.

Concentration of pesticide aldrin (mg/l)	0.01	0.65	0.30	0.50	0.70	0.40	0.80	1.0	0.9
Mortality (%)	6	72	16	48	65	36	78	98	91

4. Formulate regression equation for the following data on supply and price.

Supply	80	82	91	83	85	89	96	93	90	92
Price	146	140	130	117	133	127	115	95	100	97

5. Formulate multiple regression equation for the following data on the variables X, Y and Z.

X	112	125	118	118	121	125	131	135	140	145
Y	106	102	102	104	98	96	90	85	86	82
Z	115	125	192	193	168	145	150	155	156	157

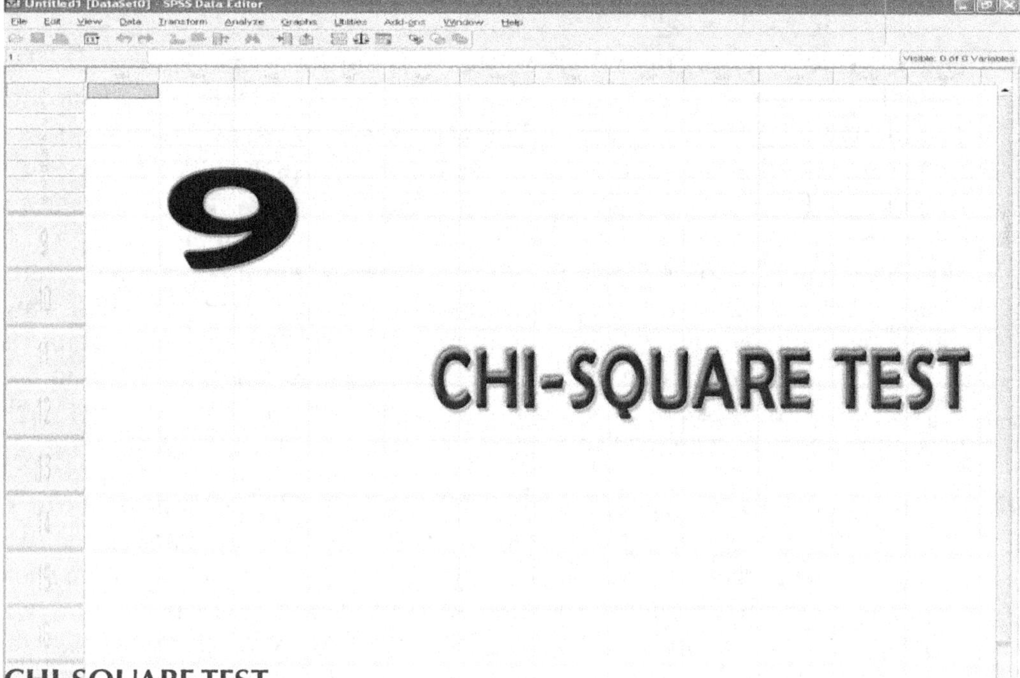

CHI-SQUARE TEST

Karl Pearson in 1900 developed a Statistic procedure for testing the significance of discrepancy between experimental values and theoretical values obtained under some theory or hypothesis. This test is known χ^2 (Chi-square) test. It is a test of goodness of fit and is used to find whether the deviation between observation (experiment) and theory may be attributable to chance (fluctuations in sampling) or any other factor. Chi-square test is applicable to enumeration data (the data obtained by counting) and not to data collected on measurements on continuous scale (quantitative continuous variable).

The formula to calculate chi-square value is

$$\chi^2 = \Sigma \frac{\left(O_i - E_i\right)^2}{E_i}$$

where,

Σ—sum

O_i—observed frequency

E_i—expected frequency.

Data Applicable to Chi-square Test

i. **Qualitative or categorical variables**   There are a number of qualitative variables in human population such as colour of the skin, eye, hair, etc. The individuals possessing these characters are counted and the number of occurrences in the sample is given in the form of frequency (called observed frequency). These characteristics are expected to occur in certain frequencies, called as expected frequencies. Similarly, there are a number of categorical variables such as blood group, education level, employment level, etc. These variables are categorized and the number of individuals possessing these characters is counted and the number of occurrences in the sample is given in the form of frequency against each category. For example, number of persons with the same blood group are counted and given against each category like A, B, AB and O.

ii. **Qualitative or categorical variables given in contingency table**
Sometimes the investigator may be interested in finding out whether two qualitative characters tend to occur together in a given population. In such a case, the individuals are counted for the presence or absence of two specific characters and are given in the form of a contingency table.

Hair colour	Eye colour	
	Black	**Brown**
Black	50	10
Brown	9	51

An environmentalist may be interested in finding out whether two species tend to occur together in a given ecosystem. A pharmacologist may be interested in finding out whether a new drug is effective in curing a disease, a clinician may be interested in finding the association between two diseased conditions in patients. In all these cases, the data are presented in the form of a table with variables, one each in row and column and under each category the observations are placed in two categories. This table is a 2×2 contingency table, since data are presented in two rows and two columns. Depending upon the number of categories for each variable the number of rows and columns vary.

iii. **Qualitative or categorical variables in the form of proportions**
A demographer may be interested in finding out whether the proportion of marital status of men in four different cities is the same. He counts the number of persons—married and single and presents it in the form of proportions like married/Total and single/Total against each city.

Conditions for Validity of Chi-square Test

Chi-square test can be used only if the following conditions are satisfied:

i. N, the total frequency should be reasonably large, say greater than 50.

ii. The observations in the sample should be independent. This means no individual item should be included twice or more in the sample.

iii. No theoretical frequency should be small. Preferably, each theoretical frequency should be larger than 10 but should not be less than 5.

iv. The data should be given in original unit.

Applications of Chi-square Test

i. *Chi-square test of goodness of fit or Chi-square test with a priori hypothesis* Goodness of fit is a generic term used to indicate how far an observed frequency distribution fits well with the expected frequency distribution based on some theory or expectation. Since the expected frequencies are calculated based on some theory or hypothesis, it is also called Chi-square test with a priori hypothesis.

   In this case the null hypothesis (H_0) is "There is no difference between observed frequency and expected frequency". The alternate hypothesis (H_A) is "There is difference between observed frequency and expected frequency".

ii. *Chi-square test for association between attributes or independence of attributes or chi-square test without a priori hypothesis* It is used to find whether two characters have the tendency to remain together or remain independently. For example, whether a patient suffering from a disease is cured because of the drug or the recovery from illness is independent of the drug. In this case, the frequencies are given in the form of a contingency table.

   Hence, the null hypothesis (H_0) is "There is no association between two characters", i.e., the drug is not effective in curing the disease. The alternate hypothesis is "There is association between the two characters". i.e., the drug is effective in curing the disease.

iii. *Chi-square test to test the equality of proportions* In addition to the above, chi-square test enables one to find out the significance of difference between two or more population proportions. As stated above, if an investigator is interested in finding out whether the proportion of married men is same in four major cities. The null hypothesis (H_0) is "The proportion of married men is the same in four major cities. The alternate hypothesis (H_A) is "The proportion of married men is not the same in four major cities".

iv. *Chi-square test of homogeneity*   Sometimes we need to compare samples taken from two populations differing in some characters. For example, samples are drawn from two populations namely "normal" and "liver disease patients"; these two samples are then classified into two:

1.   persons with hepatitis and

2.   persons without hepatitis

Here Chi-square is used to find out whether two populations from where the samples were taken are homogenous or not. In this case the null hypothesis (H_0) is "The two populations from where the samples are drawn are homogenous". The alternate hypothesis is "The two populations from where the samples are drawn are not homogenous".

Though, four different applications are given for χ^2 test, all these tests are basically same as these tests find whether the observed frequency fits well with expected frequency, i.e., null hypothesis $(H_0) = O_i - E_i = 0$ but the statement of null hypothesis differs.

Procedure to Carry out Chi-square Test

i.   Propose Null and Alternate hypothesis

ii.   Calculate expected frequencies

iii. Find the deviations between expected and observed frequencies

iv.   Square the deviations and divide by respective expected frequencies

v.   Substitute in the formula

vi.   Write the degrees of freedom

vii. Refer the tabulated test values for the specified degrees of freedom at 0.05 (or 0.01) probability level

viii. Compare calculated chi-square values with tabulated χ^2 chi-square values

ix.   Interpret the results.

The above procedure is routinely done to work out any problem manually or with calculator. But when we use SPSS, there is no need to do any of the steps from ii to viii, we need to propose the hypotheses, enter the data correctly, run the analysis and interpret the results.

CHI-SQUARE TEST WITH SPSS

Chi-square Test for Goodness of Fit with SPSS

Chi-square test for goodness of fit allows us to test

  i.   whether the observed frequencies for a categorical variable differ from expected frequencies based on some hypothesis or theory and

  ii. whether the observed frequencies of a particular variable follow theoretical distributions like binomial or Poisson distribution.

Goodness of fit for a categorical variable

Example 9.1

It is believed that the general human population in a region consists of 10% Hispanic, 10% Asian, 10% African–American and 70% White folk. In a sample survey it was recorded that there were 24 Hispanic, 11 Asians, 20 African–American and 145 White folk. Test whether the observed frequencies differ significantly from the hypothesized values. (Expected ratio for this category of human race is = 10: 10: 10: 70)

Null and alternate hypotheses:

H_0 There is no difference between observed and expected frequencies.

H_A There is real difference between observed and expected frequencies.

Step 1 Open a new data file in SPSS.

Step 2 Name the variables in **Variable View**: Click **Variable View** and name the variable in the first row as "Race", select numeric under **Type**, select 0 under **Decimals**, label the variable under Label column as "Races of human population" (This will appear in the output). In the **Values** column click the grey area to get **Value Labels** dialog box and assign value number and label as 1 for Hispanic, 2 for Asian, 3 for African–American and 4 for White and click OK (Figure 9.1).

Type Frequency in the second row under the head Name, select Numeric under Type, select 0 under Decimals, label the variable under Label column as "Frequency of different races in the population" (This will appear in the output). There is no need to label the values column (Figure 9.2).

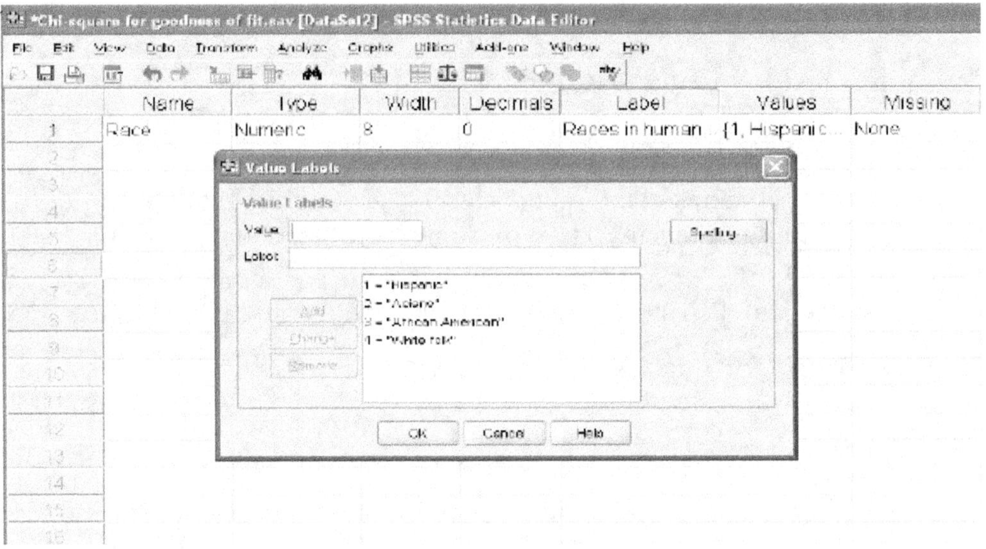

Figure 9.1   **Variable View** with **Value Labels** dialog box

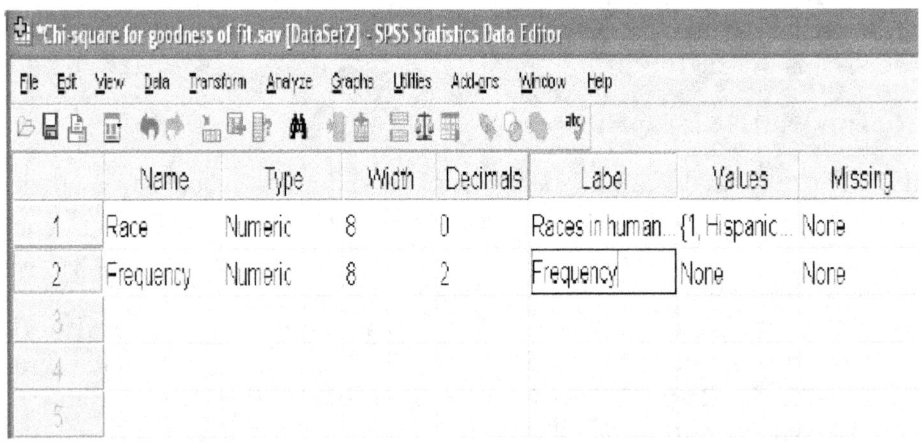

Figure 9.2   **Variable View** with variable name and frequency

Step 3 Click **Data View** tab to switch to data view. The file appears as in Figure 9.3 and enter data.

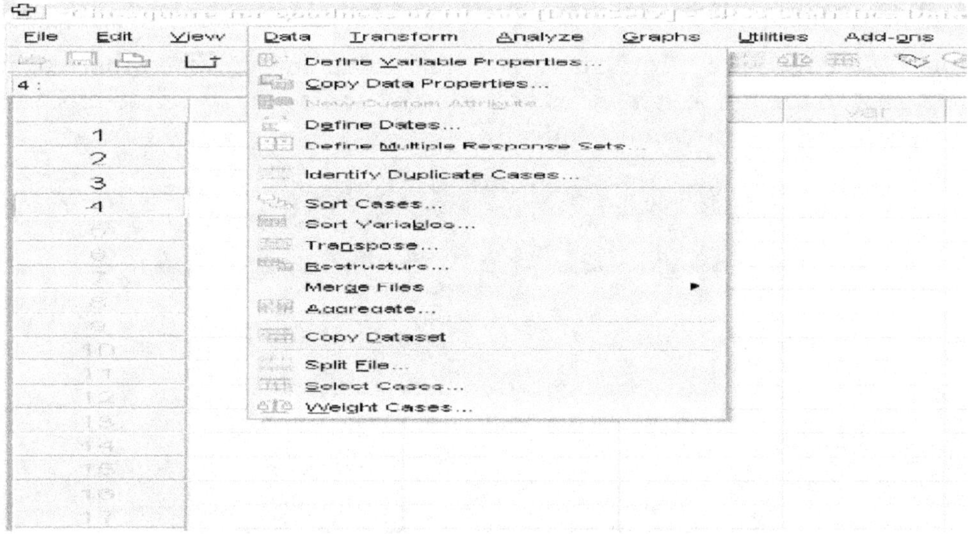

Figure. 9.3   Data View with data entered

Step 4 Click **Data** in the main menu, then click **Weight Cases** (Figure 9.4).

Figure 9.4   Selecting **Weight Cases** from main menu

This opens the **Weight Cases** dialog box (Figure 9.5).

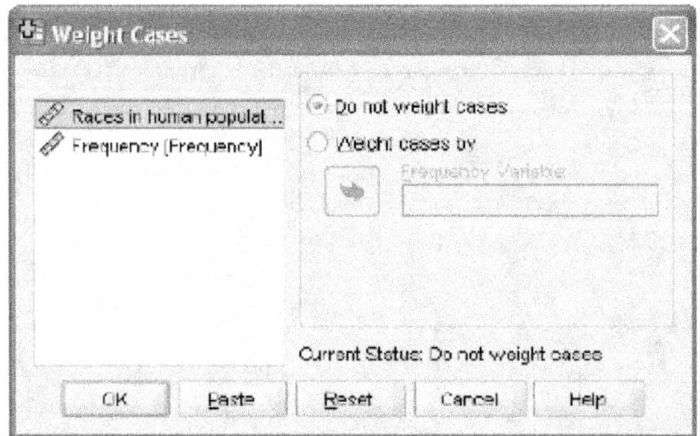

Figure 9.5   Weight Cases dialog box

Step 5   Select **Weight Cases** by radio button, click on the name "Frequency of different races" and transfer to **Frequency Variable** box (Figure 9.6) and click OK.

(***Note:*** If the data are recorded case by case in the data file then there would be no need to use the weight cases procedures because the cross tab procedure would count up the cases automatically.)

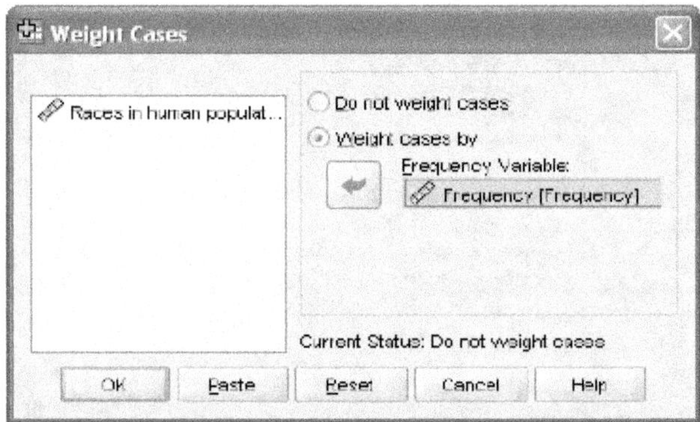

Figure 9.6   **Weight Cases** dialog box with frequency transferred under **Weight Cases by**

Step 6   Select **Analyse** from the main menu, click **Nonparametric** and then **Chi-square** (Figure 9.7). A window appears as in (Figure 9.8).

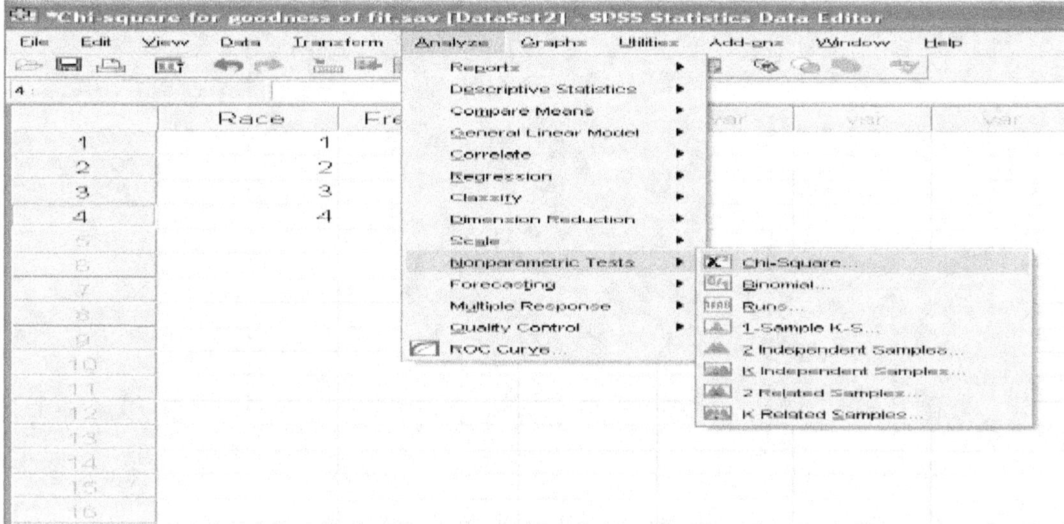

Figure 9.7   Selecting **Chi-Square** from main menu

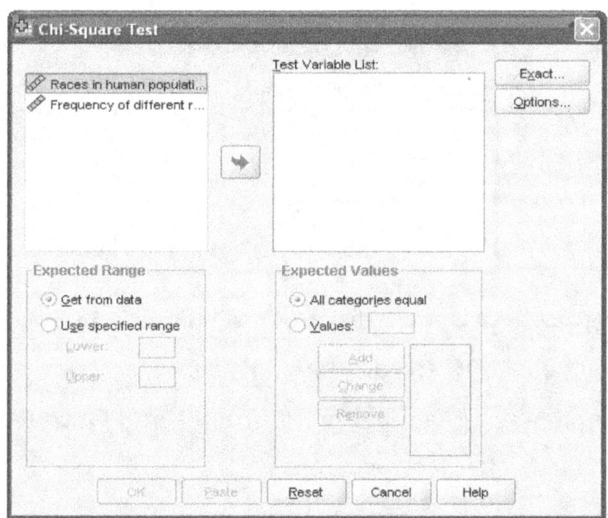

Figure 9.8   **Chi-Square Test** dialog box to transfer the variable

Step 7 Transfer "Races in human population" from left pan to **Test Variable List**. Then select **Values** radio button under Expected Values and type the ratio 10: 10:10:70 one by one and add by clicking on **Add** each time and complete as shown in Figure 9.9. Now select **Get from data** under Expected Range and check whether everything is completed as shown in Figure 9.9. Click OK to return to Chi-square Test and click Options.

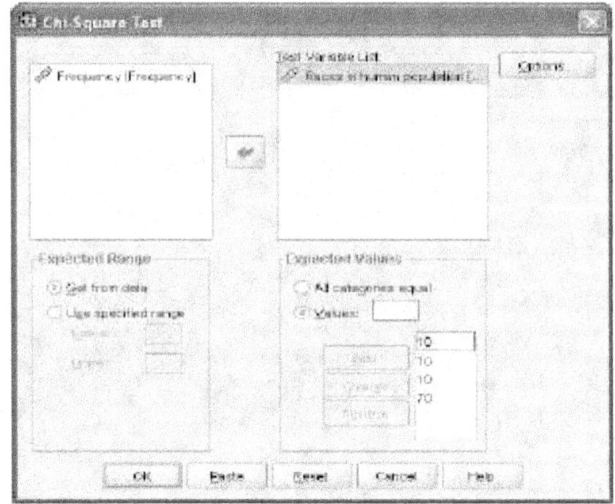

Figure 9.9   **Chi-Square Test** dialog box with expected values typed

Step 8 Chi-square Test: Options appears as in Figure 9.10. Select Descriptive and then click **Continue**.

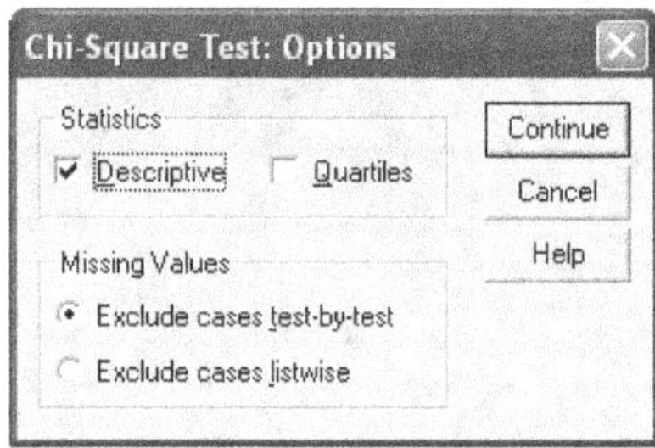

Figure 9.10   **Chi-Square Test: Options** dialog box with **Descriptive** selected under **Statistics**

Step 9 Finally click **OK** to run the analysis.

The outputs appear as given below (Output 1 and Output 2)

Output 1

Frequencies

Races in human population

	Observed N	Expected N	Residual
Hispanic	24	20	4
Asians	11	20	-9
African American	20	20	0
White folk	145	140	5
Total	200		

Output 2

Test Statistics

	Races in human population
Chi-Square	5.03[a]
df	3
Asymp. Sig.	0.17

a. 0 cells (.0%) have expected frequencies less than 5. The minimum expected cell frequency is 20.0.

Interpretation

The observed and expected frequencies are given in output 1. The Chi-square value is 5.029 for 3 *df* and asymptotic significance is 0.170, (i.e., *p*-value) are given in Output 2. Since, the *p*-value 0.170 is greater than 0.05 ($p > 0.05$), the difference between observed frequencies and expected frequencies is insignificant. Therefore, the null hypothesis (H_0), i.e., there is no difference between observed and expected frequencies is accepted at 5% level of significance. The answer to our problem is that the racial composition of our sample does not differ significantly from the hypothesized values for human population in that region.

Example 9.2

The theory of genetics predicts that the proportion of pea plants in four groups A, B, C and D should be in the ratio 9:3:3:1. The number of plants in the four groups are $A = 365$, $B = 130$, $C = 125$ and $D = 47$. Do these experimental results support the theory that the results are in the ratio of 9:3:3:1?

Null and alternate hypothesis

H_o There is no difference between observed and expected frequencies.

H_A There is real difference between observed and expected frequencies.

> **Step 1** Click **Variable View** and name the variable in the first row as "Plant", select numeric under **Type**, select **0** under **Decimals**, label the variable under **Label** column as "Characters in pea plant". In the **Values** column click the grey area, to get **Value labels** dialog box and assign value **number** and **Label** as 1 for A, 2 for B, 3 for C and 4 for D and click **OK**.

Step 2 Enter **Frequency** in the second row under the head Name, select Numeric under **Type**, select **0** under **Decimals** and label the variable under **Label** column as **Frequency**.

Step 3 Click **Data View** tab to switch to **Data View** and enter data.

Step 4 Click **Data** in the main menu, then click **Weight cases**. This opens the **Weight cases** dialog box. Select **Weight cases** by radio button, click on the name "Frequency" and transfer to **Frequency Variable** box and click **OK**.

Step 5 Select **Analyze** from the main menu then click **Non-parametric** and then **Chi-square**. A window appears as in Figure 9.8. Transfer "Characters in pea plant" to **Test Variable List**. Select **Values** radio button under **Expected values**. Type the ratio 9: 3:3:1, one by one and add by clicking on **Add** each time and complete. Now select **Get from data** under **Expected Range** and check whether everything is complete as shown in Figure 9.11.

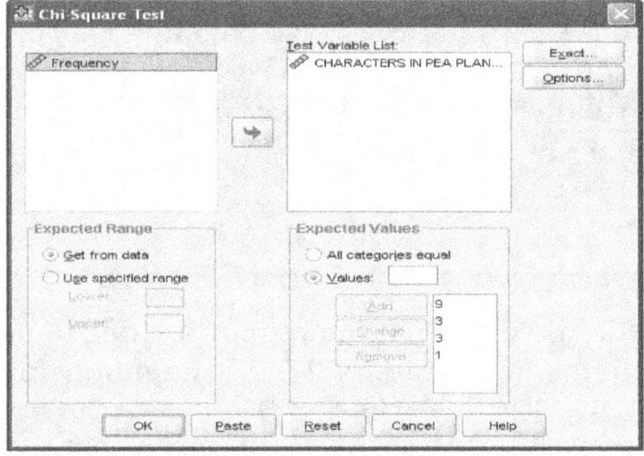

Figure 9.11   **Chi-square test** dialog box with **Test variable** transferred, **Expected range** selected and **Expected values** typed

Step 6 Click **OK**. The outputs appear as given below

Output 1

Characters in pea plant

	Observed N	Expected N	Residual
A-Round yellow	365	375.19	-10.19
B-Round green	130	125.06	4.94
C-Wrinkled yellow	125	125.06	-0.06
D-Wrinkled green	47	41.69	5.31
Total	667		

Output 2

Test Statistics

	Characters in pea plant
Chi-Square	1.15[a]
df	3
Asymp. Sig.	0.77

a. 0 cells (.0%) have expected frequencies less than 5. The minimum expected cell frequency is 41.7.

Interpretation

Output 1 gives observed and expected values. Output 2 gives the Chi-square results.

The χ^2 value for 3 *df* is 1.15. The *p*-value given against Asymp. Sig. is 0.77. Since the *p*-value is greater than 0.05 ($p > 0.05$), the difference between observed and expected frequencies is insignificant and therefore the null hypothesis is accepted. The experimental results support the theory and the results are in the ratio of 9:3:3:1.

Goodness of fit for Poisson distribution with SPSS   There are a number of events such as getting a girl or a boy in a single birth, number of emergency admissions in a hospital at a given interval of time, number of accidents in a place at a given interval of time, etc. The distribution of these variables can be given in the form of probabilities of occurrence. We can fit the given distribution to model distributions like Poisson or Binominal distributions and test the goodness of fit.

Before starting to work on the examples let us first understand the basics, conditions and data to which Poisson law is applicable. Poisson distribution is a discrete theoretical distribution. In Poisson distribution, the occurrence of events n is not known, therefore one can count the number of times an event can occur but not the number of times the event fails to occur.

An event is said to follow Poisson distribution when the probability of occurrence is very low, but the number of occurrence of such events are large and the events are independent of space and time.

Examples of poisson events with respect to time are number of accident deaths per year, number of earth quakes per year, number of emergency admissions in a year and so on. Some poisson events with respect to space are number of "moss plants" in a hill side, number of organisms in a counting chamber, number of yeast cells in the squares of a haemocytometer in a sample of curd, number of emergency admissions in a hospital, number of printing errors in a page, etc.

In these examples one can find out whether the occurrences of the events are random or otherwise.

Example 9.3

The following table gives the distribution of yeast cells over 400 squares of a haemocytometer in a sample of curd. Find out whether the distribution of yeasts follows Poisson law or Poisson distribution.

Yeast	0	1	2	3	4	5	6
Frequency	103	143	98	42	8	4	2

We need to compute the mean, find Poisson probabilities and test the goodness of fit.

1. *To find the mean of the distribution*

Step 1   Click **Variable View** from the tabs at the bottom left. Type "Yeast" under **Name**, choose **Numeric**, select **0** under **Decimals** and type under **Label** as "Number of yeast/square". No need to fill the Value column. In the next row type under **Name** as "frequency" and fill the rest as in (Figure 9.12).

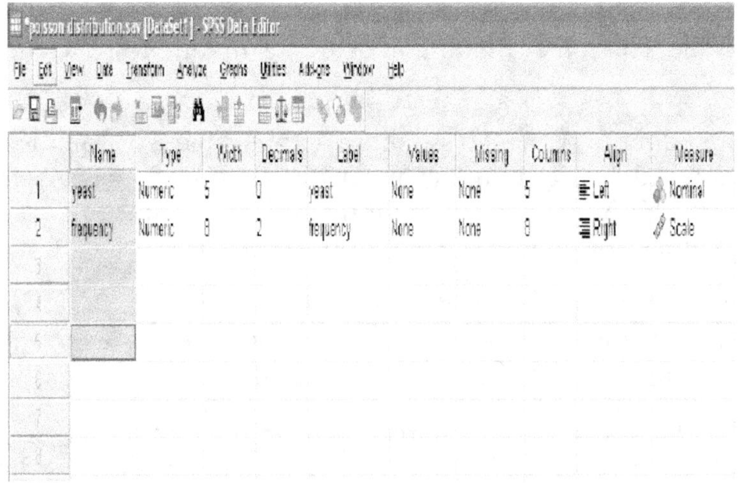

Figure 9.12   Variable View with discrete variable entered

Step 2 Click **Data View** from the tabs at the bottom and type data as given in Figure 9.13.

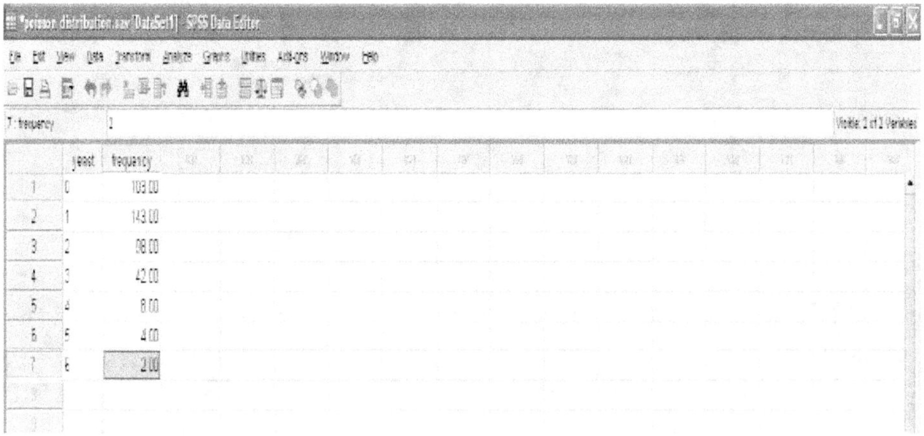

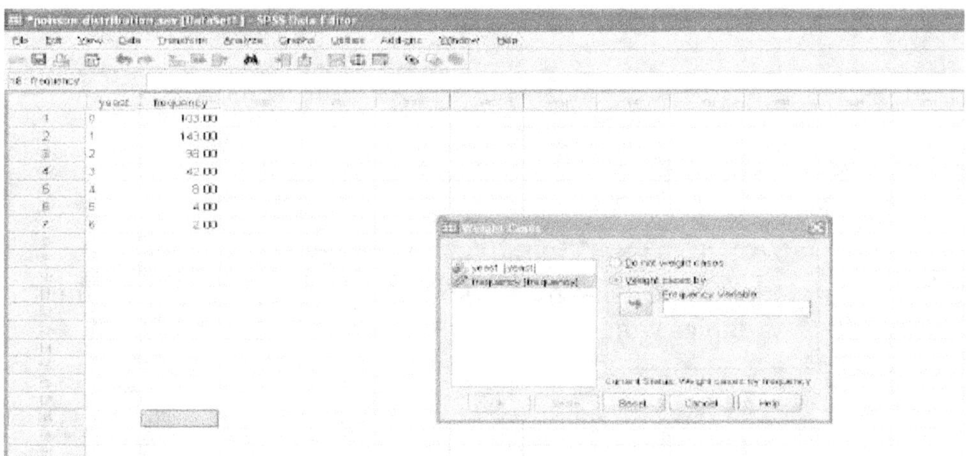

Figure 9.13   Data View with discrete frequencies entered

Since the variables are grouped, we need to weight cases. Yeast is our test variable, weightage for each variable is frequency. Therefore assign weightage as follow.

Step 3 Go to **Data** and select **Weight Cases**, a dialog box appears as given in Figure 9.14.

Figure 9.14   Weight Cases dialog box with **Data View**

Now click the radio button Weight cases by in the left hand window. Select Frequency from the list and click on the arrow to transfer it to the box labelled Frequency Variable and click OK (Figure 9.15).

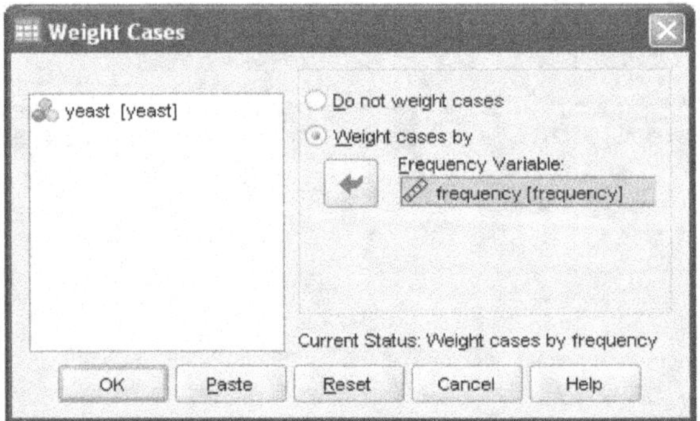

Figure 9.15   **Weight Cases** dialog box with frequency transferred under **Weight cases by**

Step 4 To calculate mean of the distribution, click **Analyze**, then **Descriptive Statistics** and than **Frequencies** (Figure 9.16).

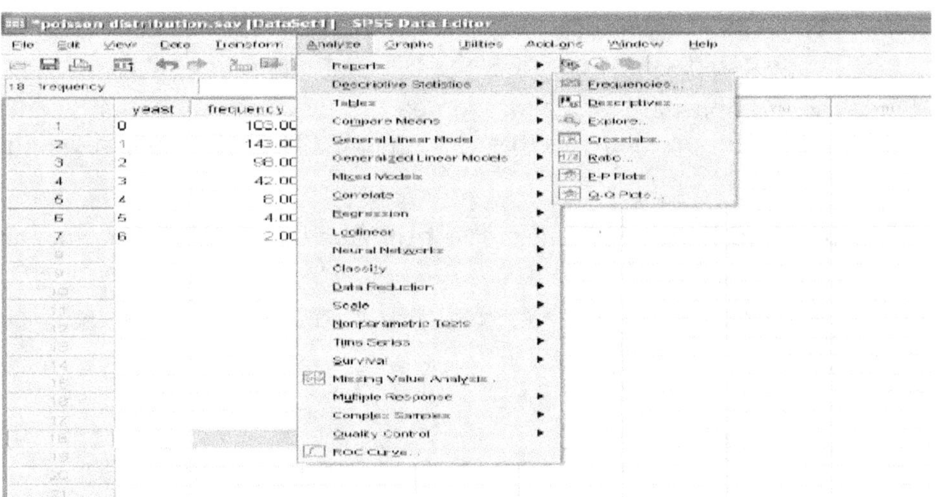

Figure 9.16   Selecting frequencies from main menu

A pop up window appears as given below. Select yeast and click on the arrow to transfer it to Variables window (Figure 9.17).

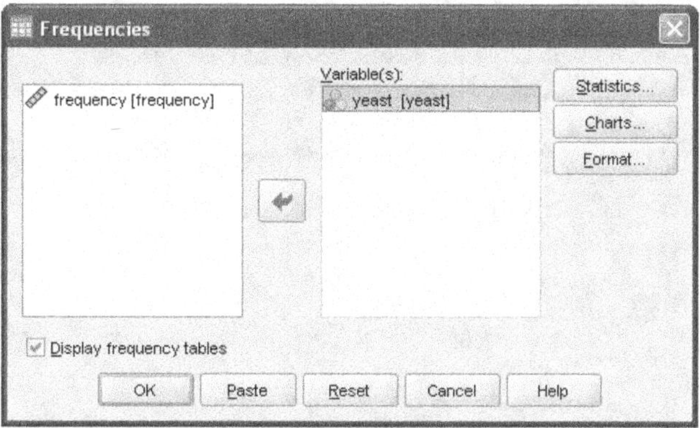

Figure 9.17   **Frequencies** dialog box with test variable selected

Step 5 Click on **Statistics** and select **Mean** under Central Tendency (We need to calculate mean of the distribution to calculate Poisson probability distribution) (Figure 9.18). Click Continue and click **OK**. The result appears as given in Output 1.

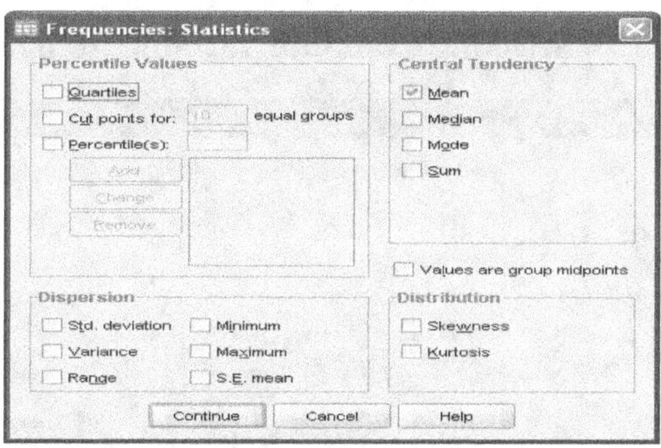

Figure 9.18   **Frequencies: Statistics** with mean selected under **Central Tendency**

Output 1

Statistics

yeast

N	Valid	400
	Missing	0
Mean		1.32

2. *Calculation of Poisson probabilities*

Step 6 Select **Transform** from the main menu and then **Compute Variable** (Figure 9.19).

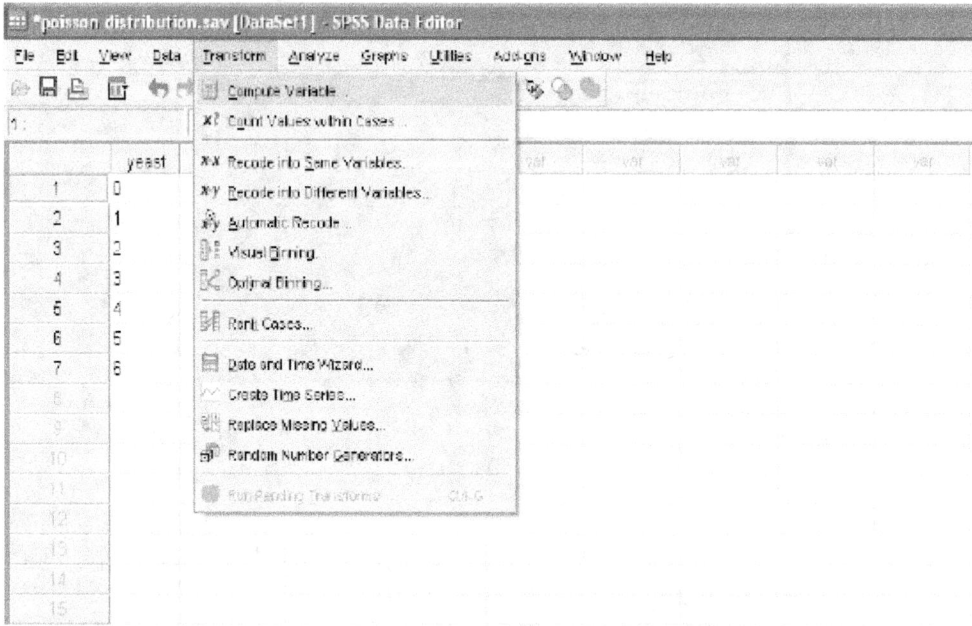

Figure 9.19   Selecting **Compute Variable** from main menu

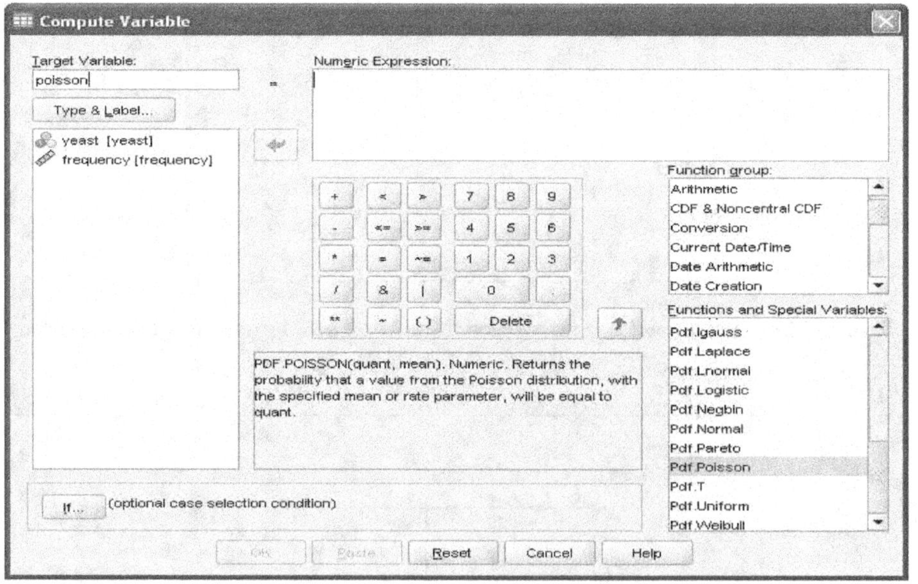

Figure 9.20   **Compute Variable** dialog box to type **Poisson** and select **Pdf Poisson**

In the **Compute Variable**, dialog box type the name **Poisson** under **Target Variable**. Now, scroll down **Function group**: and select PDF and Noncentral PDF.

Then, scroll down **Functions and Special Variables**, and select Pdf. Poisson. Pdf stands for "Probability density function" (Figure 9.20). Click on the upward arrow to move this into the top right window named as **Numeric Expression** (Figure 9.21).

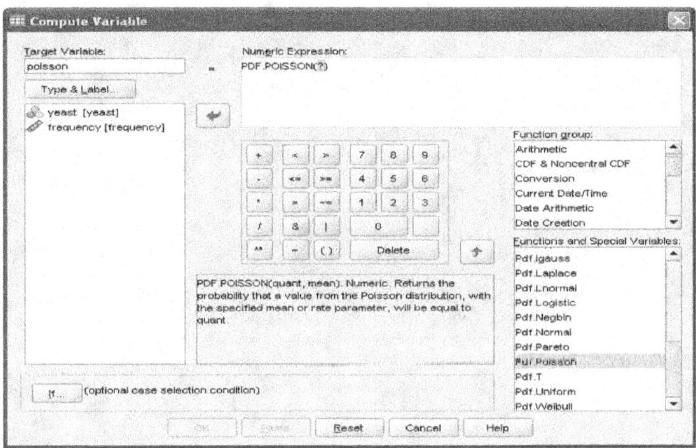

Figure 9.21   Compute Variable dialog box to transfer the **Variable** and type the value of **Mean**

Now the **Numeric Expression** window has **PDF. POISSON(?)**. Select yeast from the left hand window and click the arrow to transfer it to the right hand window. Type the value of mean (1.3225) from Output 1 (Figure 9.22). Check this procedure very correctly, as this is the basis for the calculations of Poisson probabilities. Finally click **OK**.

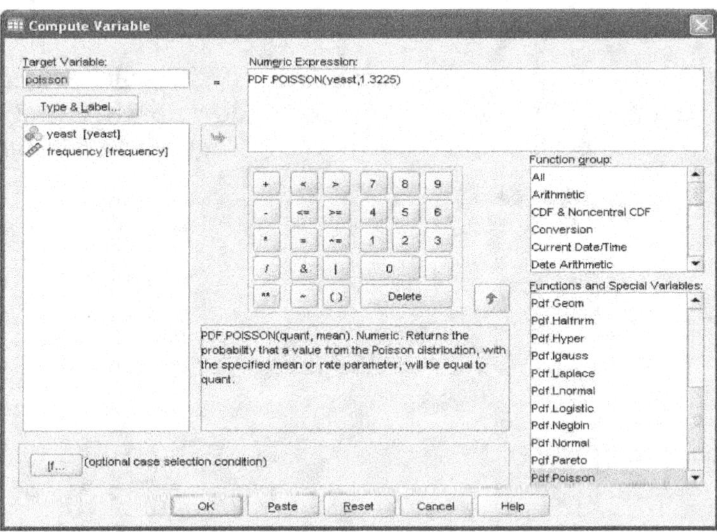

Figure 9.22   Compute Variable dialog box with all options complete

The output appears as given below with Poisson probabilities in the SPSS data view along with the data entered already (Figure 9.23). Now, delete the entire row (7th row) where poisson value is 0. (In problems involving Poisson law, if Poisson value is '0' then e cannot enter that value.)

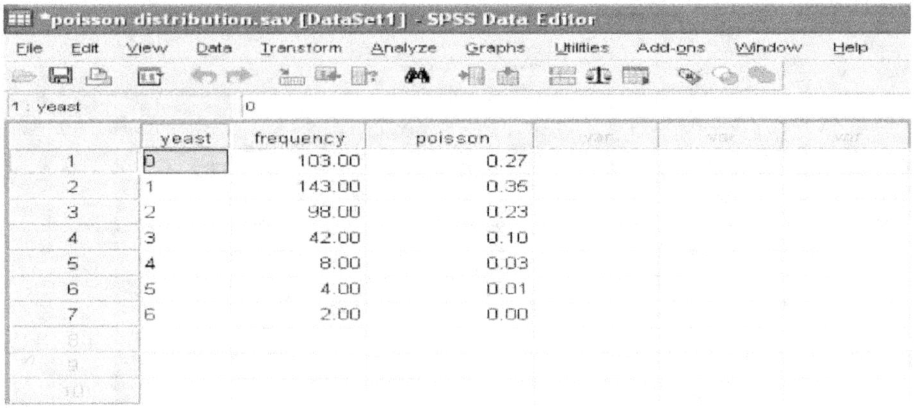

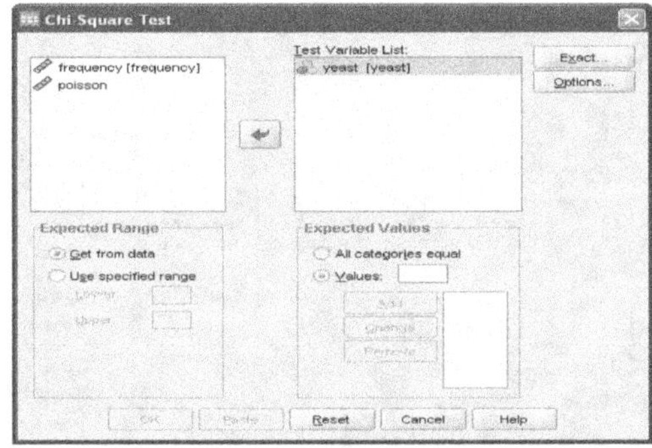

Figure 9.23   **Data View** with Poisson probabilities computed from **Transform** option

3. *Analysis of Goodness of fit*

Null hypothesis   There is no difference between the observed and expected Poisson theoretical frequencies.

Alternate hypothesis   There is real difference between the observed and expected Poisson theoretical frequencies.

Step 7   Select **Analyze** from the main menu, then click **Nonparametric** and then Chi-square. A pop up window appears as given in Figure 9.24, select yeast and transfer it to **Test Variable List**.

Figure 9.24   Chi-Square Test dialog box

Step 8 Select **Get from Data** radio button under **Expected Range**. Select **Values** radio button under Expected Values.

Enter Poisson probabilities from **Data Editor** into the **Values** box and add one by one and complete as in Figure 9.25.

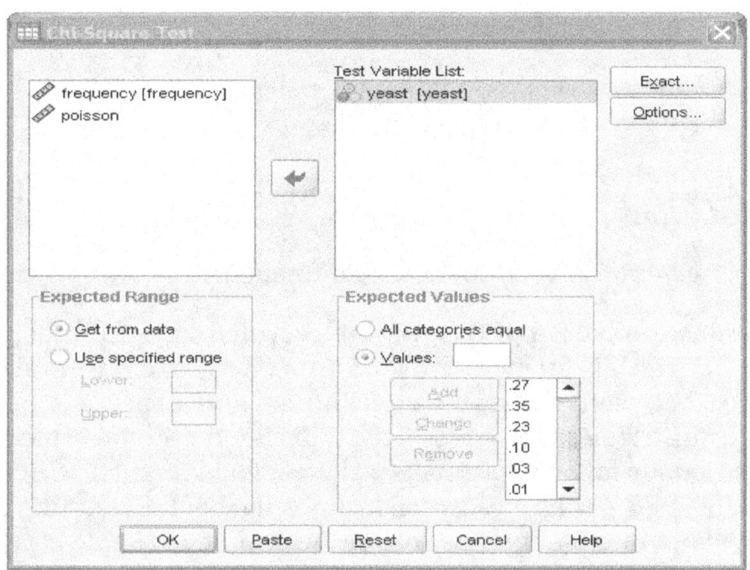

Figure 9.25   **Chi-Square Test** dialog box with **Test Variable** and expected values (Poisson probability)

Step 9 Click **OK**. The output appears in the output window.

Output 2

Frequencies

yeast

	Observed N	Expected N	Residual
0	103	108.55	-5.55
1	143	140.71	2.29
2	98	92.46	5.54
3	42	40.2	1.8
4	8	12.06	-4.06
5	4	4.02	-0.02
Total	398		

Output 3

Test Statistics

	yeast
Chi-Square	2.1[a]
df	5
Asymp. Sig.	0.84

a. 1 cells (16.7%) have expected frequencies less than 5. The minimum expected cell frequency is 4.0.

Interpretation

Output 1 gives observed and expected frequencies.

The Chi-square value is 2.100 for 5 *df* and asymptotic significance is 0.835 (Output 2), which is greater than 0.05 ($p > 0.05$). There is no significant difference between the given distribution and expected theoretical probability distribution. Therefore, the null hypothesis is accepted and the given distribution follows Poisson law. There is goodness of fit. Scientifically, the probability of getting a yeast cell in any square of the counting chamber is very low but the total number of yeast cells in the sample is very high.

Chi-Square Test for Independence of Attributes with SPSS

The Chi-square test for independence is a test to find out whether two categorical variables are associated with each other. To conduct a Chi-square test of this kind we need two categorical variables that can reasonably be given in a bivariate table (i.e., with a limited number of categories).

Example 9.4

A group of students were classified in terms of gender (male and female) and blood group (A, B, AB and O). Find whether there is association between gender and blood group.

Sex	Blood group				
	A	B	AB	O	Total
Male	28	16	7	49	100
Female	25	13	8	54	100
Total	**53**	**29**	**15**	**103**	**200**

Two groupings of categorical variables are

   i.   Gender—male and female

   ii.   Blood group—A, B, AB and O.

Null and alternate hypotheses

H_0 There is no association between gender and blood group.

H_A There is real association between gender and blood group.

Step 1 Open a new data file in SPSS.

Step 2 Name the variables in **Variable View**. Click Variable View, type the variable in the first row as "Gender" under **Name**, select **Numeric** under **Type**, select **0** under **Decimals**, label the variable under **Label** column. In the **Values** columns click the gray area, to get **Value labels** dialog box and assign value **number** and **labels** as 1 for male and 2 for female. In the second row, type the second variable as "Blood group" under the column **Name**, select **Numeric** under **Type**, select **0** under **Decimals**, label the variable as "Blood group" under **Label** column. In the **Values** column click the grey area to get **Value labels** dialog box and assign value **number** and **label** as 1 for A, 2 for B, 3 for AB and 4 for O (Figure 9.25).

Step 3 In the third row type **Frequency** under **Name**, select **Numeric** under **Type**, **select** 0 under the column **Decimals**, label column as "Frequency". There is no need to give value labels under **Values** (Figure 9.26).

	Name	Type	Width	Decimals	Label	Values	Missing	Columns
1	Gender	Numeric	8	0	Gender	{1, male}..	None	8
2	Bloodgroup	Numeric	8	0	Blood group	{1, A-group}..	None	8
3	Frequency	Numeric	8	0	Frequency	None	None	8
4								

Figure 9.26 **Variable View** with variables named

Step 4 Click on **Data View** and enter data under the respective variables as labelled in **Variable View** as in Figure 9.27.

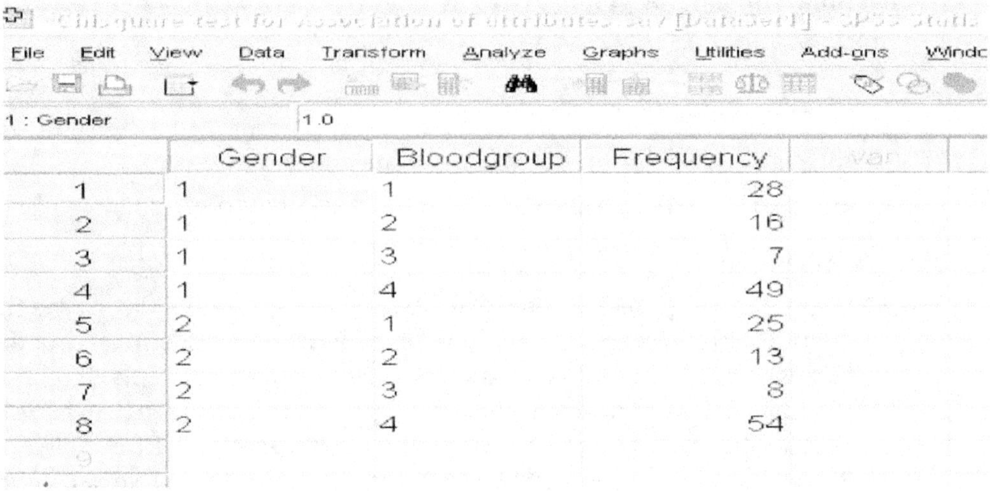

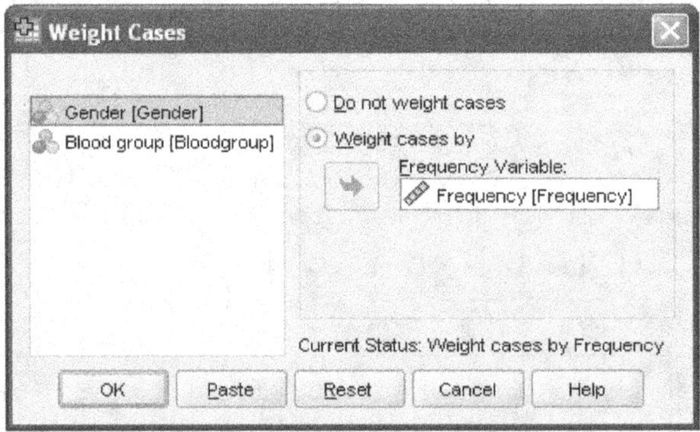

Figure 9.27   **Data View** with frequencies entered for two categorial variables

Step 5 Select Data from the main menu and then click **Weight cases**. This will open the **Weight cases** dialog box (Figure 9.28), select **Weight cases** by and transfer Frequency to **Frequency Variable**. Click OK. Now the entire display will disappear.

Figure 9.28   **Weight Cases** dialog box

Note: As previously stated if the data had been recorded case by case in the data file then there would be no need to use the weight cases procedures because the cross tab procedure would count up the cases automatically.

Step 6 Select **Analyse** from the main menu then click **Descriptive statistics** and then click **Crosstabs**. **Crosstabs** appears as in Figure 9.29. Transfer Gender and **Blood group** in rows and columns boxes respectively. If you want bar diagram select **Display cluster bar chart**. Click the **Statistics** button.

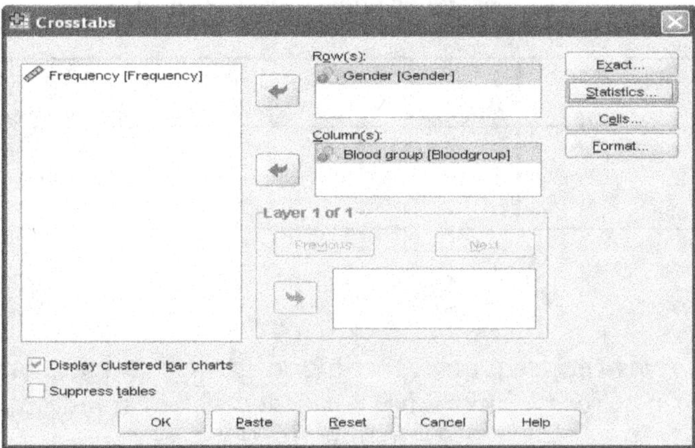

Figure 9.29   **Cross tabs** dialog box to select categorical variables in Rows and Columns

Step 7 **Crosstabs: Statistics** window appears as in Figure 9.30. Choose Chi-square and other options as needed. Click **Continue**.

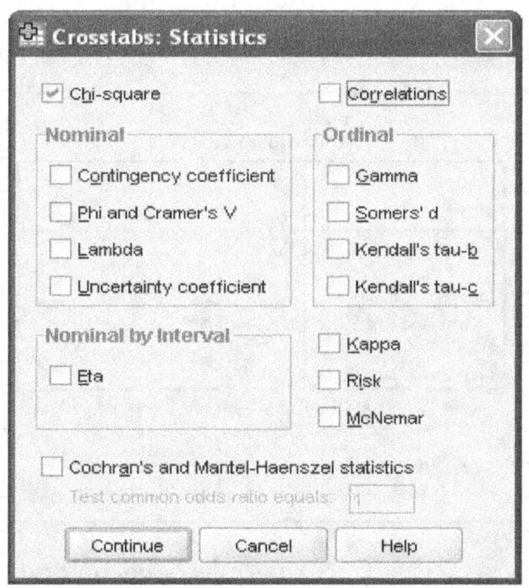

Figure 9.30   **Crosstabs: Statistics** with **Chi-Square** option selected

Step 8 Finally click **OK** to run the analysis. **SPSS output** appears as given below and interpret the results.

Output 1

Gender * Blood group Crosstabulation

Count

		Blood group				
		A-group	B-group	AB-group	O-group	Total
Gender	male	28	16	7	49	100
	female	25	13	8	54	100
Total		53	29	15	103	200

Interpretation

Output 1 gives the frequencies of blood groups in male and female in the table form (Cross tabulation). For 3 degrees of freedom i.e., $[(r-1)(c-1)] = [(2-1)(4-1)] = 3$, the p-value 0.852 is greater than 0.05. The difference is considered insignificant. The null hypothesis is accepted and therefore, there is no association between sex and blood group. In other words, the gender and blood groups are independent in human.

Output 2 gives the results of Chi-Square tests.

Output 2

Chi-Square Tests

	Value	df	Asymp. Sig. (2-sided)
Pearson Chi-Square	0.79[a]	3	0.85
Likelihood Ratio	0.79	3	0.85
Linear-by-Linear Association	0.58	1	0.45
N of Valid Cases	200		

a. 0 cells (.0%) have expected count less than 5. The minimum expected count is 7.50.

Example 9.5

Two groups A and B consist of 100 people each having a particular disease. A drug is given to group A and not to group B. Otherwise both are treated identically. It is found that in group A and B, 80 and 65 persons have recovered from the disease. Test the hypothesis that the drug helps to cure the disease at 0.05 level of significance.

Null and alternate hypothesis

H_0 The drug is not effective in curing the disease.

H_A The drug is effective in curing the disease.

Step 1   Open a new data file in SPSS.

Step 2   Name the variables in **Variable View**. Click **Variable view**, name the variable in the first row as "Group" under **Name**, select **Numeric** under **Type**, select **0** under **Decimals**, label the variable under **Label** column. In the **Values** column click the grey area, to get **Value labels** dialog box and assign value **number** and **label**, 1 for group A and 2 for group B. Name the second variable as "Drug" in the second row under the column **Name**, select **Numeric** under **Type**, select **0** under **Decimals**, label the variable under **Label** column. In the **Values** column click the grey area to get **Value labels** dialog box and assign value number and label as 1 for cured and 2 for not cured (Figure 9.31).

Step 3   In the third row type "Frequency" under **Name**, select **Numeric** under **Type**, under select **0 Decimals**, **Label** column as "Frequency". There is no need to give value labels under **Values**.

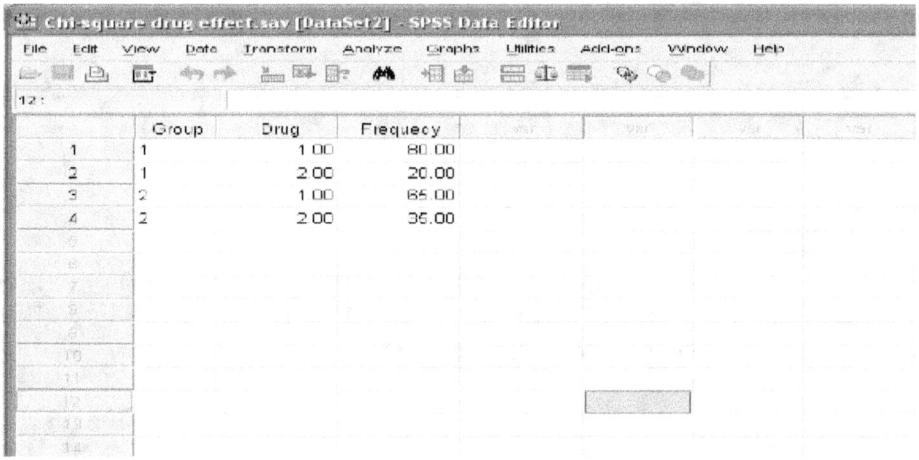

Figure 9.31   Data View with frequencies for two categorical variables

Step 4 and **5**   Refer previous example and complete weight cases.

Step 6   Select **Analyse** from the main menu then click **Descriptive statistics** and then click **Crosstabs**. In the **Crosstabs**, transfer **Group** and **Drug** in rows and columns boxes respectively. If you want bar diagram select **Display cluster bar chart** and click the Statistics button.

Step 7 Crosstabs: Statistics window appears, choose Chi-square and other options as needed. Click **Continue** and **OK**. The output appears a given below.

Output 1

Group * Drug Crosstabulation

Count

		Drug		
		Cured	not cured	Total
Group	Group A	80	20	100
	Group B	65	35	100
Total		145	55	200

Output 2

Chi-Square Tests

	Value	df	Asymp. Sig. (2-sided)	Exact Sig. (2-sided)	Exact Sig. (1-sided)
Pearson Chi-Square	5.643[a]	1	.018		
Continuity Correction[b]	4.915	1	.027		
Likelihood Ratio	5.698	1	.017		
Fisher's Exact Test				.026	.013
Linear-by-Linear Association	5.614	1	.018		
N of Valid Cases	200				

a. 0 cells (.0%) have expected count less than 5. The minimum expected count is 27.50.

b. Computed only for a 2x2 table

Interpretation

Pearson's $\chi^2 = 5.643$ for 1 degrees of freedom, i.e., $[(r-1)\,(c-1)] = [(2-1)\,(2-1)]$. The p-value 0.018 is less than 0.05. Therefore, null hypothesis is rejected and the drug is effective in curing the disease ($p < 0.05$).

Review Exercises

1. In guinea pigs, black is dominant over white colour, and short hair is dominant over long. When F1 hybrids with black short haired guinea pigs are crossed, the F2 hybrids are in the ratio of 315 black long: 105 black short: 108 white long: 35 white short. Test whether these values agree with the expected genetic ratio of 9: 3: 3:1.

2. Fit a Poisson distribution for the following data on number of plankton from the water samples and test the Goodness of fit.

Number of plankton	0	1	2	3	4	5	6
Number of samples	93	105	89	42	11	8	2

3. The following data gives the response of a particular drug in curing a disease. Find whether the drug is effective in curing the disease.

	Cured	Not cured
Drug	300	200
No drug	50	250

4. The following data gives eye colour of the father and the eye colour of the son. Find whether there is any association between eye colours of the sons with their father.

Eye colour of father	Eye colour of son	
	Dark	**Light**
Dark	230	148
Light	150	471

5. Student from a college were graded according to their IQ and their economic conditions. Find whether there is an association between IQ and economic conditions.

Economic conditions	I Q	
	High	
Rich	460	140
Poor	240	160

Glossary

Adjusted R² A measure of the loss of predictive power in regression analysis. The adjusted R tells us how much variance in the outcome would be accounted for, if the model has been derived from the population from which the sample was taken.

Alternative hypothesis Any statement (hypothesis) which is complementary to null hypothesis. This states that the sample mean and population mean are not equal.

ANOVA Analysis of variance. It is an inferential statistical procedure that examines the difference or variance between control and treatment groups in an investigation.

Bivariate correlation A correlation (relationship) between two variables.

Categorical variable Any variable that consists of categories of objects or entities. Test results in a class is a good example because it is classified into pass and fail.

Chi-square distribution A probability distribution of sum of squares of several normally distributed variables. It is used to test hypothesis about categorical variable.

Chi-square test Generally refers to Pearson's Chi-square test. It is used to find the discrepancy between observed and expected frequency based on some model or to test the independence of two categorical variables.

Confidence interval A range of values around that statistic (for example, mean) that are believed to contain, with a certain probability (95%), the true value of that statistic (i.e., mean of population).

Contingency table A table classifying the individuals with respect to two or more categorical variables. The levels of each variable are arranged in rows and columns and the number of individuals falling into each category is noted in the cells of the table. For example, if the students in a college are classified with respect to gender and blood group, the contingency table will show the number of males in blood group A, the number of females in blood group B and so on.

Correlation coefficient A decimal number between 0 and 1.00 that indicates the degree and direction to which two quantitative variables are related and represented by r.

Covariance A measure of how much the deviations of two variables match.

Covariate A variable that is related to the outcome variable that is measured. Basically, anything that has an impact on the dependent variable and that cannot be controlled for by design can be a covariate.

Criterion variable The outcome variable (dependent) that is predicted in regression analysis or correlation research.

Data editor The main window in SPSS to name the variable, enter data and carry out analysis.

Data view One of the two ways to view the contents of the data editor. The data view has a spreadsheet for entering data.

Degrees of freedom A difficult thing to define in the glossary. It is the number of items that are free to vary when estimating some statistical parameter. Degrees of freedom (df) are given by the number of independent observations minus the number of parameters estimated. If there are n observations in a sample and deviations of all n items are estimated from the mean of the sample and only one parameter mean is estimated then df $= n - 1$. This is a term borrowed from physical science, in which the degree of freedom of a system is the number of constraints needed to determine its state completely at any point.

Dependent variable A variable that is measured in a study with respect to the variable that is manipulated by the experimenter. It is otherwise called as outcome variable. This term is used in any study to determine cause-and-effect relationship.

Descriptive statistics The statistical procedures that simply describe different characteristics of the data rather than trying to infer something from the data.

Factor Another name for independent variable or predictor that is used in describing experimental designs.

F-Ratio A test statistic with known probability distribution (F-distribution). It is the ratio of average variability in the data that a given model can explain to the average variability unexplained by the same model.

Goodness of fit An index to find how well a model fits the data from which it was generated. Chi-square test is one of the tests to find the goodness of fit.

Grouping variable   If the observations in a study are assembled according to similarities or resemblances, each forms a group. In SPSS, a set of code numbers is given to indicate each group in variable view.

Hypothesis testing   A statistical procedure for testing the null hypothesis against alternate hypothesis. The statistical procedures in hypothesis testing include t, F and χ^2-square tests.

Hypothesis   In statistics, a hypothesis is a statement about a population, such as the nature of the distribution. (There are two kinds of hypothesis, Null hypothesis and Alternate hypothesis).

Independent variable   A variable under study, to determine whether it has a causal effect on the dependent variable. In regression studies, the term is used to denote a predictor variable or regressor.

Inferential statistics   Includes a set of statistical tools which enable the researcher to infer or reach conclusions about the data.

Kendall's tau   Correlation test for use with two ordinal variables or an ordinal and an interval variable. Prior to computers, rho was preferred to tau due to computational ease. Now that computers have rendered calculation trivial, tau is generally preferred. Partial Kendall's tau is also available as an ordinal analog to partial Pearsonian correlation.

MANOVA   Multivariate analysis of variance. It is an analysis of variance (ANOVA) applicable to multivariate (a multivariate data set containing observations on three or more variables dependent variables) situation, for two or more independent variables.

Mean   The average of a set of numbers or scores in a distribution. To get the mean, all the values are added up and the sum is divided by the total number of all the values.

Measures of central tendency   Single numbers that are used to describe a larger set of data in a distribution of scores. The measures of central tendency are mean, median and mode.

Median   The score or number, which falls directly in the middle of a distribution of numbers or divides the data into two equal parts.

Mode   The number or score, which occurs most frequently in a distribution of numbers.

Multiple regression   An extension of simple regression in which an outcome is predicted by a linear combination of two or more predictor variables.

Multivariate analysis   Analysis of variance that involves more than one outcome variable that have been measured.

Mutivariate Analysis of variance involving more than one outcome variable (multivariate = many variables)

Negatively skewed Skewness is asymmetry in a distribution. A negatively skewed distribution has most of its scores bunched up at the higher end (right side) of the distribution.

Nominal data A data set in which the numbers merely represent names, the numbers have no meaning other than the name.

Non-parametric tests Statistical tests or procedures that do not assume that the data have come from a normal distribution. Tests such as Mann-Whitney test and χ^2-square test are non-parametric tests.

Normal distribution Another name for the bell-shaped curve; this distribution forms a very important concept in statistics and research. It has certain distinct characteristics, which make it a very useful tool for descriptive and inferential statistics.

Null hypothesis A hypothesis made by the investigator on the problem under investigation. A null hypothesis is a statement of 'no difference'. The H_0 states that there is no significant difference between sample mean and population mean, or between means of two populations, or between means of more than two populations.

One-tailed test One-tailed test is used to test if the sample mean is significantly greater than population mean or if it is significantly less than that, but not both.

p-value The probability value (p-value) of a statistical hypothesis test. It is the probability of getting a value of the test statistic as extreme as that observed by chance alone. Small p-values suggest that the null hypothesis is not true. The smaller the p-value, the more convincing is the rejection of the null hypothesis. p-value indicates the strength of evidence for rejecting the null hypothesis H_0.

Percentile Any distribution could be described in terms of percentiles. 10th percentile is the value in a distribution below which 10% of the values lie. 90th percentile is the value below which 90% of the values lie. So 50th percentile is the median in a distribution.

Positively skewed Skewness is asymmetry in a distribution. A positively skewed distribution has most of its scores bunched up at the lower end (left side) of the distribution.

Post-hoc comparisons Unplanned comparisons, one wishes to make after the data have been gathered. It is usually carried out if there is significant difference between two groups (pairwise comparisons) covering the different levels of the variable under study.

Predictor variable The variable from which the criterion variable is found out in a prediction study.

Probability The term probability does not allow a concrete definition; it can be defined in different ways. In simple, probability is the ratio of favourable number of outcomes divided by total number of outcomes in any one trial or experiment.

Qualitative variable A character or property, such as blood group, gender or nationality, which can be expressed in kind and not in numbers. It is an attribute and is descriptive in nature.

Quantitative variable A variable whose differing status can be expressed in numbers. Characteristics like height, weight, length, etc. are measured quantitatively.

Regression The mathematical process of using observations to predict a target-dependent (criterion) variable from other variables known as regressor or independent variable. The prediction is made by constructing a regression equation or a regression line, the line of best fit through the data.

Sample A smaller collection of units from a population used to determine the charcterstics or truth of the population.

Sampling distribution The probability distribution of a statistics. If a large number of samples are drawn from the population and some statistics calculated, for example mean, we would create a frequency distribution of mean. The resulting distribution will form the sampling distribution of means.

Scatterplot A scatterplot is a plot of points on coordinate axes (X and Y-axis) used to represent and illustrate the relationships between two quantitative variables.

Skewed A distribution is skewed if majority of the scores are bunched up at one end or the other.

Spearman's rho The most common correlation for use with two ordinal variables or an ordinal and an interval variable. Rho for ranked data equals Pearson's *r* for ranked data.

Standard deviation An estimate of average spread (variability) of a set of data measured in the same units of measurement as the original data. It is the square root of variance.

Standard error The standard deviation of the sampling distribution of a statistic. For example, mean is a statistic, standard error tells how much the sample means differ from the population mean. The larger the standard error the greater is the possibility that the sample may not be an accurate reflection of the population from which the sample came.

String variable Variable involving words, i.e., letter strings (e.g., gender, blood group, etc.).

Sum of squares An estimate of total variability of a set of data. First the deviation for each score is calculated and then this value is squared and summed up. It is denoted by SS.

Syntax Pre-defined written commands that instruct SPSS what the user would like to do.

Total sum of squares An estimate of total variability in a data set. It is the total squared deviations between each observation and from the overall mean of all observations.

t-test A statistical procedure to find the significance of difference between two groups. The means of both groups are compared to each other.

Two-tailed test A two-tailed test means that the level of significance 0.05, is equally distributed on both the sides of the tail. 0.025 is in each tail of the distribution of the test statistic. A two-tailed test will test if the mean is significantly greater than μ or if the mean significantly less than μ.

Type I error Rejecting the null hypothesis when it is actually true. The probability of a Type I, α error is the level of significance and is also known as α-rate or α-level

Type II error Accepting the null hypothesis when it is actually false. The probability of a Type II error α is known as beta-rate or beta-level. Beta-level is decided by a number of factors like sample size and significance level.

Univariate Means only one variable. The term usually refers to a situation where only one variable has been measured.

Variable view One of the two ways to view the contents of the data editor. It has a spreadsheet for entering the name and details of the variable.

Variable A property or characteristic on which the data are collected. There are qualitative and quantitative variables.

Variance The average amount of dispersion or spread in a distribution. The deviations from the mean are squared and summed up to find variance.

Wilcoxon signed-rank test A non-parametric test which is used to test the difference between two related samples. It is a non-parametric equivalent to a matched pair *t*-test

Z-score A conversion of a raw score on a test to a standardized score represented in units of standard deviations. This is a commonly used statistical procedure that is used to compare scores of tests that might not be measured on the same scale.

References

Andy Field. (2005). *Discovering Statistics using SPSS*, 2nd edition. Sage Publications, London.

Eelko Huizingh. (2007). *Applied Statistics with SPSS*. Sage Publications, New Delhi, India.

Elhance, D.N. and Prasan Prakash. (1975). *Fundamentals of Statistics,* 16th edition. Kitab Mahal, Allahabad.

Gupta, S.C. (2007). *Fundamentals of Statistics,* 6th revised and enlarged edition. Indra Gupta (ed.). Himalaya Publishing House, Mumbai.

Gurumani, N. (2005). *An Introduction to Biostatistics*, second revised edition. MJP Publishers, Chennai.

Ipsen, Johannes and Feigl, Polly. (1970). *Bancroft's Introduction to Biostatistics*, Harper International Edition. Harper and Row Publishers, New York.

Jacobson, Perry E. (1976). *Introduction to Statistical Measure for Social and Behavioural Sciences*. Dryden Press.

Jerrold, H. Zar. (1999). *Biostatisticial Analysis*, 4th edition. Prentice Hall International.

John, E. Freund, (1981). *Statistics: A First Course*, 3rd edition. Prentice–Hall, Inc. Englewood Cliffs, New Jersey.

Mandal, R.B. (2001). *Statistics for Geographers and Social Scientists*. Concept Publishing Company, New Delhi.

Paul, R. Kinnear and Colin, D. Gray. (2006). *SPSS 14 Made Simple*. Psychology Press, Taylor and Francis group, Hove and New York.

Sivathanu Pillai. (1973). *Elements of Statistics.* Progressive Corporation Ltd., Allahabad.

Sokal, R. Robert, and Rohlf, F. James. (1973). *Introduction to Biostatistics.* W.H. Freeman and Company, San Francisco.

N

O

P

Q

R

S